Shoshanna's Story

Shoshanna's Story

A Mother, a Daughter, and the
Shadows of History

Elaine Kalman Naves

National Library of Canada Cataloguing in Publication

Naves, Elaine Kalman
Shoshanna's story : a mother, a daughter and the shadows of history /
Elaine Kalman Naves.

ISBN 0-7710-6730-5

1. Holocaust, Jewish (1939-1945)–Personal narratives. 2. Holocaust,
Jewish (1939-1945)–Hungary. 3. Holocaust survivors–Canada–Biography.
I. Title.

DS135.H9N38 2003   943.9'0099   C2003-902565-9

We acknowledge the financial support of the Government of Canada through
the Book Publishing Industry Development Program and that of the
Government of Ontario through the Ontario Media Development
Corporation's Ontario Book Initiative. We further acknowledge
the support of the Canada Council for the Arts and the
Ontario Arts Council for our publishing program.

Parts of this book were published in *Saturday Night*
in May 1998, under the title "Hair."

Typeset in Bembo by M&S, Toronto
Printed and bound in Canada

This book is printed on acid-free paper that is
100% recycled ancient-forest friendly (100 post-consumer recycled).

McClelland & Stewart Ltd.
The Canadian Publishers
481 University Avenue
Toronto, Ontario
M5G 2E9
www.mcclelland.com

1   2   3   4   5   07   06   05   04   03

For Archie Fineberg

Every memory is turned over and over again, every word, however chance, written in the heart in the hope that memory will fulfill itself, and become flesh.
— Marilynne Robinson, *Housekeeping*

CONTENTS

ACKNOWLEDGMENTS

I gratefully acknowledge the financial assistance provided by the Department of Canadian Heritage, by the Conseil des Arts et des Lettres Québec, and by the Canada Council.

This book could not have been written without the unstinting cooperation of my mother, Anna Kalman. My wholehearted gratitude goes to her for laying open her life before me and for giving me free rein to write about it as I saw fit. *Shoshanna's Story* is her book as much as mine.

I wish to thank Bryan Demchinsky, Donna Bailey Nurse, and Linda Schwartz for reading early versions of the manuscript and for their helpful comments. Michael Ignatieff and Don Obe, along with my fellow participants in the Creative Non-Fiction Program at the Banff Centre for the Arts in 1998, gave me excellent editorial advice on an early draft of Chapter 6. Marvin Orbach of the Vanier Library at Concordia University provided me with invaluable research support, as did the reference staff of the Eleanor London Library. Special thanks to John Rimmer of the Purley Library for sending me photographs by e-mail of Purley in the 1950s.

I am grateful to Daphne Hart, my agent, for her wise counsel; to Barbara Czarnecki for her meticulous copy-editing; and to Adrienne Guthrie for all-round helpfulness. By her own outstanding commitment and sensitivity to the subject matter of this book, Jan Walter, my editor, challenged me to produce the best I was capable of. I cannot thank her enough.

Finally, to Archie Fineberg, who kept abreast of the manuscript at every step of the way, and whose love and encouragement helped me to keep faith with it, I can only proffer the fullness of my own heart.

Elaine Kalman Naves
February 14, 2003

AUTHOR'S NOTE

Some names have been changed to protect the privacy of members of my family, but this is a true story, based on interviews with my mother, my late father, and members of our extended family, and on secondary research. However, it is my rendering of real events, my version of "the truth."

Out of consideration for English-speaking readers, I have taken liberties with the spellings of certain Hungarian names. Thus Iluska, Mariska, Nanus, Tuntus, and Menyus became Ilushka, Marishka, Nanush, Tuntush, and Menyush. Guszti became Gusti. Spelling of place names has not been altered. To remain authentic to the cultural references of my family, I have used spellings that reflect the old Ashkenazi pronunciation of Hebrew words. Thus *Shabbos* instead of Shabbat, *tzitzis* instead of tzitzit, *zmires* instead of zmirot.

one

ROSE

When we still lived in Budapest, before the Revolution, I once asked Shoshanna how a baby gets inside its mother's tummy. Shoshanna was leaning over the kitchen table, which had been covered with a crisp white sheet. She was tugging paper-thin dough over its floured surface. A small tear formed in a corner of the parchment-like pastry near the edge of the table. Shoshanna jerked her head back abruptly in annoyance. A white smudge marked her cheek, ruddy from the heat of the oven or perhaps from emotion.

"Don't ask me about this," she said. "When you're old enough, I will tell you all you need to know."

The next day it rained, and Shoshanna sang me her rainy-day song. The tune was from a musical version of *Cinderella* in which she had played the lead when she was twelve. It started out, "Oh, cream cakes are just so delicious."

A later line made tears trickle down my face every time Shoshanna sang it in her heart-rending soprano. Cinderella mourns the cream cakes she can't have because she has no Anyu or Apu to buy them for her. What a very terrible

1

thing, to have no Mummy or Daddy to bring you a cream puff when you so long for one. Shoshanna ended the rainy-day song and began to comb my hair for the third time that morning.

Shoshanna was an orphan and so was Gusti, if you thought about it carefully, though they weren't child orphans. My Anyu and Apu had met in an orphanage; he was forty and she twenty-seven. They didn't consider themselves orphans, only as having been orphaned.

How they had met was like this. Shoshanna and her sister Vera came back from the camps together. They returned straight to Hungary after the end of the war, to Budapest. Vera stayed with distant relatives who didn't treat her very well. Shoshanna travelled alone to the small town where they had been born. There she found the family home stripped of all its furniture; only a portrait of her sister Magda remained, and this she took with her, back to Budapest. Vera left Hungary soon after and eventually ended up far away in Canada. Shoshanna was able to get a job in an orphanage since she had been a teacher before the war.

One morning when Shoshanna was pouring kerosene on the heads of the orphans to get rid of the lice, Gusti came looking for her. He carried a message from a relative who lived in the country, in the same village where Gusti himself was an important man.

"Your brother-in-law has learned that you are here in Budapest, working in an orphanage," Gusti said to Shoshanna as he watched her emptying a keg onto the head of a small boy. "How can he sleep nights knowing his brother's widow has to live among strangers when he and his wife have a roof they can share with you?"

Yes, Shoshanna had lost her husband, who had disappeared in the war. Gusti too was alone; his wife and daughter had died.

After a little while the arrangements were made and Shoshanna left the orphanage with Gusti Weinberger. They travelled by truck to the village where her brother-in-law lived. Not long after that, Shoshanna and Gusti fell in love.

And that, Shoshanna concluded briskly, putting away the brush and comb, was all I needed to know about how I got into her tummy.

WHEN THE NURSES LAID ME in a bassinet by Shoshanna's bedside right after I was born, she couldn't take her eyes off me. Though it was midnight, she had them leave the lights fully blazing. She wasn't disturbing anyone else; hers was a private room in a private clinic, before everything was nationalized. Gusti still had money.

In the morning Gusti, wreathed in smiles, brought her tea roses. Roses in November! Out of a small velvet box emerged a surprise, a thick gold ring, with her initials in high relief. He slipped it onto her ring finger. He kissed her finger, then her mouth, and whispered against her neck about the wedding ring that would come later, as soon as such a thing was possible. He lifted me from the bassinet and wept for joy. "To think . . . ," he said. "To think I could have a child again."

Shoshanna and Gusti kept a diary of my every ingestion. They laid me on the scales before and after each nursing, subtracted the difference, and entered it in a ledger. "2.80 kilos at birth," wrote Gusti neatly in pencil; 2.70 kilos ten days later when they took me home. Net weight at the end of the month: 2.91 kilos. On this day Shoshanna inscribed in her slapdash scrawl, "1/4 grated apple + 5 mocha spoonsful lightly sugared orange juice once a day."

Blanka Néni, my pediatrician, paid us our first house call. We called her Blanka Néni instead of Doktor Kertész, it being the Hungarian custom to refer affectionately to any older person as "Aunt" or "Uncle," whether related or not. Shoshanna released me from the *pólya*, swaddling, on the dining room table and removed my tiny undershirt and diaper.

"Her legs are bowed," Shoshanna observed.

"Nonsense," retorted Blanka Néni, "all babies have bow legs. It's the way the fetus folds itself up in the womb. Actually..." Blanka Néni glanced at Shoshanna suggestively. "Actually, she has the shapeliest thighs I've ever seen on a baby girl."

"I'm not talking about her thighs," argued Shoshanna, who never ceded a point easily, "but her calves. They are so, too, bowed, Blanka Néni."

Shoshanna had the most beautiful legs in the world: long and firm calves, patrician ankles. Gusti called them the legs of a gazelle. In the camp where Blanka Néni and Shoshanna had first met, Shoshanna had taken first prize in a beauty contest. It wasn't a formal contest, just something the girls had invented to pass the time. There they were, about a hundred women, herded together in a cavernous hall with their bald heads and not a stitch of clothing among them. They had recently arrived, so they still had shapes. And they awarded each other "prizes" for best shoulders, best breasts, best buttocks. Shoshanna took the prize for best legs. Blanka Néni and her friend Hedy, another doctor, had been the judges.

Blanka Néni was stout and lumpish and wore mannish suits of tweed worsted. Her chin-length hair, pushed back behind fleshy, large-lobed ears, seemed shellacked in place. Though she was as Jewish as Shoshanna and Vera, in the camp Blanka Néni had had power and privileges on account of being a doctor. Nothing official, of course. To exercise them she had had to take risks.

Once, in the dinner line, Vera didn't take the bowl of soup that should have been her due. The soup had nothing in it, not even the carrot chunk that ought to have floated in its scummy broth. Vera reached instead for the bowl next in line. A guard plucked her out of the queue and beat her.

"Raw," Shoshanna told me. "Her buttocks were raw."

Shoshanna dragged Vera off to show her buttocks to Blanka Néni. Blanka Néni applied salve to them without a word. But afterwards it was whispered that Blanka Néni had let loose a torrent of invective at the camp commandant, no less. And would you believe, the commandant sent for the offending guard, chewed him out in front of Blanka Néni, and transferred him to another detail. But it could just as easily have gone the other way, Shoshanna said. Blanka Néni had been lucky. She had risked her life for Vera's buttocks.

Shoshanna looked up from her sewing. She was embroidering a smocked dress that Vera had sent me from Montreal. "Blanka Néni loved women, you know, but she was a plain good friend to me and Vera," she said. "That's why she's your doctor now."

AFTER TEN DAYS lying in at the *klinika*, Shoshanna brought me home to the apartment on Ó Utca, Ó Street, in the poorer Jewish district of Budapest, where she and Gusti were then living with his uncle and aunt, Jani Bácsi and Cirmi.

To Shoshanna's horror the bedbugs were back in droves. Before going into labour she had thoroughly fumigated her and Gusti's room with scouring powders and gasoline. But in her absence, the aunt and uncle, bitten and exhausted, had taken refuge in the former maid's room that the younger couple shared and into which a crib had recently been placed in anticipation of my birth. Jani Bácsi and Cirmi must have carried in the scourge with their own bedclothes.

Shoshanna and Gusti brought me home swaddled in Georgetta's *pólya*. Georgetta had been Jani Bácsi and Cirmi's only child. Had she lived, Georgetta would have been twenty years older than me. Her layette was still in mint condition: embroidered undershirts, starched bibs, little white nighties with lace trim, elaborate *pólyák*, all stored between layers of fine tissue paper. Shoshanna had only to buy new diapers for me.

Jani Bácsi was the only one of Gusti's father's siblings to have survived the war. He was a Budapest Jew, not a country Jew; that's why he and Cirmi had been spared. There had been no systematic deportations from Budapest, as there had been in the countryside. There was a ghetto, there were atrocities — at times in the last year of the war, Jewish blood had dyed the Danube crimson — but the chances of getting through it alive were far better in Budapest. Jani Bácsi and Cirmi had muddled through somehow. But eighteen-year-old Georgetta *elpusztult.* She perished.

Their high-ceilinged apartment was aromatic with pipe smoke, for Jani Bácsi was never without his pipe. There were two large rooms, one of which served as his office, and a narrow kitchen. A small square room off the kitchen was meant for the maid they no longer had. Here Shoshanna disobeyed her pediatrician's strictures about letting me cry. Blanka Néni had been very clear on the subject: feed her amply, make sure her diapers are clean, but don't pick her up until the next scheduled feed. No, not even if she howls for the duration: it's good for her lungs. But, Shoshanna reasoned, you couldn't let a baby howl at night in a household with other people. You couldn't let a baby disturb the slumbers of Jani Bácsi and Cirmi. She dared not bring me into bed with her and Gusti, lest the bedbugs attack me. She dared not rock me in the upholstered armchair, in case they had ensconced themselves there too. She sent Gusti to the kitchen for a hardback wooden chair. After she had fed me sitting bolt upright, she crawled back under the eiderdown and tried to sleep. But all she could think of was how to escape to a place of her own. A place free of bedbugs. And free of Jani Bácsi and Cirmi, whose pain over the loss of Georgetta seemed to have intensified with my arrival. Shoshanna felt she should hide her joy in me.

No one called Cirmi "Cirmi Néni." It was always "Jani Bácsi and Cirmi," because Cirmi was much younger than Jani Bácsi, who at that time was approaching sixty. They had met when he was an up-and-coming lawyer, short but dapper in his double-breasted suits, his dark hair slicked back from his hairline with its widow's peak, no hint of the out-sized hernia that would double him over a cane in his later years. Cirmi's past was a bit murky. Her first husband, it was said, had beaten her. She had a mother whom she called Muttika, but there was no father in the picture. One day in the early 1920s she had simply materialized in Jani Bácsi's office, a picture of elegance with her alligator shoes and matching purse. Tall, thin, and sinuous, she was gorgeous despite two oversized front teeth separated by a gap that in others would have been unsightly but in Cirmi merely added to her allure.

Jani Bácsi counselled her through her divorce. Some months later she came to see him again, seeking advice. What did he think of such-and-such a person, who had asked for her hand in marriage? Jani Bácsi got up from behind his desk and bent over the hand in question. Surely, he said, kissing it, she didn't think he had helped part her from her husband in order that she might marry someone other than himself? Cirmi took this for the proposal it was meant to be.

Georgetta was an exceptionally pretty child with bee-stung lips and deep, dark brown eyes. Jani Bácsi and Cirmi spoiled her shamelessly. They actually placed her potty on the gleaming dining room table. This was in their Szécheny Utca apartment beside the Danube, not on down-at-the-heels Ó Utca, where they lived when I was born. Jani Bácsi was still practising law then, before he took it into his head, egged on by Cirmi, that though you could make a decent living from the law, you would get rich only in business.

Georgetta grew from being a spoiled, pretty child into a beautiful, headstrong girl. There was a boyfriend. He may have been Jewish, but perhaps he was not. She met him during the German occupation. Her parents pleaded with her not to go out nights to see him, but she wasn't in the habit of listening to her parents. She was wilful, she was wild, she broke curfew regularly. One night she simply did not come home. *Elpusztult.* Perished.

Once when Shoshanna returned to Ó Utca after taking me in the carriage for a quick walk, Jani Bácsi and Cirmi came into our room as Shoshanna was removing my clothes, Georgetta's clothes. They wept over me in the crib and invoked the memory of Georgetta, whom they said I resembled. Shoshanna didn't know what to say, so she said the first thing that popped into her head. "You must forget Georgetta. Why torment yourselves?"

She meant to be helpful. She herself was trying very hard to forget, to live in the present that, even with its manifold hardships and inconveniences, offered her such rich blessings. But the two old people – for suddenly Cirmi, too, looked old, her hair all at once more grey than black, her face haggard, the protuberant teeth catching her lower lip in a rictus of sorrow – stared at her for an instant in disbelief. Then as if by prearrangement their hands met and they backed out of the room together.

That night when she lifted me from the crib for a feeding, Shoshanna began to shriek. It was teeming with bedbugs.

IN 1947, THE APARTMENT SHORTAGE was still acute in Budapest, which is why we were living in a cramped maid's room near the Dohány Utca synagogue. But, after the bedbug scene, Gusti finalized the transaction that saw us move to our own place on Róna Utca, with singular haste.

The Róna Utca apartment had many advantages. It was in the suburbs, in the fresh, cleaner air of the fourteenth district, not far from the spacious park called the Liget, an ideal place to wheel a baby in a carriage. ("You may take her out on even the coldest days," Blanka Néni instructed, "but not if it's windy.") It was close to the grocery store on Thököly Út that my father had purchased in partnership with Zoli Bácsi, his one surviving uncle on his mother's side. That made it possible for Shoshanna, after she had hired a girl to look after me and the house, to run down to the store for a couple of hours a day, to sit at the cash and keep an eye on things. And it afforded privacy. Finally Shoshanna could follow Blanka Néni's child-rearing rules to the letter.

That Blanka Néni was an excellent pediatrician was supported by the fact that what she asked of parents was so difficult to follow. Her advice went against the grain and therefore must surely promote sound health.

Shoshanna and Gusti lay in the dark in the new apartment, which was large enough to accommodate matching sofa beds along opposite walls of the living room. Their eyes were wide open, their muscles tensed, their eardrums vibrating.

"Go and feed her, *please*," Gusti begged.

"Blanka Néni says only once every four hours."

"But she's hungry."

"No, she isn't. Last night when I went to check her diaper, she stopped as soon as I picked her up."

"So then *I'll* go pick her up."

"*No*, Gusti! Blanka Néni says it's good for her lungs."

I hollered in the crib six feet away, near the warmth of the tile stove. When Shoshanna, worn out by sleeplessness and frustration, finally came to fetch me, she uttered a familiar shriek, higher-pitched than my own. That same oily stench, the crib once again alive with the brown-red plague. The bedbugs had migrated in it from Ó Utca to Róna Utca.

Nanush was called in. Nanush was the senior of Gusti's three surviving aunts. She was a brick, a real auntie, someone to depend on. Shoshanna summoned Nanush in tears and told her that she would jump out of her skin if she saw another bedbug.

Nanush was a squat little woman with slightly bowed legs and an air of immense competence. She took the crib apart, slat by slat, in a matter of minutes. She hauled the washtub down from the attic and carried it to the kitchen, the way the washerwoman did on laundry day. She fed the oven with firewood and boiled vats of water in the largest of our cauldrons. First she placed the slats in the washtub and poured boiling water on them not once, not twice, but three times. Then she repeated the procedure with the crib mattress. That was the end of the bedbugs.

Nanush had a habit of taking charge in a crisis. She had been the voice of reason at my birth, too, the only person who had kept her head, according to Shoshanna.

Gusti had a previous model for birthing. To him birth was a hideous process made up of equal parts blood, suffering, and unbearable noise. Above all, it was about unaccountable waiting. His first little girl, Évike, had come into the world after no less than ten months of gestation. He was fully prepared for me to do the same.

Shoshanna had woken up to labour pains at five in the morning at Jani Bácsi and Cirmi's on November 9, some ten days before I was due. Gusti tried to hide his agitation by timing the contractions, at first ten minutes apart, then seven, then five. Cirmi, elegant and slinky in a grey silk peignoir even in the morning, knocked discreetly on their door at ten. This was a reversal of custom in itself; usually it was Shoshanna who called on Cirmi to say that the café au lait was ready.

With the exception of Georgetta, Cirmi had never looked after anyone. Not only did she not know how to cook, she almost didn't know how to eat. She could digest nothing but the finest foodstuffs; cream cakes for breakfast if they were to be had, otherwise nothing. And nothing but the freshest and choicest of any comestible. When Shoshanna served a cauliflower soup twice in a row, Cirmi declined. She simply gagged at the sight of leftovers.

Impractical as she was, Cirmi sized up the situation in the maid's room swiftly. "It's time," she said to Gusti, who argued feebly that it was ten days early and that Évike had taken ten full months to arrive.

"It's time," Cirmi repeated, and she fetched Jani Bácsi to speak to the concierge about a cab. Cirmi was above speaking to the concierge herself.

The *klinika* was on Szoby Utca, only minutes away by car. Shoshanna had no sooner arrived than her waters burst with a rush on the *klinika* floor. Doktor Vágó was called. But then, before he could get there, the pains stopped. By noon Shoshanna was back at Ó Utca. She and Gusti walked home, with Gusti's protective arm around her. He assured her that it would be another six weeks at least before I made my appearance. "My children," he joked, grateful for the temporary reprieve, "are cautious types, like their father. Never in a great hurry."

Shoshanna heated the bean soup she had made the day before and tucked in. In fine appetite after the morning's travail, she put away the large goose drumstick Nanush had brought her the day before. And then, overcome with sleepiness, she lay down for a nap. She woke with a jolt at four in the afternoon with her belly alive with pain.

Gusti wouldn't hear of returning to the *klinika*. "I've been a laughing stock before," he said. "In 1938 for a full month Mancika and I moved into Debrecen from the country, waiting for Évike to choose her moment. And waited and waited and waited, till the whole town was snickering at me."

Shoshanna stood in the large room of Jani Bácsi and Cirmi's apartment, her back to the warmth of the ████. "It hurts," sh██ ████ ████ ██ ████ ██ ████ ██ Gusti that Ma█ ████ ████ ████ ████ ████ ████, had howled, i█ ████ ████ ████ ████ ████ ████, and noble co█ ████ ████ ████ ████ ████ ████iled, so Gusti ████ ████ ████ ████ ████ ████ 'like a pig bein█ ████ ████ ████ ████ ████ █r by temperam██ ████ ████ ████ ████ ████ ████

Nanush█ ████ ████ ████ ████ ████ ██ery afternoon ████ ████ ████ ████ ████ ████on towards supper, which she usually stayed for. She took one look at Shoshanna and asked, "Why is she here?" Gusti explained the situation and made a quip about that morning's "false labour."

"Nonsense," said Nanush. "She lost her waters. The *klinika* had no business sending her home. Look at how she's suffering. For a cautious man, Gustikám, you're being quite irresponsible."

So the taxi was called again. Nanush went along, as did Jani Bácsi, though it wasn't clear whether they were there to lend support to Shoshanna, who was biting her lips but was otherwise calm in the front seat, or to Gusti, whose hands shook uncontrollably as he mopped his brow with an out-sized handkerchief in the back.

The physician on duty, an older man in white, examined Shoshanna. "It hurts, does it, my dear young woman? It's going to have to hurt a lot more, I'm afraid. You're not opening up much yet. Sister will take you to your room. Walk around as much as you can. A first baby takes its own sweet time."

Pronouncing herself satisfied with the course of things, Nanush departed, leaving Gusti in Jani Bácsi's charge. They sat down in Shoshanna's room while she walked in circles in front of them, stopping her perambulations as each contraction hit and clutching either the bedstead or Jani Bácsi's hand for its duration. Sister came by to give her a pill. "This will make the pains better, sweetie." By this Shoshanna understood that her pain would ease, but no: by "better," Sister had meant stronger. It seemed the pills were designed to intensify the waves of pain into one solid wall, without the slightest respite.

She couldn't walk around any more and sank down on the bed. Gusti began to cry softly. Shoshanna lost her temper. "Jani Bácsi," she said, "take him away, please! Go home, Gusti, so I can suffer properly." She needed to scream but wasn't about to do so in front of him. She had resolved to best Mancika in childbirth: here was one chink she had been able to intuit in her predecessor's armour. Now the urge to cry out was elemental, and Gusti mustn't hear her.

Gusti left in tears, but he couldn't stay away. He came back a couple of hours later at ten, composed, though his eyes were red. Doktor Vágó arrived, a well-built, extraordinarily good-looking man who had been recommended to Shoshanna by Cirmi. (Any man Cirmi recommended was invariably handsome and was almost certainly a former or current lover.)

"My good woman," he said, "I want you to push that baby out now."

Shoshanna stared at him. She had almost forgotten that this was about a baby.

"You look as if you need help. I'm going to help you get that baby out."

Shoshanna felt an instant of profound gratitude, then a clamp descended on her belly as the doctor's hands fastened onto her. "Push," Vágó ordered. She tried to push against the vise of pain that was immobilizing her. The doctor seemed to be lying on top of her, pressing on her belly so hard that she felt as if her soul were being ripped out along with her innards.

"Push!" Vágó commanded and repeated the manoeuvre, bearing down on her abdomen with his whole weight.

Shoshanna screamed. "Don't you dare do that to me again! Kill me before you do that again!"

Someone placed a mask over her face. Then she heard a baby crying. "What time is it?" she asked, thinking hours had gone by and it must be morning. "Almost midnight." Vágó smiled down at her. "Your daughter is a night baby. It's still November 9."

"Where is she?" Shoshanna demanded, completely restored to strength and impatience. "Give her to me."

She began to grill the doctor. Was the baby all right? Did she have all her fingers and toes? She wasn't going to be lame, was she? On the street where Shoshanna had grown up, there had been three lame girls. Was he hiding the baby from her now because of some defect?

"My good woman," Vágó said, his voice rough, as he continued to stitch her up carefully, "that child has everything possible that a female could have after crawling out of her mother. The one thing she's missing is what all women lack, and she'll get that in due course when she's twenty."

Shoshanna fell into an outraged silence.

SHOSHANNA BENT OVER ME, untying the rags in my tautly wound hair. "I hope I can disguise the bald spot," she murmured as she combed out my locks. In the mirror, my reflection was so fetching I could barely recognize myself. Fluffy curls framed my chubby face, but Shoshanna remained unsatisfied. She heated a curling iron on the stove till it was red hot. She wet the ends of my hair slightly so they sizzled at the iron's touch.

Parting my hair at the centre, Shoshanna tied white

silk ribbons on either side of the part. She pulled the smocked white dress from Vera out of the wardrobe, took out brand new knee socks, and laced up my freshly polished two-tone boots.

At the studio, the photographer asked Shoshanna to remove my dress and undershirt. He was a young man who made funny faces at me, and when I didn't laugh, he took a feather duster and touched it to my bare shoulder. That photograph would depict me with an adorable dimple, my tongue between my teeth, head screwed coquettishly around my shoulder. The other picture that Shoshanna sent to Vera had me posed in a low chair, the white dress hoisted high to show my panties. My legs were crossed and a large picture book rested on my knees. I gazed at the page, serious and absorbed.

"The photographer posed her so as to disguise the extent to which her legs are bowed," Shoshanna wrote to Vera. Her letters catalogued my many illnesses and visits to orthopaedic specialists who, though they found no fault with the shape of my legs, diagnosed flat feet, for which the treatment was customized arch supports. I sat with my feet in wet clay, ribbons of gauze wound up to my knees. Plaster moulds were taken, exercises prescribed. All this and more Shoshanna wrote to Vera who, when she finally met me in person, expected to greet a cripple.

I LAY ON THE SOFA for my afternoon nap, right thumb in mouth, a clump of my hair twirled around my index finger. Surreptitiously my left hand slid down the back of the sofa and surfaced with more precious treasure: a secreted hair ball that I transferred to my right fist. The rough canvas back of the sofa was upholstered with additional tufts of hair.

Shoshanna threatened to have my hair shaved off if I didn't stop pulling it out by the handful. I glowered and said nothing. When the booty behind the sofa lost its delicious softness, I somehow obtained a fresh supply. Pulling the strands never hurt. Handling them gave an inexpressible comfort.

Above my head in the landscape on the wall, the sheep grazed beneath the benevolent eye of a mustachioed shepherd, staff in hand. On the opposite wall hung a portrait of Mancika holding Évike on her lap. I closed my eyes and twirled the hair ball beneath my nose.

When I awoke, I headed downstairs to play, first asking Shoshanna to lift me up so I could touch the mezuzah on the front doorpost, then bring my fingers to my lips as Gusti had shown me to. Shoshanna obliged but without enthusiasm.

Downstairs, my friends were sweaty and hoarse from running around. I tagged along as they headed for the Catholic church, a favourite hangout for catching our breath. The boys in the group doffed their caps in the vaulted doorway. Following their example I shucked off my kerchief. I dabbed droplets of holy water from the font onto my forehead like the others and inhaled the sweetish scent of mystery compounded of old wood and incense and must. In the chapel I crossed myself and knelt. I feasted my eyes on the play of sun through the stained glass. The blood-flecked statues and the crucified, sinewy Christ both repelled and fascinated me.

Back upstairs Shoshanna confronted me at the front door. "I watched you from the window, missy. Since when does one kiss the mezuzah and then head off to church?"

"I can't believe it," she said, as she prepared supper and tempted me with sugared tomato slices. "I can't believe that the namesake of my sister Magda would go into church after kissing the mezuzah." My middle name is Magda, my first is Ilona, and I am nicknamed Ilushka.

"Your Aunt Magda was a remarkable woman," she continued, slicing off small pieces of *kolbász* and placing them almost out of my reach. She smiled to herself as I reached for a piece, thinking I didn't notice her ploy.

Magda Néni's portrait hung in the narrow room where we ate our meals when Gusti was away on business. Shoshanna continued her monologue below Magda's smiling face during supper. "Magda was beautiful. I had a reputation for being a beauty, too, but I didn't even come close to her. Her hair was gold and her eyes green as a cat's. The artist really hasn't caught the refinement of her features, nor the flawless quality of her skin. And she was devout, too."

I slurped my cocoa noisily and punched holes in the bread with my finger till Shoshanna noticed and got mad at me for playing with food.

WHEN I CAME DOWN with whooping cough, the city lay under a thick pile of snow. Blanka Néni nonetheless upheld the view that fresh air is the only treatment for whooping cough. So, despite the bitter January cold, Shoshanna and I set out like summer day trippers. We climbed Gellért Hegy all the way to the monument at the peak. We went to the zoo. We visited Margit Sziget, the isle in the middle of the Danube.

On the island we followed the most exposed paths along the shoreline, for Blanka Néni had decreed that wind in particular is beneficial for whooping cough. When I coughed, the cold air entered my lungs with the sure thrust of a blade. Shoshanna stopped at a small promontory and tried to distract me from a bout of wheezing by pointing to a spot in the distance, a bay in the slate-coloured river. The orphanage used to be there, she pointed out, the orphanage where she first met Gusti.

Absently she said, "If my parents had lived, I would have waited."

"Waited for what?" I gasped.

"Waited longer to see if Márton would come back."

"Who's Márton?"

"No one . . . I just wouldn't have taken up in such haste with your father. If my parents had lived."

"Why not?"

Shoshanna didn't answer, didn't tell me how I came to be born. Instead she told me how she acquired the name Shoshanna. Her real name is Anna, but since that day on the island I have always thought of my mother as Shoshanna, the Hebrew word for rose. That's what the orphans called her. The orphans whose hair was thick with lice. The orphans who sobbed in the night and whom she comforted. They thought the name Shoshanna suited her because she reminded them of a vivid red rose. Shoshanna was a fitting name for a passionate, raven-haired pioneer who dreamed of going to Palestine. That's what she would have done if she hadn't met Gusti. She would have gone to build a new country with her orphans.

She wouldn't have had me.

two

DEMITASSES

My birth was the fulfillment of the seemingly impossible dreams of both my parents.

Immediately after the war, when she was working at the orphanage, my mother almost bled to death. In the camps, a powder had been added to the bread of female inmates to suppress their periods. Shoshanna didn't menstruate for more than a year. When she suddenly hemorrhaged one morning at the orphanage, the doctor wouldn't allow her to get out of bed for a week. He told her she would never be able to have children. She didn't tell Gusti. She didn't tell anyone. She refused to believe it.

There were days when Gusti's nerve failed him. His round face seemed pinched, his full square lips set sternly. On those days, he wondered out loud if, after all that he had been through, he was permitted to love a vibrant young woman like Shoshanna. Or, more disturbing, he declared that, having been married to a woman the calibre of Mancika, he didn't know if he could ever fully love anyone else again.

Shoshanna not only felt chilled in her heart by these doubts, she experienced them as profoundly unjust.

But then all such resentful and heavy thoughts could be dispelled in an instant. They'd be walking along a street in town, and Gusti would spot a child, and take Shoshanna's hand in his, and smile his full-faced, cherubic smile and say to her that the thought that he might once again have a child filled him with a joy akin to what God must have felt at the beginning of time.

When her pregnancy began to show, at four and a half months, Shoshanna couldn't work at the orphanage any more. It was then that Gusti, in partnership with his uncle Zoli Bácsi, bought a grocery store on Thököly Út. Shoshanna had some savings, too. No matter how straitened her circumstances, she always managed to put a little aside, and she gave the money to Gusti for the business.

The summer of 1947 was a time of such hope, such promise. In two years Hungary had transformed itself. When Shoshanna came back from Germany in the summer of '45, the mode of travel was, as it had been on the way out of the country, a cattle car or an open freight wagon. Liberation notwithstanding, the voyage was fraught with danger almost equal to the earlier one, at times requiring young women to fling themselves off moving trains to escape the slant-eyed Russians, reincarnations of Genghis Khan, bent upon rape. In the capital, if you could lay your hands on bread, it was almost certainly made of crumbly yellow corn flour and inedible. If you managed to get yourself a job, table salt was the currency of your wages.

But two years later the country was humming with energy. Though the Soviet army was omnipresent, the Communist Party had not yet established its stranglehold on power and the country was governed by a coalition. Minions of the Russians, Hungarian Communists made reassuring pledges of full democracy and free commerce. In the countryside, peasants had been given land to till and, believing they would be allowed to keep it, actually harnessed themselves to plows to produce bumper crops. At election time, posters proclaimed, "The Communist Party Defends the Property of the People." In Budapest even luxury items were available by this time, and a well-stocked delicatessen on Thököly Út, near the embassy district, held real promise. All the attachés – Italians, English, Americans – would shop there; so would ordinary Hungarians who lived in the blocks of large flats nearby.

In his former life Gusti had been a gentleman farmer, used to farming from the seat of a carriage, not atop a tractor. He had worked a huge estate with a large overhead and extensive staff. He was accustomed to doing things on a grand scale, and only the choicest merchandise sat on the shelves of his grocery store: fine bottles of Tokaj wine, crisp rolls in wire baskets, cheeses, cold cuts. It went without saying that Gusti paid high wages to his employees: how could he do otherwise, since they were all family? He hired Cirmi's cousin Marishka to be store manager, and Zoli Bácsi and Marishka took turns rising early to go to the farmer's market to buy fresh produce and perishables. Gusti never meddled with that – he managed the books and the credit, labelled merchandise, oversaw deliveries. Yes, there was a delivery boy and a shop's assistant; sometimes Zoli Bácsi's daughter came in as well to sit at the cash.

Gusti waited on customers with exquisite manners and fussy precision. Once, the janitor of the building next door, a fat woman with frizzy, luridly yellow hair, took Shoshanna aside while Gusti carefully wrapped her cheese slices, making neat corners in the wax paper and tying the package beautifully with best-quality string.

"My good woman, tell me," the janitor lady asked Shoshanna loudly, "is your husband this slow in bed, too?"

Cirmi occasionally swept in, wearing a long muslin scarf wound around her head turban style, her wispy grey bangs peeking out in the front, the ends of the scarf trailing fetchingly down her back. "Friendship, comrades!" she'd declare, using the greeting of the Social Democrats. Cirmi had, after the war, unaccountably turned into a Soc-Dem. She and Gusti got into heated discussions about the upcoming elections. Gusti said the Soc-Dems were the thin edge of the wedge; they'd be eaten up by the Communists in no time. If she wanted to be on the side of the winners, she'd vote for the Smallholders, like him. Yes, of course, he too wanted a better, more equitable world, but you couldn't trust the Communists an inch, and besides, Zoltán Tildy, the leader of the Smallholders, was a decent man, one of a handful of decent politicians in the country.

At night, he'd say to Shoshanna that Cirmi had taken leave of her senses, that she was losing her mind in her grief; a more unlikely socialist than her, with her penchant for cream cakes, couldn't be found in Hungary. Shoshanna would respond that while he had been arguing politics with Cirmi, the cash had gone seriously short.

Soon it wouldn't matter that they were losing on the store, that Zoli Bácsi, hardly a soul of probity in his former life, would skim off profits in the new enterprise, that money regularly disappeared from the cash. A year later there would be no private property, the peasants would have to give back the precious land, and the store was nationalized, when Hungary became the satrapy of Stalin's Hungarian imitators. Having been a man of property in the former life now meant you couldn't get a job — any job at all — without *protekció*, the patronage of someone in cahoots with the new regime. And if you couldn't get a job, your wife and child wouldn't eat. They would be better off without you and the burden of your propertied past.

In the nights during this time, Gusti sometimes whispered he would do away with himself. He would do Shoshanna and the baby the favour of exiting from their lives.

WHEN I WAS about three months old, in February 1948, rumours concerning the return of Hungarian prisoners of war from Russia were revived. The deputy prime minister made a speech promising their repatriation in the coming year. At around the same time, Shoshanna's older brother, Iszku, who lived in Palestine, wrote to her, cautioning her not to build her life on the burned-out hulk of a ruined ship. He was referring to Gusti, of course. He thought she should try again with Márton.

Márton Weinberger (what curious act of fate had bequeathed the identical surname to the two – unrelated – men in her life?) was thirty-five to her twenty-eight at this time. They had married and lived together as man and wife for just eight days before he was called up and sent to the Russian front in the summer of 1942. She had not seen him in six years. When she first took up with Gusti, she had not known Márton was alive in Russia. But when she received news of him, and then heard from him, some time in '46, she didn't send Gusti packing. It wasn't that she'd stopped loving Márton; she thought she did love him. But she couldn't even picture his features in her mind's eye. Gusti, on the other hand, was right in front of her. She needed someone beside her, she needed someone in the flesh. And then she got pregnant.

She couldn't bear to tell Márton any of this in the twice-monthly postcards she sent him. Her notes became increasingly rote and tepid. She knew that his brother was also writing to him. She expected that his family had thoroughly blackened her name. She couldn't fault them for it.

She dreaded Márton's return, yet she longed for it too. It would bring some kind of clarity. She was curious about him. He had been a very good-looking man. Short and fair, not like her previous beaux; not at all her type, she would have said, until he began courting her. Memories of her wedding night flooded back whenever the repatriation rumours surfaced. As she read the headlines about prisoners of war, her breath quickened imperceptibly, her eyelids snapped down like shutters, her knees wobbled. He had left his stamp on her.

Márton arrived back on Hungarian soil in June 1948. His next card – addressed to "Mrs. Márton Weinberger" and forwarded to her from the orphanage – while terse, still expressed hope. "Dearest Anna, I have arrived from prison camp. I shall reach Debrecen in a matter of days. I would like you to meet me in Debrecen. Otherwise write about the settlement of all pending matters. I am well and healthy and kiss you, Márton."

Another card, six days later, carried the return address of his home village and was addressed to her care of Mr. Gusztáv Weinberger, Greengrocer, on Thököly Út. He had clearly been briefed on the state of affairs by his brother in the village. "Dear Anna, I hope it has come to your atten- tion that I have returned from prison camp. With view to the dissolution of our marriage, please submit the necessary documents to your lawyer and kindly notify me of his name. Upon receipt of this information, I too will advise you of my legal representative. After a short rest here, I will take up a position in Budapest. I kiss you, Márton."

Their first meeting was in the lobby of a hotel in Budapest. The last time she had seen him, he had been in the fatigues of a Jewish labour serviceman attached to the Hungarian army, and now he was in uniform again, a Hungarian colonel's, crisp khaki and high, gleaming boots. He didn't look as if he had been through a bad time, he looked wonderful. His face was weathered into fresh seams, it's true, but the bronze of his tan made his fair hair sparkle, his blue eyes even more intense. They drank her in with a wariness that didn't disguise his hunger. They embraced, kissed cheeks. He and Gusti shook hands, after just a flicker of hesitation. They had met during a bout of labour service early in the war; Márton had been Gusti's squadron commander, something of a hero in one particularly fraught action. Gusti admired him, which made the present situation both excruciating and yet somehow congenial.

Jani Bácsi was introduced as Shoshanna's counsel, and Cirmi stepped forward, her scarf tails fluttering. "Friendship, comrade," she trilled coquettishly, waving away the obligatory hand kiss as a form of bourgeois indulgence, soliciting instead a more informal greeting from him since, after all, they were practically family. Márton looked momentarily taken aback, then, recovering quickly, planted a single peck on her cheek.

There was a quality of homecoming about the occasion. They asked if he had suffered much in Russia. He replied, looking only at Shoshanna, that compared with what others had been through, he did not feel entitled to complain. He had spent a lot of time in the labour camp office, doing political work. He hoped that they realized that whatever religious rigamarole was required for the divorce, he'd only go through it if he didn't have to swear on any Bible. He had become a member of the Party in the Soviet Union; was it Marx or Lenin who'd said that religion was the opiate of the masses?

"It was Marx," Gusti observed dryly. And no, Márton wouldn't be obliged to swear on anything. Old promises would be dissolved, not new ones made.

Jani Bácsi broke in, defusing the brittleness of this exchange by explaining that the whole divorce process would be handled expeditiously since it was taking place by mutual consent. There would be a hearing at the courthouse, followed by another at the Jewish congregational offices. Then, for bureaucratic reasons, the child would briefly have to be declared illegitimate. Since Shoshanna had been married to Márton at the time of Ilushka's birth, technically Márton was Ilushka's father. Later the child would be declared Gusti's and legitimized.

Márton asked if he could have a moment alone with Shoshanna. Gusti, Jani Bácsi, and Cirmi trooped out, Gusti casting worried glances over his shoulder. Shoshanna studied the dregs in her demitasse. They had been sitting in a small alcove around a coffee table. She and Gusti had occupied one loveseat, Jani Bácsi and Cirmi the other, with Márton in an armchair to the side. He now moved over and took the seat next to her. "Look at me," he said.

Shoshanna raised her eyes from her lap where they had been intently scrutinizing the floral print of her summer dress.

"The child is legally mine. You have my utter assurance that if you come back to me, I will raise her as my own. I will never reproach you for anything. I still love you regardless of everything."

Márton's future, Gusti's, her daughter's, not to mention her own, all rested with her at that moment.

She shook her head slightly. "I can't."

"Tell me just one thing. When did the two of you become man and wife?"

She thought for a second. "About two years ago."

"So I would have had to come back two whole years ago, for this not to have happened?"

Shoshanna sat there thinking. When should he have come back to prevent this from happening? When she first met Gusti in the fall of 1945? When they had begun sleeping together in June of 1946?

"Ilushka was born on the night of November 9 last year. Count back nine months from that. That's when you should have come back. Before I fell pregnant."

They were both weeping by this time and continued weeping when they left the lobby together.

They met one more time a year and a half later. He was still in uniform, looking as if born for command. The red star on his hat, the hammer-and-sickle pin in his lapel didn't bother her. Nor the fact that he had become an atheist. You had to move with the times, compromise some beliefs if need be, something Gusti seemed unwilling to do.

Gusti didn't come with her for the divorce ceremony, he was minding the store. It was a mellow October day, but for some reason the windows of the congregational offices on Sip Utca were shuttered, and a dismal murkiness permeated the stuffy room. The rabbi was hunched over his desk in shirtsleeves, his black jacket flung over the back of his chair. The ends of his *tzitzis* flapped against his dark pants as he stood up when she entered with Jani Bácsi. The room smelled fusty from the books that lined all four walls and were piled up in little off-kilter heaps at the base of the shelves. At a small side table there dozed a man in a black suit and square black skullcap and thin, wispy beard: the scribe. The *shammus* and Márton were engaged in conversation in a corner of the room, waiting. She heard the beadle suck in his breath at the sight of her. "How can you divorce such a beautiful woman?" he whispered loudly to Márton.

She knew she was beautiful. Her sister Vera, who had left Hungary for Israel in the spring but had got off the train in Paris and stayed there, had sent her the camel hair suit she was wearing. The dressmaker had taken it in slightly so that it accentuated Shoshanna's every curve. Her black hair tumbled in shiny waves to her shoulders, contrasting dramatically with the pale gold of the wool jacket.

The rabbi motioned to her and to Márton to sit in the two chairs in front of his desk. "It is my solemn duty to ask you if there is any chance you may be reconciled. What do you say, Mrs. Weinberger?"

"It is impossible," Shoshanna said in a clear voice.

"And you, Mr. Weinberger?"

"Likewise."

"Then I will ask the scribe to write out the *get*."

They sat in interminable silence as the scribe scratched away with his nib, chanting under his breath the incomprehensible words in Aramaic. When he was done, the rabbi took the pages from him and began to translate.

"This is the gist of it, Mr. Weinberger, this is what you're effectively saying to your wife: 'Thus I set free and release you, put you aside, in order that you may have permission and authority over yourself to go and marry any man you may desire. No person may hinder you from this day onward, and you are permitted to every man. This shall be for you from me a bill of dismissal, a letter of release, and a document of freedom, in accordance with the laws of Moses and Israel.'

"Mrs. Weinberger, Mr. Weinberger, I asked you both before we started if your minds were made up. I cannot but notice that both of you are crying. It is still not too late to change your minds . . . No? Then we will proceed."

The rabbi motioned to the *shammus* and to Jani Bácsi to come forward to witness the document. When they had signed, he began folding the parchment in an elaborate manner – the way you would a *béles*, Shoshanna thought, opposite ends of the pastry towards the centre to make a neat pouch. He took a pair of scissors out of a drawer and neatly snipped off the four corners. Then he motioned her to rise.

"Now," he said, "you must place it in your armpit."

"My armpit?" Shoshanna exclaimed.

"And you must walk away. Take twelve steps away to the far corner of the room. Your husband has given you the *get*, and once you receive it in the intimacy of your body and walk away, you are a free woman."

Shoshanna felt herself flushing. It was a warmer day than she had realized, a little too warm for a wool suit. Beneath it she had on a silk blouse. She had begun to sweat. Through the fabric of the suit, the *get* would be imprinted with the fluids of her body. Would it smell of sweat when she handed it back to the rabbi?

She knew Márton was setting her free, but she didn't feel free. In this roomful of men, she had been marked out, branded. She was being sent away. No one had reproached her by a word, but as she took the obligatory steps with the wad of paper wedged in her armpit, she felt not only downcast but outcast.

And then it was over. She and Márton stood on the Körút, the Ring Boulevard, having said goodbye to Jani Bácsi. They were both waiting for the Number 6 tram, heading in opposite directions. "I've met somebody," Márton said.

"So soon?"

He let that go. "Her name is Zsuzsanna. She is lovely but very young."

"How young?"

"Seventeen."

"But that's less than half your age, Márton! I don't think that's very wise."

He picked his words carefully. "Do you think anything worse can happen to me than has already happened? I have no hard feelings against you, Anna, but I don't want you to take me to task, either. Or to give me advice."

I WAS THE GLUE that held my parents together. On Sunday mornings I clambered over the sides of my crib near the foot of their beds and scampered over their sleeping bodies, burrowing between them. On Sunday mornings they were invariably to be found together in Shoshanna's bed. I was the glue that bound them, but as I insinuated myself into the folds of their sleeping embrace, I was also the wedge that pushed them apart.

I was sick often with the usual childhood diseases: chicken pox, measles, whooping cough, scarlet fever. But it was my first attack of tonsillitis that terrified Shoshanna the most. It was winter and we slept in the living room, because the apartment was too large to heat fully. In the middle of the night I woke them with my whimpering.

I had known how to walk for months but was now crawling around the crib like a listless puppy trying to chase its tail. Shoshanna put her hand to my cheek: it felt fiery. Little tufts of hair were plastered in damp clots to my forehead, my lips were cracked. I gazed apathetically at Shoshanna, then lit on the objects in the china cabinet, the crystal and silver knick-knacks dancing inside in the sudden light.

"This baby doesn't look normal," Shoshanna cried. "Look at her, Gusti, she looks vacant. Oh, God, her eyes are crossed."

"No, no," Gusti said, standing beside her in his white night shirt. "You've dazed her with the lights."

Panic rose like a geyser within Shoshanna. Not even in the bombing raids in the German *Lager*, when she had been lifted off her feet and then pitched back to earth, spread-eagled, her mouth full of soil and debris, had she felt like this. What would happen to her if the baby died?

"Go get something from the pharmacy," she ordered Gusti, steadying herself with a plan. "Go get something fast."

"What, right now?" Gusti said stupidly. "It's two o'clock in the morning, I can't disturb the pharmacist."

"Disturb him?" Shoshanna shrieked against her constricted throat. "You're worried about disturbing a pharmacist when your child is in this state? Look at her, for God's sake – she's a helpless little creature, a little crazed animal."

Pointing her finger at me, Shoshanna looked beyond the crib to the large table covered with a Persian carpet throw on which a silver tray held two cups with the remains of coffee from earlier in the evening.

"She's fading before your eyes and you're worried about the pharmacist?"

In a rage, she bounded towards the table and grabbed the tray. For an instant she held it aloft, adopting a heroic pose like a statue from classical antiquity. Something in Gusti's gaze deflected her from pitching the tray at his head, perhaps a vestige of dignity even in his absurd garb, his nightshirt baring ropy veined legs at mid-calf. She let her arms fall back to her side.

The tray crashed amid a tinkling of china and silver. The demitasse cups, cobalt blue with a rim of gold, shattered, splashing coffee onto the golden parquet.

I began to cry in a thin, powerless wail.

THE NEED TO DIVORCE Márton was not the only obstacle to my parents' marriage. My father could not legally marry until Mancika had been declared officially dead. By law, five years had to elapse from the time she was swallowed by fate. Her death certificate was issued on December 14, 1949; two days later my parents were married in a civil ceremony.

My birth certificate registered me as my father's daughter, Ilona Kálmán. Friends in the know had advised him that the regime frowned on people with Jewish names. Though reluctant to give up his Weinberger identity, once he'd hit on the idea of adopting his father's given name – Kálmán – he made his peace with the change. Shortly after, a dear college friend who had joined the Party and become influential provided him with the requisite *protekció* that landed him a job as an inspector of state farms with the National Cattlebreeding Trust.

During the show trials of the early 1950s Márton was purged from the Party and sacked from the army. He and his wife fled Hungary during the first days of the Revolution of 1956 and found their way to Chile, where he became a wealthy lumber merchant.

Cirmi died of syphilis before the Revolution. No one ever told me she was dead – children had to be shielded from the sorrows of the present, if not of the past – until we were living in Canada and I asked why the letters that my father read out loud from Jani Bácsi made no mention of her. After we left Budapest, Jani Bácsi spent his days at the Zéman coffee house, sucking on his pipe and making one espresso last the whole morning, and a second one the afternoon. When he died sometime in the early '60s, there were three uncashed cheques in his desk drawer in the $50 amounts that my father sent him every month from Montreal. He may have starved to death.

My parents counted the beginning of their marriage not from the date of the civil ceremony that united them in 1949, but from the day in June 1946 when they first made love together. Their union lasted forty-four years and was marked by loyalty rather than understanding, devotion more than sympathy. When, in their later years, they stung and bit each other with bitter words, my mother would frequently lash out in frustration, "We're just like Jani Bácsi and Cirmi!"

I had never been aware that Jani Bácsi and Cirmi had bickered; either I was too little or I hadn't been around them enough to notice. Nor would I have thought to compare the two couples, although my father in old age certainly resembled his uncle in appearance, both of them bald, bespectacled, large-nosed. But my mother tended to believe in the existence of a previously written script. She seemed to think that traits as well as events repeated themselves, that people's lives somehow fell into patterns established by earlier blueprints. Like Cirmi she was a flamboyant and beautiful woman married to an older man. Both of them had been divorced; Jani Bácsi had arranged both divorces. In the lives of each couple there had been a dead child.

But their paths diverged there. My mother wasn't the sort to take lovers. She and my father were prudent and thrifty, not profligate like Jani Bácsi and Cirmi. And yet she saw some similarity. It was with an air of defeat, not her usual needling or belittlement of Gusti, that she declared, "We fight like Jani Bácsi and Cirmi. When we lived with them, I vowed I'd never sink to that."

When she made the occasional reference to Márton over the years, Shoshanna suggested that she would like to have a chance to talk over things with him again. She transmitted this desire to me. Like Shoshanna, I entertained the fancy of one day sitting down with him on a loveseat and speculating about what might have been between us. He had offered to bring me up. I wanted to thank him.

Had he come to Montreal, I would have served him an espresso out of the remaining pieces of the blue and gold demitasse set that adorn my china cabinet.

three

SHAME

"D'you know where babies come from?" Attila Takácsos asked. Attila lived one floor below us.

Our address was easy to remember: Róna Utca 232, Second Floor, Apartment 2. If I ever got separated from Shoshanna, I would be able to recite it *okosan*, cleverly, to a policeman or good stranger. I mustn't talk to bad strangers, but then again if I ever got lost or separated from Shoshanna, it would be necessary to speak to someone so I could find her again. Knowing the address was important.

"Yes, of course," I flung over my shoulder at Attila, throwing the pebble in the chalk-marked square on the sidewalk. I wished he would go away. I was perfecting my hopscotch game and didn't want him catching me out if the pebble landed on a line instead of in the square. I didn't trust Attila. He had tricked me before, more than once.

It wasn't that long ago that he'd gotten me in trouble with Shoshanna. Not big trouble, not *Intézet* trouble, but trouble enough. The kind of trouble in which the words *hülyeség* and *marhaság* might figure. Shoshanna never said that I was a *hülye* or a *marha*, she said my behaviour was *hülyeség* or *marhaság*. Idiocy. Stupidity. *Hülyeség* and *marhaság* were not the same as badness. Being *rossz*, bad, was the worst of all.

Mouthing these words out loud to get to know their distinctions wasn't such a good idea either. They must never be aimed at Shoshanna. Gusti said I had to love Shoshanna, always, because she was my mother, and no one else in the world loves a child as much as her mother. Yes, even though Shoshanna was allowed to say these words to me. That was because I belonged to Shoshanna, and she loved me that much.

"So if you know, tell me," Attila said to my back as I straddled the twin boxes in the middle of the hopscotch court.

It would be best not to answer Attila. I had been awfully silly, really *bolond*, to be frightened by what he had said the last time. That had been when I was still scared to come downstairs alone, before I knew the rules for hopscotch or how to draw on the sidewalk with chalk. Shoshanna had walked down the staircase with me, then told me to stay in the sunshine where she could keep an eye on me from the kitchen window. Two storeys up. Two whole flights of stairs.

There wasn't anything to do in the sunshine. Shoshanna had promised to come down later with my tin bucket and take me to the park. But first she needed to study her Russian grammar in peace for a while. I was to amuse myself.

Attila appeared from behind the bushes that separated the yard of our house from the one next door.

"Your mother's dead," he said.

"She isn't. She's upstairs."

"Your mother's dead," he repeated flatly.

I tilted my head back and searched for the rectangle of the kitchen window high up on the second floor. The sun shone so bright the glass gleamed black against the yellow-ish stucco.

"Anyu," I shouted, "Anyu, where are you?"

"You see?" Attila said, "she's dead. And you know what happens to children whose mothers are dead."

I knew, but not precisely. A dead mother was Mancika Néni, whose pictures were in the living room. Her little girl was dead, so maybe that's what happened if your mother died. But there were orphanages, too, for the children of dead mothers. And then there was the *Intézet*.

"Anyu," I shrieked, "are you dead?"

Shoshanna's face appeared in the rectangle. Her hair was tied back with a kerchief. Leaning forward, she peered out.

"Dear God, what ever do you want?"

"Attila said something bad happened to you."

"Ilushka, don't be *bolond*. I'm up here studying my Russian. Attila, stop this *hülyeség* and leave Ilushka alone."

Shoshanna disappeared from sight.

I sat down on the step at the doorway to the apartment. The ridges in the stone felt rough against the backs of my thighs. I hugged my flowered skirt around my knees and scrunched forward. When would Shoshanna come with my bucket to take me to the park?

Attila sat down beside me on the step.

"Your mother's dead."

"She isn't! I just saw her."

"She is so. *Meg-halt.*"

Terror gripped me. It was true that I had just seen her. But something might have happened to her in the meantime. Attila might have ways of knowing. I stood up and tried to open the front door. The metal latch wouldn't yield.

"Anyu! Anyu!" I shrieked again, not caring that I was crying in front of Attila or that my nose was running the way his always seemed to do. I just wanted Shoshanna to come to the window. "Attila says you're dead!"

That was the kind of trouble I could get into by talking to Attila. And now he was pestering me about babies.

It was self-evident where babies came from. They came from their mummies' tummies. Shoshanna's tummy was very fat and inside was the baby I had been begging for ever since I could remember. She had always said, No, one child is plenty. But now there was a baby, under the brown chequered dress that was tightening around her middle day by day. A baby girl, I kept on telling her.

"They come from their mothers' stomachs," I said to Attila, as I pivoted on the double boxes at the top of the court, stood on one leg, and aimed the pebble at the first square.

"*Jézus, Mária és József, te marha!* How stupid can you be? Everybody knows that! But how do they get in there?"

I put the other foot down. This question had not occurred to me until this instant. Couldn't something start by itself? Grow on its own?

Attila planted himself in front of me and blocked me from jumping again. In spite of being a year younger, he was the same height as me. His older brothers picked on him and called him a snot-nosed bastard. He had light brown hair that fell over his forehead in jagged swatches. One of his eyes, which were also brown, wandered towards the bridge of his nose with troubling regularity.

"What d'you think? You spit on a wall and a baby grows in your stomach?"

I pictured a great gob of spit against the wall of the dining room.

"No," I said uncertainly.

"That's right, no." Attila moved his face so close to mine that I could smell his stale breath. A narrow crust of green caked one of his nostrils. His malevolent eye floated inward. "The father takes his thing and puts it in the mother's thing and they rub themselves together up and down, up and down, up and down, that's how."

"That's not true!"

"They do it in the toilet standing against the door. And sometimes in bed in the dark."

Tall, quiet, silver-haired Takácsos Bácsi in his grey suit rounding the stairs, a leather briefcase tucked under his arm? And Takácsos Néni in her apron, forever scolding Attila's twin brothers?

It couldn't be true. Not my parents, not Gusti and Shoshanna. Not to make me, or the baby in Shoshanna's tummy. Which had better be a girl.

"Anyu," I said to Shoshanna upstairs, "how does a baby get inside its mother's tummy?"

"Don't ask me about this," Shoshanna said, her hands coming to rest on the mound of her belly. "When you're old enough, I will tell you all you need to know."

I was almost six. I was old enough to know about lots of things. How to handle the grown-up silverware whose high ridges around Mancika Néni's initials imprinted themselves in my palms when I clutched them in my fists. (The baby spoon and fork had been put away for the baby.) How to wipe my own behind. Who the dead children were in the photographs in my room. Évike, who had been Gusti and Mancika Néni's child, was the one with the straight hair. Marika, who had been my Uncle Pali's little girl, was the one with the ringlets.

IT WAS FALL, so I was sleeping in my own room. At this time of year, the air in it was fragrant with the scent of apples. Shoshanna and I had shopped for them at the market and brought them home in a horse-drawn cart. The market was a busy place, crowded. I had to hold Shoshanna's hand tight. She had me recite our address. Slowly, clearly, *okosan*, like a clever child, so I could be understood by someone who didn't know me. In a place like that, if we weren't careful, we might be separated from each other.

At home, I watched Shoshanna in the kitchen as she cut newspapers in squares with scissors, then wrapped the red *Kanadai Jonatán* apples in newsprint. On the weekend, when Gusti was home from his business travels, he'd climb up on a chair and place them on top of the long wardrobe in my room for storage the winter long. That's where other photos of Évike and Marika were kept. As he arranged the apples he'd pick up the frames and dust them off, before tenderly replacing them. In one picture the children wore white rabbit coats, hats, and muffs, and were giggling at each other in the snow. In the other it was summer and they were in short skirts.

I liked sleeping in the summer room. The balcony opened from it, and the large picture window gave light late into the evening. The bathroom was also off my room. Before the baby started growing in Shoshanna's tummy, I used to bathe with her all the time. Gusti hauled in coal from the shed at the side of the house, then made a fire in the bathroom boiler. He brought in fresh towels so they would warm as the bathroom heated up.

Shoshanna was already in the tub when Gusti brought the towels, which was strange. Girls and boys weren't supposed to show their bodies to each other, Shoshanna had told me. Once I had been very *rossz* because Shoshanna found me lying naked in the small room off the kitchen while Gyuri from next door examined me. He was playing the doctor that time and had his ear to my chest. That was never to happen again. But of course Gusti was my Apu and it was all right that he helped me out of my clothes, and towelled me off after my bath, and dressed me in pyjamas. Shoshanna didn't mind that. I was glad she didn't, because I loved it when he tickled me and carried me all bundled up to bed, and sang a special tuneless song he had composed for just this ritual.

If boys and girls weren't supposed to show each other their bodies, why was it all right for Gusti to come into the bathroom when Shoshanna was in the bathtub? Still it couldn't be true. Not my parents. It was impossible.

And why did Shoshanna say, "When you're old enough"? Why didn't she think I was old enough already?

SHOSHANNA HAD BEGUN to pin her hopes for having a normal child on the fetus within her. It was increasingly evident that either Blanka Néni's rules for bringing up children were wrong-headed or I was. At almost six, and despite being toilet trained at one, I was still regularly wetting my bed. No matter that Shoshanna didn't allow me to drink anything after six in the evening, that she woke me before retiring for the night and took me to the toilet, that she even roused herself from sleep to take me once more. All that Shoshanna had accomplished by these stratagems – undertaken at Blanka Néni's express instructions – was to disrupt her own sleeping patterns and wake up every morning with jittery nerves. And yes, in the morning, there was the inevitable reek of urine, wet pyjamas, and a soaked mattress. Shoshanna decided that she would devise her own methods of rearing the next baby.

This baby, like all of her pregnancies, had not been planned. Although she had always meant to have babies galore – she remembered wanting six when she was a girl – not one of her pregnancies had been intended. Me – well, I had been a special case.

I had been a mistake, like the others, but a clarifying one. I made her mind up for her: until she became pregnant, Shoshanna's head had buzzed perpetually. Márton, Gusti, Gusti, Márton. She had walked along the streets seeing double: she beheld, coming towards her, her husband in the fatigues he had worn when she said goodbye to him in '42. And beside him she saw Gusti in his white summer knicker-bockers, as he was in '46, a portly figure, thinning on top, his moon face alight at the sight of her. She would go to the movies and the male lead was a chameleon that in one frame wore wire spectacles over a jutting nose like Gusti's, and in the next had gold curls and dancing blue eyes like Márton's.

Her pregnancy with me had resolved that double vision in the streets, that split screen at the theatre. I had deter-mined the future for Shoshanna and I was a miracle for both her and Gusti: for her, the child she feared she might never be able to carry; for him, a message from above that the vast cataclysm hadn't annulled the precious forward thrust of life. It was just that I didn't act like a miracle. I cried when I was supposed to sleep, wet the bed when I was meant to stay dry, tore my hair in the pattern of a tonsure, talked back in front of company. Lately, Shoshanna had concluded, her child's behaviour had become truly bizarre.

When I started to toddle, Blanka Néni had decreed, "Put away the nighties, it's time for pyjamas. Make sure that her hands are on the counterpane when you put her to sleep. And when you check on her at night, replace them on the coverlet. Hands always above the covers!"

All this Shoshanna had done. Night after night, she chastely placed and then replaced my fingers on a counter-pane adorned with white satin-stitched hearts enclosing Mancika's initials. But what was the point of doing that now, when, at the age of six, I sat in bed, bedclothes and pyjama bottoms flung aside, legs bent at the knees like a frog, with my head sunk between them, as I contemplated my genitals while chanting a little rhyme: "*Rózsa, rózsa, te vagy az én rózsám.*" Shoshanna could not bring herself to tell Blanka Néni about this. How to describe the scene, the child singing an ode to her private parts, calling them a rose? And not stopping, not allowing herself to be distracted, when Shoshanna came into the room?

Shoshanna didn't know what to do. Blanka Néni had not prescribed a rule for this. Blanka Néni had not told her what to say when the child asked about conception, either. And come to think of it, this preoccupation with the rose began after the child had asked about babies, after Shoshanna's pregnancy became visible.

The earliest intimation of this pregnancy – her fourth – came in the spring of 1953, even before she missed her first period. A travelling carnival had pitched its tent in the fields behind the house. The three of us had gone with all the other neighbours for a little diversion, but once I had exhausted the possibilities of the merry-go-round, I began to campaign for the Ferris wheel. Gusti urged Shoshanna to go up with me. The big hero, Shoshanna muttered to herself; he has no intention of being whirled in the sky. But she had allowed herself to be persuaded even though from childhood she had been afraid of heights. Once we were cranked up on high, it turned out that I had no more taste for altitude than she did. I began to blubber that I wanted down. There was no getting off, though. Twirling gently, the cars climbed and descended their allotted time and course while Shoshanna tried to pacify me and to quell rising waves of nausea in herself. When we touched ground, Shoshanna was barely unbuckled before she began retching bile with the peculiar vehemence she recognized from previous pregnancies.

These were alarming times to bring any child into the world, let alone a Jewish child. It was only a few months since a political war of nerves had been unleashed by the Doctors' Plot in Moscow. Nine prominent physicians were arrested and charged with poisoning leading government and party officials. The doctors, at least six of whom were Jews, were also accused of being spies for the British and American governments and of serving the interests of international Jewry. Zealously following suit, Hungary purged its Communist Party of a number of prominent Jewish members. One of those taken into custody was a cousin of Gusti's who, anticipating the outcome of his interrogation, leaped to his death – or was he pushed? – from his seventh-floor holding cell.

A climate of such fear reigned that Gusti panicked and destroyed his secret affidavit. Immediately after the war, a cousin in New York had sent him a guarantee of sponsorship should he decide to come to America. That precious document had been his clandestine insurance policy. Tucked away in his tallis bag was the hope of life remade in America should things become impossible in Hungary. But in the atmosphere of paranoia generated by the Doctors' Plot, he deemed that discovery of the affidavit might cost him his life, and he shredded it into tiny strips before flushing it down the toilet.

In the meantime – the Almighty be praised – Stalin had croaked. But this was still no time to consider more children. Who knew when the Russians, as anti-Semitic under

Communism as ever, would change their minds again? Who knew when Hungarian Nazis reborn as Communists would rap at the door of a former landowner, a former *Jewish* landowner?

The trouble was that Shoshanna and Gusti seemed fated to procreate. A year after me, there was a pregnancy that Doktor Vágó terminated in his office – without anaesthetic, since abortions were illegal. The pain had been so severe that when, a few months later, she fell pregnant again, Shoshanna decided to have the baby rather than face a second abortion. By the time she miscarried, she had got used to the idea of another child, was looking forward to it, and so was sorry to lose it in the end. Blanka Néni had not helped matters, scolding her roundly for daring to iron when she was four months gone. Ironing was heavy work; Shoshanna should have known better. But Shoshanna didn't think it had to do with ironing. Vágó must have tampered with her during that excruciating abortion; he may very well have done her permanent damage. That's what had gone wrong.

In the spring of '53, there was no possibility of being sentimental about a baby. Both she and Gusti were desperate to find a doctor who would abort her. None could be found. This was one of those periodic moments when producing children was a comradely obligation in the Soviet Union. Hungary fell into line, too. The child in Shoshanna's womb was therefore another sort of miracle, as much the result of thirty-year jail sentences for performing abortions as of some slip-up during a tired act of love. Shoshanna resigned herself to carrying the child to term. And in the process she became secretly happy.

She communed with the baby within, promising not to heed Blanka Néni on every count. She vowed to have no more babies, even if it meant forgoing sex forever. No more pessaries that made her insides feel as if they were about to fall out. No more coitus that was never interrupted soon enough. She would indulge herself with this child. She wouldn't let it cry for hours. She would do what felt right, even if that meant spoiling it. Let Blanka Néni go hang.

Maybe then this child wouldn't grow into another Ilushka. Shoshanna couldn't understand how such a beautiful baby could have become such a trying little girl. Always demanding: why, at the market, after Shoshanna had bought me peaches and apricots and pretzels and corn on the cob wrapped in tissue, I had demanded some coal when we passed by a pile of the stuff. And had clamoured the length of the walk home at not getting my way. Finally we arrived at the phone booth in front of the Közért grocery on Erzsébet Királyné Utja and Shoshanna, enraged and at her wits' end, had ducked in and pretended to call the *Intézet*.

Shoshanna's threatening references to the Institute for Bad Children always had a sobering effect on me. If I was whining or defiant, mention of this figment of Shoshanna's beleaguered imagination would elicit immediate tears of contrition. If I was hollering and mulish returning from the market, it would make me fall gratifyingly silent in mid-sob. For a clever child, I was remarkably credulous. Not only did I have a wholehearted conviction of the existence of the *Intézet*, I believed in Shoshanna's telepathic power to summon its agents. There was no telephone at home with which to call forth the *Intézet*'s lackeys. Still, all Shoshanna had to do to win instant compliance was to lift one hand to her ear, while miming the act of dialling with the other.

I suffered from other surprising shortcomings. Not only did I refuse to be good, I didn't seem to understand what being good meant. Gusti's friend Vili, whom we had visited *en famille* recently, had been so exasperated when I repeatedly tore up and down his apartment emitting war whoops that he had made a great show of removing his belt to beat me. To which – cheeky child – I had responded boldly that my Apu and Anyu never hit me and wouldn't let anyone else do so either. Then on the trip home, when a seat became vacant on the tram, I had slid into it with a sly glance at Shoshanna. Gusti had bent over and whispered something about giving up my seat for my mother. I had simply turned my head away to look out the window, fixing my gaze on the illuminated embankment, the Danube swimming with the reflection of street lights and the Lánchíd, the Chain Bridge, looming over the river, while Shoshanna stood with her quickening belly and aching legs, remembering how much she had once wanted to be a mother.

But the most astonishing thing after all this was that when they had put me to bed that night and bent over to kiss me, I had actually asked, "And was I a good girl tonight?" Because of course I had been instructed by both Gusti and Shoshanna, but especially by Gusti who had a habit of begging me, to behave myself when we went to Vili Bácsi's. I had no idea of how awful I had been.

THE VISIT TO VILI was about the pregnancy. My parents had already canvassed everyone else. Even Gusti's crazy aunts,

Bóba and Bazsa, who couldn't be counted on to think straight on an ordinary day, let alone in a crisis, had been consulted. No one had a good word to say about it: not Nanush, whom Shoshanna adored most of the time, not Nanush's daughter Ibolya, who was living with us temporarily just then, nor Gusti's college chums László and Zsiga. The only person who had given a nod of encouragement had been Gusti's tailor, Mozart, a man in his early thirties, a good fifteen years younger than Gusti, who treated him with the exaggerated respect due someone of venerable age.

Shoshanna didn't know what had possessed Gusti to discuss such a private matter with Mozart when he went for a fitting for a new suit. But Mozart had responded with complete candour as he draped the dark grey worsted across Gusti's shoulders. "Gusti Bácsi," he had said through pins dangerously held in the corner of his mouth, "I look at it this way. I'm only passing this way once. I'm not about to change my plans. The wife and I have always wanted to have three kids. We have two sweet little fellows now, and we're hoping for a girl one day. Well, I'm not about to do anything to stop a baby from coming along. It makes no difference to me what the penalty for abortions happens to be, nor what the leadership of the Soviet Union has up their sleeves for us. I have a life plan, and I'm sticking to it."

Which was an unusual slant on the current situation, and not as disheartening.

Gusti took courage from what Mozart said. To think of it, the wisdom of a young man, when everyone else had oozed pessimism. Here he was, nearly forty-eight, the age his grandfathers had been when he was born, with a young wife, a young child, a skimpy income, and ever-present uncertainty, about to become a father for the third time. But the baby was coming, along with the winter. He had to take action. He must try to acquire more coal, more firewood, in case the winter was especially severe. January was absolutely the worst time of year to have a baby, but that was the time this child had picked. With a newborn in the house – perhaps a boy? – to be without heat would be almost as bad as being without food.

Food wasn't usually a problem, but with Nanush and Ibolya staying with us and Ibolya's fiancé János taking his meals with us as well, things were tight. But Gusti couldn't say no to them, even though he knew Shoshanna was tired from the pregnancy and worn down by an annoying little girl. With him away in the country, did she need his relatives on top of her head? No, she didn't, as she had tartly pointed out. But Ibolya had fallen in love with János, a Budapest historian, and so had asked for a transfer from the University of Debrecen, where she taught, to the University of Budapest. Shoshanna surely didn't want to stand in the way of true love, he asked smilingly as he chucked her under the chin. Surely she hadn't forgotten how Jani Bácsi and Cirmi had once helped them out of a similar predicament? Nanush and Ibolya would soon find an apartment of their own, he was certain of it. Until then they would live with us, even though that meant heating the balcony room, demanding more firewood and extra coal. And anyway, it was reassuring to have them there for Shoshanna in her condition, since he was obliged to be travelling so much of the time.

"ISN'T IT TIME for Ilushka to be in bed?" Ibolya asked Shoshanna.

We were sitting around the dining room table, sipping coffee, while Nanush cleared the dishes. Ibolya and János were chain-smoking. I was fiddling with one of the remaining forks on the table. I bore down on the tines with my fingers so the handle bounced up like a seesaw.

"*Ilushka*," Ibolya and János exclaimed in unison, "stop that."

Shoshanna felt harried. I never went to bed early; I still napped in the afternoon. She needed me to nap in order to get through her own day. Shoshanna studied Russian grammar while I slept, preparing for a some-day career as a translator.

"I really think," Ibolya repeated, "that it's time for that child to be in bed."

Shoshanna was torn. Had she and I been on our own, she would have let me stay up. But she supposed that Ibolya and János had a right to have some time to themselves in the evening without a pesky child bothering them.

"Come on, Ilushka," Shoshanna said.

"I don't want to."

"Come on, I said. Let's go make pee-pee."

"No."

"Ilushka," Ibolya said, "be a good girl and go to bed already."

"I don't want to."

Nanush came in from the kitchen.

"Ilushka," she said, "come with Nanush. Nanush'll get you ready for bed and tell you a story."

Shoshanna took the heaped ashtray to the kitchen, rinsed it out, and returned it to the table. Ibolya and János were holding hands, quite oblivious to her comings and goings. Nanush returned, a smile on her seamed face.

"Thank you, Nanush," Shoshanna said.

"You know how I dote on that child," Nanush answered.

Shoshanna went to say her own good nights and to find her Russian grammar. Maybe she could study a bit more before collapsing into bed.

I was standing up in the crib. "I'm thirsty," I said in the dark.

"Not now," Shoshanna whispered as she touched her lips to my forehead and smoothed back the hair. "You'll wet in the night if you drink."

"But I'm thirsty."

"All right," Shoshanna said, giving in easily. The child felt warm, she might really be thirsty. "I'll get you some water."

She had to walk through the dining room to get to the kitchen. Appalled, she noticed that Ibolya had brought out shoe polish and was blackening her boots at the dining table. Fatigue, rather than politeness, made Shoshanna swallow her objections. She continued through to the kitchen, then came back with the glass in hand. János said, "I thought you didn't give her water so she'd stay dry at night."

"She's thirsty," Shoshanna said curtly.

"Really, you ought to be more consistent with that child," Ibolya said. "It's no wonder she can't behave."

I took two sips of water in the dark, then said, "I'm not tired. I want to come out."

Shoshanna snapped by reflex, "If you don't behave your-self, I'll call the *Intézet*!"

"You're not a good Anyu! Mancika Néni was a good Anyu! I wish she was my mother, not you."

Shoshanna's hand moved — it seemed to her — of its own volition, catching me full force across the face. I let go of the glass. Water cascaded down Shoshanna's leg. Dazed, she bent down to pick up the empty glass from the soaked carpet. "Don't you ever dare say that to me again!" she hissed.

"No," I said meekly, and lay down without being told.

Shoshanna tossed and turned the whole night long but was so upset that she didn't rouse me for the toilet. She was astonished to find my bed bone dry in the morning. Horrified, she noted the red welts on my cheeks. But I was in good spirits that whole day, and the next. I behaved like a model child. And I continued to stay dry night after night.

Gusti worked Mondays through Saturdays, inspecting the state's network of collective farms. Shoshanna expected him home that Saturday, as always, without knowing precisely which train he would catch or his exact time of arrival. But she had an uncanny ability to recognize his footsteps. Even up on the second floor, she knew the moment he entered Number 232. She always stood waiting for him by the open door when he rounded the second flight of stairs.

But on this Saturday, for the first time since late summer, she slipped downstairs to wait for him while I napped. Pacing up and down in front of the house in her thin lace-up ankle boots with the open toes, she avoided the patches of black ice on the pavement and clasped her arms about the coat that no longer fastened around her girth. When she sighted him turning the corner from Erzsébet Királyné Utja, she began to run lumberingly towards him. He too broke into a shambling run, fearing some calamity.

Long before reaching him, Shoshanna began to cry. "I hit her," she sobbed. "I'm sorry, I hit her!"

THE CURTAINS WERE TIGHTLY DRAWN in the living room as I woke woozily from my nap. They were bending over me, Anyu and Apu, one on either side of the crib. Apu reached through the slats and touched my left cheek.

"Why?" he said reproachfully to Shoshanna who just stood there, not speaking. With her drooping shoulders, big belly, brown maternity dress, and distraught expression, she looked crushed.

"Anyu hit me," I said, in a clear, fluting voice, aware both of telling the truth and of being satisfyingly at the centre of the universe at that moment. "Because I was very bad. But I haven't wet the bed for three nights in a row."

I continued to stay dry, even after Apu went back to the country and Nanush, Ibolya, and János found a new place to live. They were supposed to look in on us regularly, Apu said, because soon Anyu would be going to have the baby in the hospital, and if it wasn't on a Saturday or Sunday, he wouldn't be home and might not be able to get back to us on time from the country. Nanush or Ibolya would stay with me, if he wasn't here. Would I promise to be good?

"I promise," I said, "if the baby is a girl."

But Nanush and Ibolya never came. It was snowing on the night that Shoshanna said she had to go to the hospital. Nanush and Ibolya hadn't been to see us for two whole weeks.

Shoshanna went down to the first floor and knocked on Takácsos Néni's door. Both Takácsos Néni and Petőfi Néni, who lived across the hallway from her, came out onto the landing. They all congregated upstairs in our dining room. Then Takácsos Néni ran back down to tell Árpád, her oldest son, to fetch Ágnes Néni, our cleaning lady. Everybody kept smiling at me and saying I'd soon have a baby brother or sister.

"A sister!" I shouted, but Shoshanna shot me a quelling glance. "A baby girl," I repeated, modulating my voice somewhat. The Takácsos twins had been dispatched to look for a taxi on Erzsébet Királyné Utja but came back saying there were none because of the snow. Ágnes Néni arrived and said if Shoshanna didn't intend to have the baby at home, she'd better get herself to the hospital somehow.

There was a whispered consultation between Takácsos Néni, Petőfi Néni, and Ágnes Néni. Shoshanna was asked how she felt. Shoshanna said that she had been told when she was giving birth to me that walking was always a good idea. Takácsos Néni and Petőfi Néni went downstairs. Shoshanna was ready by the time they returned a few minutes later, bundled up in their coats and hats. Shoshanna tied a big scarf around her middle to hold her coat together. Petőfi Néni, the huskier of the two neighbour ladies, picked up Shoshanna's suitcase and they headed for the door.

"Ilushka," Shoshanna said, "be good. Do as Ágnes Néni says. I will be home soon with a baby brother or sister."

"I won't let you in unless it's a sister."

The two women flanked Shoshanna. She linked her arms through theirs and walked out the door.

Because of the snowstorm, Gusti didn't get home until the weekend. My sister was born on the Wednesday before. Children weren't allowed in the hospital, but Ágnes Néni snuck me in using a service entrance, so I saw Juditka even before my father did. Later on I would hear my mother say she was doubly disappointed: not only was the baby not a boy, but she wasn't instantly beautiful. She was covered in a kind of cheesy lather, Shoshanna said, her face red, her nose flattened. "If she was going to be plain, why couldn't she at least be a boy?"

"We are here to see the Kálmán baby," Ágnes Néni said to Sister in the nursery. With her iron-grey hair braided tightly around her head and her ramrod back, Ágnes Néni had a no-nonsense demeanour. Sister must have recognized her mettle, because she didn't tell us to go back where we came from, children weren't allowed to visit. Her starched skirts rustled as she turned on her heel and from some mysterious region beyond what was visible in the narrow glassed-in corridor with its polished linoleum and disinfectant smell, she came back with a bundle in her arms.

The baby was swaddled tight in a cream blanket, only her face uncovered. Sister held her up for me on the other side of the glass, cradling her against the ample bib of her uniform. There was a shock of hair above a ruddy little face and, as Ágnes Néni and I gaped in awed silence, the little head rolled to the side a bit and the eyes opened a crack. A tiny red tongue lolled out of the side of the baby's mouth and raised a few bubbles of spit, as if in greeting.

"Oh," I said, enchanted, "she likes me."

When Gusti came home that Saturday, he went straight to the hospital. Afterwards he didn't return to work for two weeks. When it was time, he brought Shoshanna and the baby home. They slept, just the two of them, in the little room off the kitchen, which could be kept cozy warm. There was a couch for Anyu against the wall, and a carriage beside her for Juditka.

I had never seen my Apu angry before and though he didn't carry on like Shoshanna, I knew that he was upset because of the way his lips were drawn tight when he questioned Shoshanna about Nanush and Ibolya. Shoshanna was lying on the couch, propped up on an elbow in her nightie and bed jacket, the baby under the eiderdown next to her. Gusti sat in the armchair, peeling an apple for me the way I liked, using his penknife with the mother-of-pearl handle. The rind unspooled in one long unbroken ribbon, one side the colour of white apple flesh, the other a deep *Kanadai Jonatán* red.

"But are you sure," he kept on asking her, "they didn't leave a message with someone? Perhaps they couldn't come on account of the snow?"

"They didn't come before the snow either," Shoshanna said shortly. "They didn't come and they didn't send word."

Later that day Gusti and I walked down Róna Utca to the telephone booth in front of the Közért on Erzsébet Királyné Utja. Gusti dialled and asked for Nanush. We waited a while until their neighbour lady fetched her and then he began to speak. I was surprised that he didn't sound mad. "Fine," he said. "Yes, Anna is fine. Yes. Ilushka is very well. Yes, we have enough wood. How about you?"

"Tell her about Juditka!" I said impatiently at his knee. Gusti's gloved hand closed gently over my mouth.

"Come tomorrow," he said. "I'm home on Sunday."

The next day we waited for Nanush. Apu made a big fire in the tile stove in the living room, and he let me help him wheel Juditka ceremoniously from the small room through the dining room, to the far corner of the living room, tucked away. Nanush mustn't be told when she arrived at the door. It was a surprise.

When Nanush rang the doorbell, I couldn't stop dancing around and whooping with excitement. She thought it was because I was happy to see her. I was, but I was most happy about Juditka and the fine surprise Nanush would have. Nanush took off her coat and kerchief and we hung them up in the wardrobe in the hall. Then Apu took her by one arm, and I held her free hand. And like that we walked into the living room.

Shoshanna was reclining on Gusti's sofa under the photograph of Mancika Néni, her hand resting on the carriage handle. Its hood was pulled down and the baby, wrapped in her *pólya*, lay on her back, asleep.

Nanush stopped in her tracks when we reached the pedestal table. She let go of Apu's arm and my hand, and clutched the table for support. Her big hazel eyes, magnified by the glasses, took in everything at once.

"When?" she whispered.

"Two weeks ago," Gusti said sternly.

Nanush bent over the carriage a long time. When her face emerged, it was wet. I had never seen a grown-up cry before.

"Gustikám, why ever didn't you notify me?"

"Nanushkám," Gusti said, "I am deeply disappointed. Not to look in on Anna, not to call, after all that she has done for you and yours. *Szégyeld magad.* Shame on you."

I stood transfixed. The idea that *Nanush* could have been bad, deserving of some kind of reproach – punishment even – was startling. And so too was her response. Shoulders heaving, she headed with unsteady gait for Shoshanna on the couch. At first my mother stiffened when Nanush reached for her, but after hesitating for a moment, she pulled the old woman towards her in an awkward yet enveloping embrace.

four

AUNTIES

"This is quite beyond my powers, Nanushkám," Gusti said. "I simply can't do anything about it. She's just going to have to face the music."

"But, Gustikám, we can't let her go to jail!" Nanush wailed. "We can't sit idly by without intervening."

Nanush had come to visit, yet she wasn't playing with me. More disappointing, she hadn't brought me a present. She and Apu were sitting at the big dining room table, both of them agitated and raising their voices. Shoshanna was in the kitchen, preparing Nanush's favourite snack, toast rubbed with goose fat and garlic, and tea with rum – a medicinal treat for non-specific ailments. I was squatting under the table, untying the laces of Nanush's black oxfords. The shoes shone and smelled of polish, though the leather was cracked and wrinkled all over, a bit like the network of thin, purple veins I could just make out on Nanush's legs through the lisle stockings, artfully darned with beige silk.

Bazsa Néni had got herself into trouble. Again.

Bazsa Néni was my middle great-auntie, born between Nanush and Bóba, all three of them sisters of my father's dead mother. Bazsa Néni lived in Debrecen, which is where she'd run into difficulty, selling something she shouldn't have been selling, a matter I need not bother myself about.

"If she only knew what she was doing!" Gusti growled, bringing his fist down on the table so the china rattled above my head. "Or at least had the sense to deny it, when questioned!"

"She is ill, Gustikám, how often must I repeat this for everyone?" Nanush sniffled. "Some are afflicted with TB, some with diabetes. The two of them have this. And just as we once looked after the ones who had TB and diabetes, now Bazsa and Bóba have to be looked after in their affliction."

I didn't know how Bóba Néni had suddenly found her way into the story, nor what "affliction" meant. Maybe whatever it was accounted for the fact that I didn't feel the same way about the other two great-aunties as I did about Nanush.

"But she's broken the law and been sentenced," Gusti retorted. "What on earth do you expect me to do?"

"She's your aunt. She's my sister! She can't go to jail like a common criminal, along with common criminals."

"She was caught selling on the black market." Shoshanna sailed in and deposited the tray with the toast on the table. It smelled interesting enough for me to crawl out from underneath.

"Hush – the child," Nanush said warningly, reaching out her arms towards me and smiling a glimmer of a smile as she pulled me into her arms. "Now, what have you done with my shoes, you clever girl?" She broke out laughing, her hair tickling my neck as she held me close. "If she hasn't tied my shoes together! And how is it no one told me you'd learned to tie bows since the last time I was here?"

NO ONE TALKED ABOUT the black market in front of me, but it wouldn't have mattered if they had, as I didn't understand any of it. The market Shoshanna and I went to was all kinds of colours. Peasant women wearing layers of skirts and head scarves patterned with red roses stood by their stalls hawking tubs of flowers, mounds of tomatoes, yellow, green, and red peppers, pale green kohlrabi, creamy vegetable marrow, purple cabbage, brown potatoes. Some of the grapes on display were black, but surely people wouldn't be sent to jail for selling them.

Usually Shoshanna and I took the tram and trolley to and from the market, but sometimes in late summer she would buy a whole wagonload of tomatoes for winter and then we'd ride home in a cart. I wrinkled my nose at the barnyard smell of the horse but admired its long blond tail, which so efficiently flicked off flies. And trotting briskly up Erzsébet Királyné Utja in the bright sunshine was quite splendid. As the wagon bounced to the click-clack of the animal's gait, I fancied myself the envy of every pedestrian we passed.

Market expeditions sometimes put Shoshanna in a storytelling mood. If she'd struck a good bargain and wasn't cranky on account of the heat, if I was good and hadn't pestered her to buy me too many things but had settled for a crisp *kifli* roll or a juicy peach, if Juditka wasn't bawling when we got home but nursed well and went down for a nap, afterwards Shoshanna might lapse into a bittersweet reminiscence sparked by the morning's activities and the pleasurable ordeal of coping with a cartload of tomatoes.

"Wednesdays were market days at home," she'd say, as she put wood in the black iron stove in the centre of the kitchen, laid newspapers on top of the wood, and set the paper alight with a match. The odour of phosphorus mingled with the sweet scent of the tomatoes as she chopped them at the table in front of the window. I sat on the table, dangling my legs off the side, great green jars waiting to be filled in a row beside me. The fire crackled, a pot of water spat on the stove-top, and the kitchen became tropically hot. Enveloped in a large apron and with a scarf covering her hair, Shoshanna looked happy as she bustled about.

"On Wednesdays Mamuka went to market, and in summer vacation Vera – your aunt Vera in Canada – and I went along to help her."

Mamuka was Shoshanna's mother. Coincidentally, like my other grandmother, she was called Ilona. I had been named for both of them, it being the custom to call a new child after someone recently deceased.

"Mamuka had to buy lots and lots of every kind of food for such a large family. We were seven children at home, you know."

"Tell me their names again."

I had begun to pay closer attention and tried to keep track of the many children in the Schwartz family. I used to mix them up, especially the girls. Shoshanna's brothers were easier to remember. Iszku Bácsi, who was a pioneer in Israel, was the oldest boy, twelve years Shoshanna's senior. He used to spook her and Vera with ghost stories by the fire in the nursery. He would make terrible grimaces, pretending to be Raskolnikov in *Crime and Punishment*, or assume a grotesque limp, candle in hand, to imitate the peg-legged man who lived up the street.

Duved was the other son. When Duved Bácsi was a boy, he was skinny and frail and had a lisp. He was a picky eater, too (just like me, Shoshanna said), and as a teenager took cold showers in the yard, even in the middle of winter, to toughen himself so no one would think he was a sissy. And now he had three sons of his own in England.

Vera was easy to remember, too. She was just a year younger than Shoshanna and the two of them had been like peas in a pod when they were small, except that Shoshanna had been tame and Vera wild. When they climbed the big plum tree in the backyard and got caught, Shoshanna had tendered her bottom for the required spanking by Apuka, my grandfather, but Vera had run off and made him chase after her, until he was too tired to punish her.

And now Vera lived in Canada and sent us parcels and photographs. I knew her from the smiling snapshot in Shoshanna's album in which she wore a broad-brimmed straw hat and skimpy bikini as she posed on a rock, her hip cocked seductively to the side.

But until recently I hadn't been able to sort out the other three aunties. I used to think they were all one and the same, a generic aunt called Magda, for whom, along with my grandmothers, I had also been named. If I'd been a boy, I would have been called Kálmán Sámuel after my two grand-fathers. But because my grandmothers shared a name and there had been such a bonanza of recently dead people to choose from, I was named after three people, Ilona Magdolna.

"Rózsika was the oldest of us all," Shoshanna said, scooping me off the table, before pouring boiling water into the green jars that would soon receive the tomatoes. "And the wisest and the most beautiful."

"What did she look like?"

"Well, people said that I looked like her. But she was more beautiful. Black hair and blue, blue eyes. Shorter than me, but with the same legs — up to her neck — and a figure sculpted like a china doll's."

Shoshanna's voice took on an incantatory inflection, as if she were reciting from a poem. "Rózsika was a treasure. She was wisdom. She was beauty. She was intelligence! She was everything the best, even the most religious among us. So that the rabbi sent *bocherek*, yeshiva students, to eat at her table. Yet she moved in the highest social circles as well, in Christian society . . . She was fine, refined, *the best*, I tell you. But she was luckless."

I didn't want to hear about luckless. I didn't want Shoshanna to turn sad. I loved her like this with her red bandana the same shade as the tomatoes, her cheeks flushed, her fingers flying as she diced. And still she managed to tell a story.

"Who came after Rózsika?"

"Iszku, the oldest boy."

"I know that. I meant of the aunties."

"Lilli was the next."

"Can I get the album to look at her?"

Shoshanna hesitated. "I can't leave off with these tomatoes now to go looking for the album."

"But I know where it is."

"Well, I don't think –"

"I'll be careful."

"Don't wake the baby, whatever you do!"

The album was in the living room. With the exception of Magda's portrait in the front hallway – the one treasure Shoshanna had salvaged from her ancestral home in the town of Beregszász – pictures of Shoshanna's family weren't on display in the apartment as Gusti's were. Magda had been painted by an artist from Paris, who had been much taken with her. On my way to fetch the album, I flicked on the hall light and drew closer to the wall to take a quick look at her. It was a shame that along with her name I hadn't also inherited her face and her clothes. She was wearing a form-fitting black velvet blouse with white lace ruffles at her neck and was seated by the grand piano that Mamuka had purchased to surprise Apuka when he was away on a buying trip in Budapest or Prague. The surprise hadn't been entirely pleasant, as Mamuka had only ordered the piano; Apuka was the one who had to pay for it. Magda's fingers rested lightly on the keys, her lips slightly parted because, as Shoshanna had told me, she was singing. Her front teeth were entirely Shoshanna's, small, flaring out at the bottom, and with a little gap at the very front. Her brown hair was parted in the centre and pulled back to reveal a wide brow. The artist had captured some essential grace, an inner charm that communicated itself as much through body language as through the regularity of her features, but perhaps had nothing to do with either.

Shoshanna's photos were in an album in the buffet in the living room, under a stack of white embroidered tablecloths. As I stooped to yank open the door, Juditka sputtered in the crib in the corner. I ignored her, hoping she'd go back to sleep, but she began caterwauling in earnest. I took out the album just as Shoshanna entered the room, complaining but without much heat about my having woken the baby. She began cooing at Juditka, who couldn't seem to make up her mind, once Shoshanna appeared, whether she was laughing or crying. Shoshanna told me to stop harassing her about the album; now she'd have to feed and change the baby. Why didn't I go downstairs to play?

SHOSHANNA SANK INTO THE FOLDS of the couch, tugging off her apron, and unbuttoning her blouse. God, it was good to get off her feet after the stint with the tomatoes. What a job! Back home, she'd always tackled tomatoes with Vera, never on her own. She remembered their first attempt with a slight smile. Mamuka and Apuka had gone to the baths in Marienbad, and she and Vera had decided to surprise them by turning a wagonload of tomatoes into juice. Some surprise: they scorched the tomatoes, and all that winter the stuffed cabbage and peppers had tasted acrid.

Shoshanna's smile broadened as she gazed at the baby suckling in her arms. Shoshanna loved babies. Mamuka had predicted she would have a dozen. She had been thirteen when the first Juditka, her sister Rózsika's little girl, had been born. Shoshanna had practically moved in at Rózsika's. Every day after school, she headed straight for her sister's apartment. The nursemaid had been quite jealous of the way she'd taken over the baby, changing her diapers, fussing over her, pushing her pram along the Korzó, the elegant promenade where the town's smart set paraded in their finery.

What an outstanding child that Juditka had been. With her olive complexion, velvet brown eyes, and blond tresses, she had taken after her father, but she had also inherited Rózsika's intelligence and distinction. Even in the Jew-baiting days, she had been accepted in the *gimnázium*, the only Jewish child in her year to be admitted to the classically oriented high school. That year Juditka was singled out to recite a celebratory poem in the main square on Mother's Day. Mamuka had sewn her a beautiful pale blue satin dress for the occasion and they had all swelled with pride that, in spite of everything that was happening, it was their granddaughter, daughter, niece who had been the one chosen. And what a credit to them she was on the podium, the whole town gathered at her feet, as she milked every syllable of drama and emotion from Sándor Petőfi's famous poem lauding his beloved mother.

Juditka had been twelve at the time she was wrested from their lives; Gusti's little girl had been six. Shoshanna and Gusti had struck a bargain on the name of their second child, should she be a girl: Éva Judit. Shoshanna had agreed to give precedence to Gusti's dead daughter in the formal first name, as long as the baby's everyday name was Juditka. It was a compromise they both found just, for Gusti conceded that it would be unbearable if every time he uttered the new child's name, her dead half-sister were to shimmer in the air around them.

Shoshanna stuck her finger in the baby's mouth to break the suction on her nipple. She giggled softly as Juditka's eyes popped open in dismayed surprise. Still, she didn't whimper. She was such a good baby, smiling now, but a little uncertainly as Shoshanna propped her in her arms and rubbed her tummy. Her round face and eyes favoured Gusti's side, a bit like Gusti's mother in the photos and – God forbid the comparison – a bit like Bazsa. But such an even-tempered child – that certainly wasn't like Bazsa! She slept well and didn't fuss over Shoshanna's thin breast milk, about which Shoshanna felt alternately grateful and guilty. Shoshanna had been having gallbladder attacks ever since the birth of the baby, and she was convinced that her milk had a greenish cast to it caused by bile. And no doubt bile was coursing in her system after all the aggravation she'd had to put up with from Gusti's aunts.

Once again, Bazsa was about to descend on them. Late at night in bed, Gusti had recounted in whispers to her the tale of Nanush's feat in staving off Bazsa's punishment. The trouble was that since she wasn't going to jail and she couldn't be allowed free rein at home, lest she lapse into some scrape again, she'd have to live somewhere else. Nanush couldn't put her up right now. Nanush was still convalescing from the effects of her efforts on Bazsa's behalf. So that left Gusti, which effectively meant Shoshanna, because who was going to be supervising and feeding and humouring Bazsa while Gusti was at work? Who else but Shoshanna?

What impossible creatures they were, the two younger aunties, Bazsa and Bóba. Shoshanna wondered if the thought had ever crossed Gusti's mind as to why, unlike the scores of his relatives who had perished, these two hapless women had been chosen for survival. How they had survived was another matter. Bazsa had the sheer luck of being in the right place at the right time. But the unfortunate Bóba, with her delicate air and sickly ways, had been among the first to be designated for annihilation. Seven times, she claimed, she had come before Mengele for selection in Auschwitz, and each time she'd had her patrons. Her very frailness and rarefied, subtle beauty had, it appeared, been a magnet for lesbian guards in the SS who persisted in smuggling her back to the right-hand side from the left. No one ever asked about the services she had had to render in return for her life.

Shoshanna remembered her first dealings with the aunties, soon after the war ended. Gusti had introduced Bóba to her at the outset because Bóba was living with him at the time in Mada. Mada — formally Nyirmada — was the village to which Shoshanna had been summoned from Budapest in the fall of '45 by Márton's brother. It wasn't Gusti's hometown; Gusti came from nearby Vaja, but he'd migrated to Mada by the time Shoshanna appeared on the scene.

If you thought about it, everything had hinged on chance. The fact that her brother-in-law had sent for her, that she'd decided to accept the invitation and had gone there to live with him and his wife. Her sister-in-law had been horrid, expecting — no, demanding — that Shoshanna scour the kitchen floor with lye in return for room and board. That arrangement hadn't lasted, Shoshanna not being one to wash the floors of others just because she was so bidden.

Around that time, she had bumped into Gusti on Fő Utca: Gusztáv Weinberger, president of the local branch of the American Jewish Joint Distribution Committee, head of the congregation, manager of farms and distilleries on his own behalf and for other Jewish landowners who were not yet returned, or would never return. Gusti Weinberger, a man of substance, kindliness, integrity, a man who inspired confidence, the eligible widower par excellence. And she an eligible widow, as was then believed by herself and everyone else. He needed an assistant, he told her on the dusty street, as bedraggled survivors queued up for communal meals at one of the larger homes that housed the aid committee. Did she perhaps have time to help him?

It wasn't long before one thing led to another, and he was stroking her long black hair as she took dictation in his office. He told her then – it just came back to him on the spur of the moment – that he had once seen a photo of her, a small square snapshot lovingly extracted from Márton's wallet. It happened in a railway station somewhere, sometime in the middle of the war, when he'd run into Márton, his former commanding officer, who was brimming over with excitement that he was engaged to the prettiest girl in the world.

Curiously, she too had an odd little scrap of information about Gusti, acquired in her previous life. Gusti, who would later regale her and their children with stories of his family in Vaja until they took on the quality of myth, never once suggested in Mada, when they were just a few kilometres from his ancestral home, that he and she take a carriage ride there together. She had to form an idea of where he had come from and who he had been from the accounts of others and from stray recollections of her own.

Shoshanna's hometown in Subcarpathia lay a scant eighty kilometres from Vaja beyond the Tisza River. When she was born, the region, which changed hands several times in the twentieth century, was part of Czechoslovakia. Gusti's paternal ancestors were like potentates in those parts. Not in Beregszász, where Shoshanna grew up, but in Munkács, where her sister Lilli had married. Once when Shoshanna was still in her teens, Lilli's husband, Izidor, had taken her and Lilli on an outing past Oroszvég, the suburb where Izidor was building a fancy house for Lilli. Izidor had pointed his whip at the rows and rows of purple-flowering potatoes by one bank of the highway. "The fields around here all belong to the Weinbergers," he observed, and then again, gesturing towards expanses of neatly furrowed land on the other side of the road, he had flung out, "and this is Weinberger country, too."

Well, she hadn't benefited from Gusti's former wealth, other than to be impressed by the idea of it at the time. Not only was it gone now, the mere fact of its erstwhile existence was enough to brand them as class enemies in the new dispensation. Still, Gusti wasn't doing badly for himself with his state job, quite a feat considering that he'd managed to secure it without joining the Party. But every time Shoshanna contrived to put aside enough for one of those splendid electric washing machines that were every Hungarian housewife's daydream, her little nest egg was wiped out by some requirement or other of the aunties.

Holding the baby against her shoulder, Shoshanna made her way to the bathroom to change her. So, yes, it was when her interest in Gusti had originally quickened that she met first Bóba, then Bazsa. Bóba was in her mid-forties then, a scant five years older than Gusti. She was still quite attractive, with high cheekbones and streaks of grey in her thick chestnut hair. Though her illness wasn't visible, it didn't take long for Shoshanna to notice her restlessness, her excessive loquaciousness, her inability to get along with people. She had a way of creating a crisis out of thin air, of stirring things up and infecting others with her own craziness. And yet, in spite of her paranoia and ultra-sensitivity, she was truly good: warm-hearted and generous, never so happy as when giving. And she often gave well beyond her means. She was an excellent cook, too, and pressed food on Shoshanna when it was hard to come by, even in the country.

Shoshanna willed herself to like her for Gusti's sake, though Gusti's instinctive response to both Bóba and Bazsa was irritation. He certainly tendered them filial love and did his duty by them, but they drove him beyond his limits. With everyone else he was the embodiment of patience, yet the two of them invariably had him clasping his head in exasperation.

It was some weeks after her arrival in Mada that Shoshanna met Bazsa. Gusti had at first tried to hide Bazsa altogether, neglecting to inform her that he had another aunt in the village. It was only when he and Shoshanna were spending practically every waking moment in each other's company – not only working together but participating, for the one and only period of their adult lives, in a feverish round of social activities – that he had shamefacedly owned up to her about Bazsa. But only because he was afraid someone else would blurt out the information first. Better she should hear the worst from him, he said.

Bazsa was the village *kurva*. No, not true. Bazsa was *a* village *kurva*. Mada had lots of whores, was notorious in the surrounding villages as the best place to procure a prostitute. Technically Bazsa wasn't a real whore. She didn't take money; she just lay down with anyone who'd have her. She lived with a peasant family, and the country boys trooped in to see her, sometimes one right after the other. And their appalled parents fretted that she'd give them the clap.

When Shoshanna finally met Bazsa, she was stunned. She had expected a hussy, not a slattern; a painted strumpet, not an old countrywoman. A huge fat face topped by a skimpy greying bun, a short dumpy body squeezed into a loud, flower-patterned dress. Clean, though, it must be admitted, and tidy: the pleated skirt of the dress was neatly pressed.

Her madness was immediately apparent and not at all the same variety as Bóba's. Bazsa was witless and confused, her conversation and behaviour scattered. She laughed a great deal, recited poetry, told outlandish stories. She had been married and divorced before the war to a man who, though at first seemingly suitable, soon turned into a wastrel. After meeting Shoshanna, she took her aside to confide that before her marriage, she had been seduced by a scion of the famous Kállay family – by a brother, in fact, of the wartime prime minister. "I was a fallen woman, that's why they married me off to Emil," she grinned.

Shoshanna originally dismissed the tale of Bazsa's purported seduction as idiotic jabber. But later, when she and Gusti were living in Budapest, he came across a photo of Bazsa in her youth. Shoshanna was astonished by the picture, taken just prior to the First World War at a spa by the Adriatic. Bazsa was almost unrecognizable, quite the beauty, with wide-set eyes shining out of a heart-shaped face. Her waist could easily have been encircled by two large hands.

In the bathroom, Shoshanna laid Juditka on the quilted changing table and dropped the wet diaper in the soaking pail. The baby kicked her legs with pleasure at being unbound and laughed out loud as Shoshanna tickled her tummy. She sprinkled powder over the plump little rump and couldn't resist making a loud raspberry against the baby's belly button.

"Men are pigs," Shoshanna announced firmly to Juditka, who was chortling with delight. "Pigs, every one of them, including your father."

Gusti may have confessed Bazsa's sins to Shoshanna, but he hadn't made a clean breast of his own until she forced the issue. Hugo Weinstock's sister had been the one to spill the beans about Gusti. Hugo was one of the many young men buzzing around Shoshanna at the drinking parties and sleigh rides; perhaps the sister hoped to advance his cause by discrediting Gusti. At any rate, the sister had inquired of Shoshanna with seeming innocence whether Zsuzsi Néni was a fixture in Gusti's household whom she was prepared to tolerate indefinitely.

Shoshanna had opened her eyes very wide but had not pursued the matter with her. She asked Gusti what Hugo's sister had been alluding to and was dismayed to see him flush to the roots of his receding hairline.

Beyond the caressing of her own hair and the occasional accidental grazing of their hands in the office, nothing of a physical nature had yet passed between Gusti and Shoshanna. Still, they were both sufficiently preoccupied with each other for her to feel entitled to an explanation. All she knew about Zsuzsi Néni was that she was Gusti's live-in house-keeper. Old enough to be his mother, and in fact, as it emerged from Gusti's halting sentences, a sister of Dobos Néni, his former wet nurse – a state of incestuous connection best left unexamined, in Shoshanna's opinion.

Shoshanna had frequently seen Dobos Néni and Zsuzsi Néni in Gusti's yard busying themselves with the slaughtering of pigs and the force-feeding of geese. Dobos Néni, still handsome and robust, her hair coiled around her head in thick braids that were practically untouched by silver, wielding a large knife; Zsuzsi Néni, huge haunches astride a goose, shovelling corn down the protesting animal's gullet. She was ugly as sin, her most prominent feature a coarse pit of a mouth filled with irregular blackened teeth.

Zsuzsi Néni was the chief madam of Mada, and Gusti's connections with her stretched way back. In his bachelor-hood on the estate in Vaja, he and his brother had shared a bedroom in an outbuilding far from parental observation. The peasant girls of their village happened to be virtuous, but there were scores of available unmarried women to be found in Mada. So if a business visitor was expected – someone to whom a special mark of hospitality ought to be shown – or if the brothers themselves had a yen for a little fun, a message would be dispatched to Zsuzsi Néni via the coachman that such-and-such a girl would be welcome for an overnight stay. And Zsuzsi Néni always made the requisite arrangements.

"Well," Gusti muttered to Shoshanna, avoiding her eyes, "it seemed natural to turn to Zsuzsi Néni in my altered circumstances." That is to say that in his widowerhood, his broken heart and devotion to the memory of his dead wife notwithstanding, a man still had certain needs. And he had spoken to Zsuzsi Néni one evening as he wiped his lips on his linen serviette after polishing off the bean soup and *tepertő*, cracklings, she had served him. "Find me a girl for tonight, Zsuzsi Néni," he had murmured. He was staggered by her answer.

"I'm not finding no one for you, honourable master. I'm right here in the flesh for you myself. What do you need a girl for? There's nothing the girls around here know they didn't learn from me."

A twinkle glinted in Gusti's eye for an instant as he recounted the story to Shoshanna. But it disappeared very quickly at the sight of the blue blaze she directed at him.

"Pigs, men are pigs! And you, you who adored your wife!"

"My wife is dead. And I was alone."

"And now?"

"I give you my word that since I laid eyes on you I have slept alone."

Shoshanna was inclined to believe him. Particularly since Zsuzsi Néni had been rather hostile towards her. And something else made sense too. A week or so earlier, that rake Hugo Weinstock had come around late at night, a Gypsy violinist by his side, and had begun to serenade her with Brahms. When she'd paid no heed, he aimed a pebble at her window. The glass had shattered into smithereens, making a terrible racket and mess. The following morning Zsuzsi Néni had been the one to carry the news flash to Gusti that all night long men had been jumping out of Shoshanna's bedroom window. He and Shoshanna had had a good chuckle over it, but now the joke was even richer.

Shoshanna, playing peekaboo with the baby in the bathroom mirror while her thoughts meandered, was suddenly brought up short by some kind of commotion downstairs. The memory of her other child surfaced as the wild barking of dogs and screeching of children reached her ears. How long ago had she packed Ilushka off to play outside?

SINCE I'D STARTED SCHOOL, I was less fearful about playing outside and less gullible. No one terrorized me these days with tales of my mother being dead. But of certain things I remained as frightened as ever. Dogs, for sure. The previous summer we had visited Bóba Néni in the country. Bóba Néni possessed an enormous German shepherd that she loved passionately. She spent a great deal of effort trying to get me to love Tuntush, too. Tuntush lived in the yard in a little house of his own, and Shoshanna, who quite liked dogs, had started carrying his food out to him there. One day, all goodness, she had taken an additional scrap of meat to him while he was still addressing the earlier contents of his dish. As she bent over him to deposit the extra tidbit, Tuntush snarled at her and tore a tidy chunk out of her calf. I saw the whole thing from a safe distance on the veranda, and despite her stoic silence after the initial scream, the sight of my mother's ripped and profusely bleeding flesh shook me up no end.

The experience left me leery of dogs in general, and of an English greyhound called Lord in particular. Lord belonged to my classmate and friend Andrea, who lived around the corner from us in Budapest. He was lean of body, loud of bark, and rambunctious in manner, given to wild lunges that Andrea tried to convince me were friendly overtures. She doted on him, so I didn't like to tell her the extent to which he terrified me. When Shoshanna sent me downstairs to play, I didn't mind, as long as Lord wasn't out playing also.

A furtive peek from the vestibule confirmed a clear coast in the yard, but when I edged past the sunflowers at the side of the house and emerged at the front, there was Lord, straining at the leash on which Andrea held him, his yellow eyes glittering. I turned on my heel and scampered back to the vestibule before they had a chance to spot me. I stayed there a good long time, breathing in the smell of mould wafting up from the cellar and the odours of food drifting down the stairwell. I counted the black and white tiles that lined the floor and sang a little ditty to myself. Rózsi, Lilli, *Magda*; Bóba, Nanush, *Bazsa*. There was a symmetry about the rhyming names that I found quite pleasing. I'd never really thought about the fact that Shoshanna had three dead sisters while Gusti had three old aunties.

After a while I tired of this game and decided to attempt another foray. This time all I did was stick my nose out, and there on the doorstep were Andrea, Lord, and Andrea's little sister, Angela.

"Come and play with us, Ilushka."

"Don't feel like it."

"What, you feel like sitting on the doorstep?"

"For now."

"Oh, come *on*. We'll get my brother and Attila and play detective."

"Are you going to take Lord home when you get your brother?"

"'Course not. He's the sniffing detective dog."

"Then I'm not playing."

"Are you scared of *Lord*?"

"Yes." I looked down at my scuffed shoes.

"But he's lovely." Andrea hugged his head close to her side.

"No, he's horrible. He growls. He'll bite."

"Lord's lovely. Look." She dragged him close to my face.

"No!" I shrieked and began to run for dear life in the direction of the street and the park.

Lord yanked himself free of Andrea and gave chase. I wavered between the need to escape and the necessity of checking on his whereabouts. I twisted my head around: he was right behind me, panting between raucous barks. I saw his pointed teeth and long pink tongue, imagined his hot breath on my neck.

"Get him away from me!" I screeched.

"Stop hurting his feelings!" Andrea yelled back. "You – you scaredy-cat! You scaredy-cat stinking Jew!"

I stopped cold. We faced each other like bantam roosters. I grabbed a fistful of Andrea's short blondish hair.

"Stinking goy!"

Andrea's open hand resounded against my cheek. Lord snarled. Angela began to whimper.

Three stories above, a balcony door opened abruptly.

"Ilushka, upstairs this minute!"

Shoshanna, with Juditka in her arms, was halfway down the stairs by the time I made it to the entrance.

"What was all that fracas about?"

"Nothing. I didn't want to play with Lord."

"And so? Is that a reason to punch Andrea?"

"I didn't punch Andrea. I pulled her hair."

"Because you didn't want to play with Lord?"

"She called me a scaredy-cat. A scaredy-cat stinking Jew."

We had reached the landing in front of our apartment.

"She did? So you pulled her hair?"

"*And* I called her a stinking goy."

Shoshanna gave me a little shove inside. I suppose she didn't want our neighbours to hear.

"Where did you ever hear that word? No one's ever said that in this house!"

"Bóba Néni did . . . once."

A hint of a smile flickered on Shoshanna's face. "Oh . . . well, that's all right then. But don't say it again."

SOON AFTER THIS EPISODE I came home from school to find Bazsa Néni ensconced in the living room, her valise open on Shoshanna's bed.

I couldn't stand Bazsa Néni's visits. She smothered me with wet kisses and asked me countless questions, without waiting to hear the answers. It wasn't just me; no one could get a word in edgewise while she was with us. She talked incessantly, and when she exhausted herself she spread a white handkerchief over her face to shut down the conversation, a signal to everyone else. She insisted that I go to bed then and there in broad daylight, otherwise she'd be unable to sleep for the noise I made.

One day I arrived home and to my joy Nanush was there as well. But after patting my head distractedly, Nanush paid scant attention to me. Bazsa Néni was weeping on the couch, clutching her head, complaining of demons. "Please, Nanushka, do something to stop them. The *bestia* has given me the evil eye," she sobbed, pointing at my mother. "There are devils warring in my head. Get rid of them with the coals, as Mother used to!"

Shoshanna and Nanush exchanged glances, Shoshanna clearly very worried, since she didn't rise to the bait about the *bestia*. (Bóba and Bazsa, when they were in their crazed states, sometimes referred to her as "the vamp." Shoshanna was rarely indignant about this, though I think it hurt her feelings. I didn't know what a *bestia* was and thought it sounded very fierce.)

Nanush asked Shoshanna if there was any coal in the house. Shoshanna said, Of course, but what was Nanush going to do with coal?

"I don't know," Nanush muttered darkly, "but I'd better do something."

The two of them left the room and I trailed after, not wanting to be around Bazsa Néni, who still had her hands clasped around her head, her brows knit, her cheeks streaked with tears. Shoshanna found some coal in a jute sack on the floor of the pantry. Nanush asked for matches and newspaper and we returned to the living room where Bazsa Néni was rocking, balled up like a hedgehog in the far corner of the sofa.

Nanush assembled her materials methodically. She placed the coals on a pewter dish and set fire to them with the matches and newspapers. By now Bazsa had quietened down as she watched the unfolding drama. A strong sharp smell began to fill the room. Using black metal tongs, Nanush carefully transferred the burning coals from the tray to a pottery jar in which Shoshanna kept flowers. I began to cough as the room filled with smoke.

"Ilushka, why don't you go wash your hands?" Shoshanna said, looking for any excuse to get rid of me. "You haven't washed your hands yet after school, have you?" I ignored her and stifled my coughs.

"All right, Bazsuka," Nanush said soothingly, "sit up like a good girl on the edge of the sofa, not so far away from me."

Bazsa Néni unfolded herself, and stuck her short, porky legs out in front of her like a stiff jointed doll. She eyed Nanush eagerly. Slowly and deliberately Nanush crossed the room with the jug in her hands.

"Forgive me, Bazsukám," Nanush said as the smoke wafted between her and Bazsa Néni. And then she spat through the smoke at Bazsa three times: "Phew, phew, phew. There, now lie down, dear, and sleep. The evil eye and the demons, they're all gone, don't you know?"

I have few other memories of Bazsa. I do remember the pained way Gusti read her rambling, disjointed letters, out loud, as was his custom with all mail from home, in later years in Montreal. He would half shade his face in misery with one broad hand, as he held the page of big looping handwriting in the other. There were, invariably, the hysterical complaints about Nanush and Ibolya and Zoli Bácsi for not doing enough on her behalf. And then, just as invariably, there were the accounts of her triumphant impromptu performances at the Vigadó restaurant in Debrecen. Egged on by the string of unsavoury young men whom she still collected, she would head for the bar to recite or sing. "I was greeted with great applause," she wrote proudly. "The Gypsies played a special fanfare just for me."

Most of what I know about Bazsa I gleaned between the lines of stories Gusti told about Nanush. Nanush may have been an exemplary wife, mother, grandmother, and aunt, but it was in her role as sister to Bóba and Bazsa that she truly showed her mettle as a human being. It goes without saying that when Bóba and Bazsa were hospitalized (Bazsa often in closed mental institutions, Bóba generally in more euphemistically named facilities and then, after she contracted intestinal cancer, in acute-care hospitals), Nanush visited them daily, wicker basket on her arm, carrying the dinners she had lovingly cooked for them. More often than not, she received a heap of abuse for her pains. On the return trip, she recited a litany of her own composition to fortify herself for the next day's ordeal: "I must think of her as if she had appendicitis or a hernia. She is sick. She is pitiful. She cannot help herself."

Once, by bizarre coincidence, both sisters were committed to the same institution. For days, they didn't recognize each other; then, in a sudden burst of enlightenment, they fell into each other's arms in a heart-rending display.

But, according to Gusti, the apex of Nanush's sisterly devotion was her stubborn resolve to save Bazsa from jail. Her infraction had been minor, but in Stalinist times, nothing was minor. Trafficking in food was prohibited to prevent prices from rising, yet since there were widespread food shortages, all sorts of middlemen engaged in a rampant black market. Poor Bazsa, not realizing she was doing anything wrong, had unwittingly taken the fall for an operation making and selling cheese without a licence.

So innocent was she in her own mind, that when she received the summons from the public prosecutor's office, where the facts of the case were to be established, she immediately gave a full if muddled account of what she had done. The trial was held at the Justice Department, where it was deemed an open-and-shut case and she was sentenced. The execution of the decree was left to the police, who were to fetch her from home to take her to jail.

It was at this juncture that Nanush had consulted Gusti. When he pronounced that she'd have to face the music, Nanush refused to give up. She began to make the rounds: to the public prosecutor, to the judge who had tried the case, to the police. She cajoled and wept but it was useless. She was shown the door everywhere. No one would intervene. Finally, as a last resort, she turned up at the Debrecen jail, where the sentence was to be served. Some of the tears she had shed before the judge and the police may have been a little forced, but when she bearded the bureaucrat in charge of Bazsa's prison file, she had come to the end of the road. There was nowhere else to go.

"Comrade, sir," Nanush began, "she is an unfortunate woman, my sister. A mentally ill woman from what we used to call, in the old days, a good family. She became embroiled in this mess . . . she didn't even know what she was doing when she was doing it. I can't count for you the number of times she's been committed to the Neurological Nursing Home. How can a person like this be held to account?"

By the time she finished this little speech Nanush was crying real tears. The clerk looked searchingly at Nanush and he was touched. Sometimes even bureaucrats have hearts.

"My good woman," he said, "listen to me. This can't be changed. She's been tried and sentenced. That's the way it is. But I'm going to help you."

He pointed to a thick docket on his desk. "You see this file?" Nanush nodded.

"That's the case against your sister. Normally it would stay here on my desk until I sent the requisition to the police to bring her here. But you know what? No one will ever see it again. The minute you're gone, I'm going to take it down to the basement archives where no one will think to look for it. No one will come for your poor sister. But for heaven's sake, make sure she doesn't do it again."

On the way back to Pest, jubilant at her success, Nanush was so elated that she threw off her overcoat and caught a terrible chill on the train. She almost died of pneumonia. But she survived to protect her sisters time and again.

IF I SCOUR MY MEMORIES, I find among them one representative scene for each of my mad great-aunts. For Bazsa it is the scene – literally like theatre – of the exorcism, a tableau so replete with hocus-pocus, I wonder if I have imagined it.

Bóba's scene is equally hysterical but far starker and scarier. Bóba Néni had come to Budapest from the country, but instead of staying with us, she had taken a room in a hotel. Why this was so, I didn't know or care. I was about seven years old, and when I heard that Apu was to call on her that evening, I wanted to go along. Both my parents demurred, but when I insisted, they gave in. It wasn't so much that I was eager to see Bóba Néni; rather, it was the prospect of having Gusti all to myself on the journey by bus and trolley that was so enticing. Shoshanna and Juditka were to stay at home.

I was of course unaware of the reason why Bóba Néni was shunning our home. Bóba Néni was currently carrying on a one-sided feud with Shoshanna, who had quite unwittingly offended her in the way that everyone around Bóba inevitably did. And as ammunition in this contest Bóba had begun to circulate the rumour that Juditka was not my father's child. Juditka – Bóba told Bazsa, who told Nanush, who felt it necessary to warn Gusti – was alleged to look exactly like the music student who boarded in our small room the spring before Juditka's birth. It was a preposterous insinuation, but because Gusti had declined even to discuss it with Bóba and because Shoshanna refused to apologize to her for the alleged slight, Bóba would not come to our place. Which didn't mean that Gusti would not pay her the respect due her as his dead mother's sister. She might not visit us, but he had to visit her.

And so the quintessential scene. Bóba Néni greeted us at the door of a room that contained overstuffed armchairs and heavy swag drapes in burgundy brocade. Her face, clouded over when Gusti kissed first her cheeks, then her hand, brightened when she noticed me. She hugged me close – too close – almost squeezing the breath out of me. As we sat down, Gusti in one of the armchairs, me on his lap, he handed over to her the butter *pogácsák* that Shoshanna had baked and carefully wrapped in a cardboard box tied with red string. Bóba's face, expectant as she undid the string, twisted when she unwrapped the plump biscuits with their shiny criss-crossed tops. Her long fingers flailed in the air during a moment of indecision, then she pitched the package to the floor.

"The *bestia* thinks to bribe me! She may fool you, but she can't take me in. She is a false, false woman!"

The word *bestia* still meant nothing to me, but the darting, mad eyes were terrifying. Still, when those eyes lit on me, Bóba's rage dissolved.

"You've brought this darling to see me! How are you, Ilushka, my sweet? The wicked one couldn't stop you two from visiting an abandoned old woman. What shall I get you, angel, what would you like?"

I stared at Bóba Néni, and for once, though I had a reputation for precocious verbal expression, I was totally dumbstruck. I was mesmerized by her mouth. It moved this way and that, a geyser of terrible accusations once more addressed to my father.

"She simply can't wait for you to clear out of town so she can cheat on you with all and sundry. I have seen the way she ogles men – and you leave her on her own with the children, you trusting chump."

I might not have understood the exact import of what Bóba Néni was saying, but that she was abusing my absent mother was unmistakable. And it was unbearable that Gusti and I should be sitting there crumpled together in the armchair in silent acquiescence to her awful slurs. Like a baby, like a crybaby scaredy-cat, I squirmed in my father's lap, twisting around so my back was turned on Bóba Néni and my face close to his. "Let's go home," I began to sniffle.

"Ilushka, sweetest angel," Bóba began to murmur, all contrition, "Bóba Néni has some candy for you."

"I don't want anything from you," I blubbered into my father's neck. "I want to go home. I want to go home to my mother right now."

POOR BÓBA, whose whole life was a misery, whose mother died when she was ten, who had stomach ulcers while still in her teens, who had to parade before Mengele seven times, died of cancer aged fifty-seven, in 1958. We were already in England. Gusti and Shoshanna received the news in a letter from Nanush, a letter whose heavy, black-inked words I wouldn't read for another forty years.

In it Nanush relayed the sad litany of Bóba's final days. Nanush had continued to minister to her with daily visits, trying to tempt her on her deathbed with treats of asparagus soup, calf's liver, cherry compote. When the delicacies disagreed with her, Bóba typically blamed Nanush. Nanush forgave her, as she had done all their lives. It was she who sewed Bóba's shroud.

Though as a child I loved Nanush more than anyone, I can't think of a single emblematic moment with her, as I can with my other two great-aunts. She was simply a welcome and uncomplicated fixture in my early life. Despite the burdens carried on her narrow shoulders, she managed to be the merriest person I have ever known. I recall her best in the most ordinary acts of play. Blowing soap bubbles through the chicken wire on our balcony, a straw between her narrow old-lady lips. Bringing me huge pastel-coloured balloons that we flew on long strings in the playground. In my mind's eye the grass in the park is always a verdant green, the sky a perfect azure blue. And I am perfectly happy.

five

LAMPPOSTS IN THE CELLAR

The final time I wet my bed, Shoshanna didn't scold me. Technically I hadn't wet the bed, just the mattress. We had dragged it downstairs into a corner of the cellar. It was three years since I'd last had an accident. I was ashamed to have one when I was almost nine, and among all these people, too.

Still, Shoshanna wasn't mad. At dawn she peeled me out of the soaking garments that clung to my cold legs, the long gym pants I wore over my pyjamas for extra warmth in the cellar. Two sets of pants to wash and the blankets, too, and still she wasn't angry. "Hush, hush," she said amid all the sleeping bodies in the chilly dankness, as the sweet reek of my pee hung in the air. "We'll go upstairs and wash you up."

The thing was, you could never tell with Shoshanna. You couldn't pin her down to hard and fast rules, causes and effects. And as far as rules went, everything was suddenly topsy-turvy anyway. That, apparently, was the real meaning of the word _forradalom_: an upside-down time. That's why we were down in the cellar with all these people, instead of up on the second floor where we belonged. We were having a revolution.

In many ways it was turning out to be a jolly thing, this revolution. In the daytime and even on many of the nights when the candles flickered and the supper smells of the various families mingled with the pervasive odour of mould, this interlude in the fall of 1956 had a faint holiday glow about it. For instance, we were eating unusual amounts of *lekvár*, plum jam, out of a huge communal jar. My father wasn't off to work in the morning, and I didn't have to go to school. A new playmate had materialized: my cousin Anna, who slept on the mattress next to mine. Well, Anna was sort of my cousin. Her father was second cousin to mine. But we were not to mention his name, nor the name of Anna's mother. (This part wasn't so jolly.) We were not to say anything about them at all, Shoshanna had said, very firmly. Anna had come to stay with us for now, and her baby sister Jutka had gone to stay with other relatives. It was better that way.

My baby sister, Juditka, was sleeping peacefully in her stroller. For sure not wetting herself. She was almost three, and good. Her nature was much easier than mine, as Shoshanna repeatedly pointed out to anyone who cared to listen. She had one calm child and one *izgága* child. Not that she loved one more than the other, she loved us both the same, of course.

A spasm of pain suddenly contorted Shoshanna's features. She turned very pale, then shook my father awake. "I have to go upstairs," she whispered urgently to him. "I'm taking Ilushka with me, to wash her up."

Gusti propped himself on an elbow and reached for his glasses under the pillow. "Stay put, it must still be dark."

My father had an amazing inner clock. He always knew what time it was, without benefit of timepieces.

"I can't," Shoshanna hissed back. "The cramps again."

HISTORIANS MAINTAIN that the Hungarian Revolution of October 1956 actually began with the death of Stalin in March 1953. The day of the funeral I remember clearly. I sat by the giant walnut radio in our living room, racked by sobs as dirges poured forth from its upholstered chest and the sombre but mellifluent voice of the announcer mourned our plight as a bereft, fatherless people. In the kitchen, Shoshanna was humming a happy tune.

Shoshanna's struggle started early too, though not as early as 1953. Her gravest preoccupation during the Revolution was not giving shelter to Anna, whose parents were hiding, with good cause, from the freedom fighters. It was not finding a place to conceal her own children when the atmosphere in the cellar became a little too fraught with freedom. It was not avoiding the crossfire between the Hungarian cannon positioned by the side of our house and the Russian tanks rumbling up and down Erzsébet Királyné Utja, a three-minute walk from the apartment. It wasn't even Gusti's disappearance for a day when he walked out into the world in search of food and news. Any of these would normally have been enough to prostrate Shoshanna with a sick headache or an attack of nerves. No, Shoshanna's biggest problem was the terrible churning in her guts which started in the summer of 1956 and for which no doctor could find a cure.

The cramps had begun shortly after we returned from a delightful holiday in the Mátra mountains. It was our one and only vacation while we lived in Budapest, partly because these were not holidaying times – people were regularly resettled from the capital into the countryside, but that didn't count – and partly because it was awfully hard to take a holiday with my father.

We had been scheduled for a vacation in the summer of 1955 and all our suitcases were packed, when Gusti heard of an outbreak of polio in a village in the area we had been about to visit. He cancelled the holiday and unpacked the bags, even as Shoshanna's blue eyes flashed, even as she tossed her head as in the days when her mane of black hair had so enticed him. These days she kept her hair short and permed it only for special occasions. Yet she continued to make that flirtatious, provocative gesture, as if her beauty alone would best him in any argument.

Not that she protested silently. What did he think, she wanted her children to get sick? He was excessive, he was mollycoddling, he was like a fussy grandmother; the polio was at least sixty kilometres away – no, look at the map, seventy! – from where we were headed.

The next summer, Shoshanna prevailed. She was off to the Mátra with me and Juditka, even when Gusti had to back out at the last minute on account of some hitch at one of the collective farms he supervised. It was a glorious vacation, despite the fact that the peasant house where we stayed was so overrun by mice that one night Shoshanna slept on top of the table rather than on the bed in order to put a little distance between herself and the wildlife on the floor. (There were lots of cats, too, predatory mousers that still could not keep the hordes of rodents in check.) Nonetheless, it was a golden interlude up there in the mountains, with splendid company. Shoshanna struck up a friendship with a young woman in a neighbouring cottage. She was also from Budapest, a pregnant newlywed who missed her husband desperately and was endlessly interested in Juditka.

On our walks in the hills my sister sang the folk songs I had performed for my school's end-of-year concert. "*Kis piricsi falu végén folyik el a kanális, enyém leszel kis angyalom ha bánja az anyád is.*" "The canal flows by the village of Kis Pirics," Juditka sang with expression, mimicking the intonations of my voice, just the way Shoshanna had coached me for the concert. "You'll be my baby, even if your mother can't abide me." The pregnant friend from Budapest was enchanted.

GUSTI'S REVOLUTION HAD STARTED far earlier, in 1944. Although he was the most unheroic, he might even have said cowardly, of men, he had saved his own skin and that of the two hundred other men in his company.

Along with their German masters, Gusti's company of Jewish slave labourers were in retreat, withdrawing before the path of the Russians who would shortly liberate Hungary from the Nazis. You didn't need to be of superior intelligence, which Gusti indubitably was, to deduce that the Germans were finished, that this was the rump of an army that had been decimated at Stalingrad, that these gallant horses, sturdy cannons, and soldiers in full regalia were taking a route that led westward back to their homeland. And, in an orderly manner, Gusti's company marched with them, in the autumn of the year, apples and pears tantalizingly ripe on the overhanging tree branches, cornstalks high in the adjacent fields. They trekked through the borderland between Romania and Hungary, following the course of the Tisza, one of the historic rivers of Hungary.

In my father's mind grew the ever-strengthening belief that as long as the Tisza was not traversed, as long as he was on its eastern bank, his life was his own. But once the river was crossed, once on the other side in German-occupied Hungary, he and the motley array of Jewish men with whom he had been serving for the last two years would be loaded on to freight or cattle trains at the railway junction at Chop. Destination: Germany.

Ironically, they were given the order to cross the river at the market town of Vásárosnamény, less than thirty kilometres from the farm where Gusti grew up. Though he knew this sandy corner of northeastern Hungary better than any place on earth, being there troubled rather than reassured him. He couldn't shake the conviction that each step towards home brought him closer to a death sentence.

The sides of the broad toll bridge were rigged with explosives cartridges, ready for the moment the Germans would blow it up before the advancing Russians. There was no way out. The company had to keep moving. And so, beneath the impassive stares of the German military police who stood at either end of the span, they marched across.

In the town's market square there was a crush of men from all ranks; German and Hungarian soldiers and Jewish labour servicemen milled about. Discipline was loose. A week earlier, on October 15, a putsch in Budapest had installed a rabidly fascist puppet government. But here, far from the centre, the knowledge that the Russians were only a few kilometres away bred an atmosphere of laissez-faire. In the mingling of the various armies, Jewish labour servicemen from assorted regiments drew towards one another. Those who had seen the Russians farther east said it was madness to continue, they must try to escape. But all Gusti could think of was that the Tisza had been crossed.

"We have to turn back," he said to a buddy.

"Turn back? With the *Polizei* on the bridge?"

"Yes," Gusti said, and he went to confer with the Hungarian sergeant who led his company.

"Sergeant, sir," my father said, "if we continue to Chop on this side of the Tisza, we will do so under German command. But if you lead us back the way we came, we can presume there'll be no more Germans because that's the direction they're retreating from, out of the path of the Russians. It would seem to me, sir, that the only thing to do is to go back where we came from."

The sergeant looked perplexed. "Back over the bridge?"

You didn't need to be of superior intelligence, which the sergeant was not, to understand that though the Germans were about to lose the war, their power to do damage to those they controlled was still boundless. The Hungarian sergeant was in little personal danger for the moment; he wouldn't be boarding the train to Germany with his Jews.

But with the imminent arrival of the Russians, his loyalty to his German superiors faltered. In such circumstances, currying favour with his Jewish underlings might actually save his neck with the Russians.

"And what am I to say," said the sergeant to Gusti, "if a German officer stops us?"

"Sergeant, sir, what you must answer is that a German lieutenant colonel stopped us in the marketplace and said to you, 'All these dirty Jews shouldn't clog the traffic here where there's no room for them. They're to go to Chop using the road on the other bank of the river!' Understand, Sergeant, sir?"

The two hundred men in the company pulled their things together and advanced towards the bridge. It was a march of some twenty minutes. Gusti's heart beat a staccato rhythm but he wore an air of studied composure. The crowds at the bridge had not abated. All traffic was still from the easterly direction. No one stopped them as they plodded back the way they had come. No one asked them where they were going.

For Hungary the ravages of liberation by the Russians still lay in the offing: the looting, the rapes, the devastating siege of Budapest in the winter to come. But, in a manner of speaking, Gusti's war was over. He would walk home in a few days a free man; shortly after, unable to bear the familiar surroundings in the absence of his loved ones, he moved to Mada.

In another manner of speaking, the war never ended for my father. Twelve years later, when the Revolution broke out, the wounds were as fresh as on the day he found out that the advice he had given Mancika had backfired. Bidding goodbye to the wife of his youth for what turned out to be the last time, he had instructed her, "Whatever happens, whatever you do and wherever you go, never let go of the children's hands."

And so when, in April 1944, a Hungarian nobleman had offered to hide Gusti's six-year-old niece, Marika, Marika's parents, heeding an older brother's advice, had courteously refused the offer. My cousin Marika and my father's daughter, Évike, had held on to their mothers' hands right to the last in the gas chambers of Auschwitz.

My father felt as much guilt on their account as if he had devised the crematoria himself.

AFTER THE WAR, after chance had brought them into each other's orbit, Shoshanna and Gusti moved to Budapest. She had grown up in a small town and he on a farm. They both disliked the dust, the grime, the hurly-burly of central Budapest, where their friends and the rest of the family lived. With some salvaged money, they bought an apartment in a suburb of Pest. There were fields in back of Róna Utca where camomile and poppies flowered in the summer. A twenty-minute walk from our house took us to the Rákospatak Canal, where you could easily imagine yourself in the village of Kis Pirics. This suburban existence proved to be both boon and hindrance during the Revolution, when the centre of Budapest was razed almost as thoroughly as it had been in 1945. Though we were relatively safe in the outlying fourteenth district, we were also isolated. It was hard to know what was going on downtown, where most of the action was taking place.

I came awake on October 23 not with Shoshanna shaking my shoulder in the dark as usual to get me ready for school at eight, but to the blaze of mid-morning sunshine and the scratch of static. Gusti was bending over me, beaming and speaking in a particularly cheerful, almost festive tone.

"You must get up, we're having a revolution!"

Over the static, the radio was transmitting a mixture of doublespeak and reassuring pap: "As reported yesterday, general meetings of students have been held in several Budapest universities." A little later: "In order to assure public order, the minister of the interior is not permitting any public meetings and demonstrations until further notice."

We didn't know that the students demanding democratization were trying to storm the radio building. By evening, sporadic volleys of machine-gun fire drowned out the broadcast. Was it that day, or the next, that Anna was delivered to our door?

Anna's father, Gusti's second cousin Ferkó, was a mid-level cadre in the ÁVO, the Hungarian secret police. His parents, who had died in Auschwitz, had had a nightmarish marriage: the father, a doctor, was known for brutalizing his wife, the mother Ferkó adored. Twenty years younger than Gusti, Ferkó came back from the extermination camps barely out of his teens. He joined the Party and was taken up by the ÁVO, which found youngsters of his type, bubbling with rage and schooled in the culture of sadism, particularly useful.

There were members of our extended family who shunned Ferkó, but my father wouldn't or couldn't. With so many gone, everyone who remained was precious. Even the scoundrels.

The ÁVO consisted of at least as many former Hungarian Nazis as concentration camp survivors, though the great majority of top-ranking ÁVO officers were Jews. One of the telling post-war Hungarian witticisms described the ÁVO as "Jews and Nazis idyllically united."

Gusti recoiled when Ferkó told him once that he had spent the previous night beating up a man under interrogation whom he well knew to be innocent of the charges against him. False charges, in fact, were the order of the day. Hundreds of thousands were arrested as enemies of the state or as wealthy kulaks, thousands were tortured, sent to internment camps, or murdered. In another popular joke, two prisoners are talking about their sentences. One asks: "What did you get?" The other replies: "Fifteen years." "For what?" "For nothing." "Impossible," says the first. "For nothing you get only ten."

There is no exact tally of ÁVO cadres who penetrated every corner of Hungarian life, spying, reporting, kidnapping, torturing, killing. According to one estimate, there were eighty thousand regulars and additional thousands of occasional agents and informants, an enormous proportion in a country of fewer than ten million.

But after the street fighting began on October 23, brutalizers quickly became victims. In Budapest, the only true atrocities of the Revolution were committed against members of the ÁVO. Lynchings became common, ÁVO officers strung up, sometimes by their feet, from trees and lampposts in the city's squares. When mob justice took hold, many ÁVO men first killed their families, then committed suicide.

Ferkó and his wife went into hiding, but not before providing for their two daughters. When they were approached about taking in Anna, Shoshanna and Gusti, who so often saw the world through very different lenses, were of one mind: naturally Anna could stay with us.

The night that Anna arrived, we were still sleeping upstairs, all of us in one room because of an anticipated coal shortage. Shoshanna and Gusti dragged their two sofa beds together from opposite sides of the living room and placed Anna between them. We woke at dawn to the rumble of heavy vehicles on Erzsébet Királyné Utja. From the balcony Gusti could make out that they were Russian tanks and trucks heading towards the centre of town. I drifted back to sleep to the drone of lumbering traffic.

At mid-morning there was a rap at the door. Shoshanna admitted a slight boy in an army greatcoat, but without any other insignia of the official military.

"*Jó reggelt, kedves nagyságos asszony.*" Good morning, dear and gracious lady.

He came into the living room and asked if he could sit. He had dark eyes and hair and just the faintest suggestion of peach fuzz at the corners of his upper lip.

"The thing is, the mates and I are going to start firing at the tanks any minute now. We're going to place the cannon by the side of your house. It's quite likely that the *Ruszkik* will fire back at us. So we'd really appreciate if you'd all take yourselves down to the cellar. When, my dear and gracious lady? Right away, if you please."

Róna Utca was a side street perpendicular to Erzsébet Királyné Utja. A row of low-rise apartment buildings faced a playground which stretched down to the main road. Our house, the last on Róna and farthest from Erzsébet Királyné, was at an ideal range for shooting at the passing cavalcade of Russian tanks.

Dragging mattresses and blankets helter-skelter behind us, we crowded the narrow stairway along with our neighbours. I had never seen the cellar before. It was like a dungeon, with a humpy earth floor, a bad smell, and a ceiling of wooden slats which Gusti, not a particularly tall man, nearly grazed with his balding head.

We were barely ensconced in a corner when the first shot, sickeningly loud and close, shook the foundations of the house. Taken by surprise, the Russians didn't respond immediately. Soon, however, the tanks began to return fire and the tinkling of glass added another note to the cacophony.

My sister's revolution began at this moment. She would not turn three until January. Not only was she as unruffled as her easy nature allowed, she was enjoying herself.

"Boom, boom," Juditka squealed in delight, clapping her small hands in rhythm to the rattling.

She didn't wet herself, she wasn't frightened, and she didn't cry.

GUSTI ALWAYS CLAIMED TO BE a physical coward, a small, soft man at home with words and numbers, frightened of risks, of change, of the unknown. But he bridled at the uncertainty and absence of hard news in the cellar, where even the radio's fairy-tale version of what was going on couldn't be heard. He itched to get outdoors to see what was happening, to make proper sense of the bursts of gunfire, to size up the situation. Besides, he told Shoshanna, who protested at his leaving, we needed to eat something in addition to *lekvár*. There must be somewhere in the neighbourhood he could find food.

Was he deliberately misleading her? Did he know that the Közért down the street was bombed out, that there was no food to be found in the shops, or did he continue on his way once he saw the local stores were without supplies, striding ever farther from home towards the centre of town?

The route he took was not towards the Közért on Erzsébet Királyné Utja, but up the lane running behind our house. He started out early in the morning on narrow, winding Dorozsmai Utca with the tactical sense of a man acquainted with the ways of war. Preferring side streets to open spaces, he set his face in the direction of the city.

When the back streets dried up, he climbed over rubbled pavement and past overturned trams. It would have taken him close to an hour to reach the Liget, with its smell of rotting leaves, its therapeutic baths, the agricultural museum, the zoo. Nothing untoward befell him until he reached Hősök Tere, Heroes' Square. In fact, it was not until he began to cross the plaza in the bright morning sunshine that he felt at all vulnerable. He suddenly realized that of all the times he had been in the square over a lifetime, he had never been alone there. This was normally a bustling place, one of the capital's distinctive landmarks. The Archangel Gabriel looked down from the central column that dominated the plaza, and Gusti was encircled by Hungary's leaders from Árpád to Kossuth. But there was not another living soul to be seen, and his footsteps echoed in the emptiness.

He willed himself forward with apparent nonchalance. He wasn't a revolutionary or a counter-revolutionary, he meant no harm to anyone. He was simply an ordinary citizen, peaceably walking to town. He was nearly across the square, nearly at the mouth of Andrássy Út, where he would once more be enclosed by buildings, safe from this huge, open space that made him an easy target, when he heard a purring motor. From the corner of his eye, for he dared not look anywhere but ahead, he caught a glimpse of a vehicle turning into Hősök Tere. A light tank, Russian markings on its side, manned by two soldiers in fur caps, each holding a machine gun.

Slowly, slowly the tank circled the great square, moving towards him. The barrels of the two guns were trained constantly on Gusti. My father plodded on towards the mouth of the street. The Russians were almost on top of him now and he felt a sensation down his spine which he was certain could only be a premonition of the end. My father was a man who, despite all that had happened, believed in God and in prayer. It may have crossed his mind to murmur the *Shema* under his breath. At the last moment the tank swerved to avoid him and rolled out of the square.

The rest of his march, which by then he had decided was to lead him to his office on St. István Körút, was uneventful but for two sights. In the middle of another square, he saw the torso of Stalin's colossal bronze statue, dragged there on the night of the 23rd, after insurgents had pulled it down from its rose marble pedestal near Hősök Tere. And in the garden of a villa on Andrássy Út (no one called this longest, most majestic of Budapest's thoroughfares by its official name, Stalin Út), he came upon a Hungarian police officer, blood congealed on his face in the October chill, kneeling rigidly, his gun propped in front of him. With a start, Gusti realized that the unfortunate man was not merely injured but dead, his body stiffened by rigor mortis.

By late morning when he arrived at the offices of the National Cattlebreeding Trust, other colleagues, too, had straggled in. In the exchange of news, the mercurial shift of Colonel Pál Maléter got top billing. On the 24th he had been ordered to lead a tank unit against the insurgents, but instead of shooting at the freedom fighters, he had joined them. Some spoke of appeals for American intervention and some of fierce street fighting. And as the conversation turned to shooting, the deafening clamour of nearby battle filled the room.

The Cattlebreeding Trust building was only a few blocks from the site where what would subsequently be known as the massacre of Parlament Tér was taking place even as Gusti and his colleagues shared their information. All that morning thousands of men and women had converged on the square around the parliament, waving the Hungarian tricolour (minus the Communist emblems) and chanting, "This is a peaceful demonstration," and "The radio is telling lies." The Russian tanks that wheeled among them were manned by soldiers sitting in open turrets and, judging by their smiles, sympathetic to the crowd. More Russian tanks were stationed in front of the parliament building. When the first volley of submachine gunfire hit the square, panic and pandemonium broke out. No one knew who had fired the first shots; according to one theory, ÁVO men posted on the rooftops of the apartment buildings in the square deliberately provoked the massacre by firing from above on unarmed civilians.

The Russians opened up and within moments the corpses of some 600 people lay strewn about. But at the Cattlebreeding Trust, to steady their nerves, my father and his colleagues took out a deck of cards. The hands of the dealer shook as he shuffled. "Gusti, what's to become of us here?" "Nothing, nothing," my father reassured him reflexively.

After a while, a pall of silence descended on the city. Carrying a small sack of potatoes that he had received at the office, Gusti headed back home later that afternoon. The return trip was uneventful, although barricades were proliferating in many sections of the city and at six an all-night curfew was imposed for the first time.

MY FATHER'S ACCOUNT of his day in the city is eclipsed in my memory by the events unfolding back home. As the days passed, we became restless underground, venturing upstairs for longer and longer stretches to use the toilet, to wash, to cook. I was always surprised by the sunshine streaming through the windows or by the wind blowing leaves or an old sheet of newspaper about outside. Somehow the string of days we had already spent in the cellar had displaced other

realities. It was the general brightness of the world above
ground, not the subterranean murkiness, that had the quality
of a dream.

Upstairs Shoshanna, her hands none too gentle in her
haste, subjected us three children to a cold-water sponge-
down; there was never enough time to heat the boiler. Gusti
towelled me briskly while Shoshanna, wearing an apron over
her winter coat, hurried to the kitchen to prepare a meal to
take below. Gusti then set up the chessboard at the little table
in front of the tile stove, out of habit, I guess, since he had
made no fire. He had recently started teaching me chess.

One day the shooting began early and we were caught
upstairs. Gusti had just shown me how the knight moved, a
strange, skewed hobble. The living room windows suddenly
cracked in a cross of artillery fire. "No one's trying to shoot
us," Gusti murmured as he pulled me to the floor close to
his warm bulk. It was only the force of an impact elsewhere
that made the windows cave in and splinter. "See," he said,
when we'd gotten up, and Shoshanna had come in from the
kitchen carrying Juditka and holding Anna by the hand.
"See, they haven't even fallen out of their frames." We were
soon repairing them, he and Anna and I, reinforcing the
cracks with tape in an intricate pattern against the force of
the wind gusting through the crevices.

Down in the cellar, it still felt cozy, still like a holiday.
The bonhomie with which we shared that small space with
the six other families in the house belied the day-to-day
frictions that, in earlier times, punctuated relations between
neighbours. For instance, Shanyi Petőfi didn't normally get

on with the Takácsos twins; now all three went demonstrating together. There was no hint of the rancour Shoshanna bore the janitor's wife, either. She and her husband were our closest cellar neighbours, in fact. Nothing in Shoshanna's manner as she offered the casserole of *sholet* beans to them betrayed her firm conviction that the janitor's wife was a thief.

Shoshanna always removed her rings and placed them on a small shelf above the kitchen table when she kneaded dough. One morning, before the cellar days, the janitor's wife had come upstairs as Shoshanna, her hands floury, mixed dough for noodles. She was trying to talk Shoshanna into buying some home-cured ham and *kolbász*, but Shoshanna wasn't having any. Not because we didn't eat pig, not at all; despite the mezuzah on our front door and our attendance at synagogue on all the major holidays, we ate everything. No, Shoshanna wasn't having any because she knew where the janitor's wife had cured those hams and sausages. She'd seen them with her own eyes from the doorway, the toilet door down the hall being ajar, and above the bowl – high up, mind you, because the ceilings in the apartments were all high – but right there in plain view hung the *kolbász*, the sausages, the *hurka*, the salamis. Shoshanna didn't say any of this to the janitor's wife, only to me after she had left, though she did wonder what there was for the janitor's wife to smile about as she went away. She understood when she discovered one of the rings missing, the ring with her initials in the shape of a butterfly, the one Gusti had given her on the day I was born.

This now seemed forgotten and so, too, was Takácsos Néni's offer to look after Gusti when the three of us went off on holiday the summer before. My mother admired white-headed Takácsos Bácsi, whom she called a long-suffering gentleman, while she frequently muttered under her breath that Erzsike Takácsos was the greatest *kurva* in the neighbourhood. "No, thank you," Shoshanna had said icily to Takácsos Néni. "Gusti knows how to look after himself."

"The cheek of her," Shoshanna had ranted to Gusti the night before we left for the Mátra. "Getting my permission in advance for her to look after you! Perhaps she got permission from Jenő's wife, too, for him to father Attila."

WHEN DID THE ATMOSPHERE in the cellar change? When did I realize that we were different from the other people below ground, that our interests were separate from theirs? Probably not for years. But I understood something of our distinctness the night Shanyi Petőfi raved about the lampposts.

Shanyi had the same name as Sándor Petőfi, our great national poet, the hero of the Revolution of 1848. Petőfi had died on the battlefield of Segesvár when he was only twenty-five, his soul throbbing with the ideals of liberty and the rights of man, the noble principles of the French Revolution. He had penned "Talpra Magyar," "Arise Hungarian," on the eve of the 1848 Revolution and it had become that conflict's anthem. I could recite "Talpra Magyar" with the best.

Arise Magyars! Your country calls you!
Now or never! Time enthralls you.

Shall we live as slaves or freemen?
Those the questions: choose between them!
By the God of every Magyar
Do we swear.
Do we swear the tyrant's handcuffs
Not to bear!

I had learned the poem from Gusti, who revered Petőfi and believed that he deserved to be known in every household on the planet. He was the greatest lyric poet who had ever lived, but only we Hungarians knew him, because he wrote in our language, the most beautiful language in the world but also the most difficult. I had a special bond with Petőfi for entirely personal reasons. The heroine of his magical epic *János Vitéz* was called Ilushka.

Perhaps, though, all of Hungary had a special bond with Petőfi. There must have been hundreds of Shanyi Petőfis, even thousands. Who knows how many of the children who threw Molotov cocktails at Russian tanks, the young people who gave up their lives in a quixotic struggle to make Hungary genuinely democratic and socialist, bore the name of Petőfi or were inspired by his genius and boldness.

During the day Shanyi didn't stay with us in the cellar. Feeling the heady freedom of his eighteen years, he didn't even bother to come home every night. But he was there on the night of October 30, when we got news that the *Ruszkik* were leaving. Our air force threatened to bomb the Soviet tanks unless they evacuated the capital, although there had been rumours for a couple of days that the Russians were going home.

Then came a startling announcement, delivered in a choked voice, on Budapest Radio:

Dear listeners, we are beginning a new chapter in the history of the Hungarian radio. For many years the radio has been an instrument of lies. It merely carried out orders. It lied day and night; it lied on all wavelengths. Not even at the hour of our country's rebirth did it cease its campaign of lies, but the struggle which . . . brought national freedom also freed our radio. Those who spoke those lies are no longer among the staff of the Hungarian radio, which will henceforth bear the name of Kossuth and Petőfi. We who are now at the microphone are new men. We shall tell the truth, the whole truth, and nothing but the truth.

The insurgents had torched Party headquarters in Buda and they had stormed the ÁVO headquarters in Pest, the members of the secret police agreeing to surrender on condition of being granted an amnesty.

"Amnesty," snarled Shanyi, who had brought a friend home with him to the cellar that night. They were lolling in the Petőfis' nook kitty-corner from ours, swigging *pálinka* from military-style canteens. "We're hoisting them onto lampposts, that's what I call amnesty!"

"Those ÁVO scum are all Jews anyway," his pal slurred.

"Well, as for the Jews," Shanyi proclaimed, "this country has paid enough already. It's too bad the great leaders of this country, the great Jewish leaders of this country, have seen fit to run off to Moscow! Otherwise, the justice of the lampposts would be far too good for them. I personally would be happy to tear them limb from limb. We'll keep the lampposts for the run-of-the-mill type of Jew, the type that didn't get finished off in '44."

I must have made some movement in our corner of the cellar. Perhaps I tugged on Gusti's or Shoshanna's sleeve. Why weren't they saying anything about Mancika Néni and Évike, about my cousin Marika, whom the good count had wanted to save? Why wasn't Petőfi Bácsi – who was known to bellow so loud at Shanyi and his pretty sister Éva that we could hear every word upstairs – why wasn't he telling Shanyi to stop? Why didn't he cuff him on the head as he was always threatening to do?

"Do you remember '44, Gusti Bácsi?" Shanyi pivoted towards us, as if he suddenly found our corner of the cellar particularly interesting. "Do you remember when Jews decorated the lampposts in town? What d'you suppose should be done to people who harbour the brats of ÁVO filth?"

"Oh, cut it out, Shanyi," Éva said softly. "Leave the children out of it."

No one said anything else that night. Not Takácsos Bácsi, whom my mother admired, not the janitor or his wife, not Petőfi Bácsi. Most surprisingly to me then, though not today, neither Gusti nor Shoshanna. Save for the occasional hiss of a candle, silence reigned in the cellar.

At dawn, Gusti shook me awake. "Would you like to come with me to visit Nanush?"

I nodded enthusiastically.

"It's going to be a long walk," he warned. "Are you up to it?"

He didn't take the back streets as he had when he walked downtown the week before. Instead, we followed our customary route alongside the park. We set out along Erzsébet Királyné Utja, where we would normally have taken a tram but now kept on walking instead. When I saw the soldier in a Hungarian uniform ahead, I wasn't scared. But when Gusti pulled me into the doorway of a strange apartment house, when I felt his convulsive grip on my arm, I became alarmed. After the soldier had passed, we turned on our heels and went home.

Gusti headed downtown by himself. Shoshanna didn't try to stop him, even though she remembered – we all did – what had happened to him at Hősök Tere the week before. That night he came home with biscuits from Nanush. He gave a barely perceptible shake of his head when Shoshanna looked a question at him. She said something about all of us going upstairs to sleep that night in case Shanyi turned up again, but he shook his head once more. "We can't risk it yet," he said. "If they start shooting, we're better off down here."

That's my last memory of the cellar until the night, a few days later, when we heard the rumble of Soviet trucks and tanks returning to Budapest. I remember Éva sobbing, "That puts paid to all our dreams."

Upstairs the next day Shoshanna said grimly, "It may have put paid to all their dreams, but it also puts paid to our future on the lampposts."

I'd always thought the end of the Revolution came at dawn on that November 4, when the Russians – taking advantage of the West's preoccupation with the Suez crisis – seized control of Hungary again. They kept it for the next thirty-three years. It surprised me later to read in the history books that this was the day on which the city became a true battlefield, that the fiercest combat actually began when the Revolution was known to be lost. Thirteen thousand Hungarians lost their lives in the fighting that continued for another six days in the capital and for months in other parts of the country.

But as I remember it, my family felt reprieved by the return of the Russians. The relief was akin to how Gusti must have felt in 1944 when he recrossed the bridge at Vásárosnamény to put himself in the path of the Russian liberators. In fact, in my parents' retellings, 1956 always sounded like a coda to 1944, Shanyi's ravings as ominous as the stomping of jackboots or the chug of a cattle train.

In fact, very little documented evidence of anti-Semitism during the Revolution is to be found. A smattering of atrocities occurred in the countryside: three Jews murdered in an industrial city, another three attacked at knifepoint in a village, some unfortunates beaten up in a provincial old-age home. Details of these events were slow to reach Budapest, the centre of Jewish life, where no pogroms occurred. Nevertheless, rumours were rife that Hungarian Nazis who had escaped to the West after the war were flooding back over a wide-open border. In the last days of the uprising, a pervasive fear, like a noxious cloud, settled upon the Jews of Hungary.

For my great-aunt Nanush, who adored my father, who adored me, that fear was enough to justify her refusal when Gusti begged her to take me for a few days, to hide me from the likes of Shanyi. Ibolya had married János, a Christian, a year earlier. Nanush's newborn granddaughter had been baptized. No one in their apartment house knew of the family's Jewish blood. Like Gusti and Shoshanna, Nanush and her family had long memories; they had all lived through 1944. Nanush wouldn't risk the baby in these times, expose her to the curiosity aroused by the inexplicable appearance of an older child, who, the neighbours might well assume, was the offspring either of ÁVO or of Jews, or both.

But then the Russians returned. The ÁVO was back in the saddle. Ferkó came to pick up Anna.

SOON AFTER, Shoshanna was bitten by a new enthusiasm. In my nine years, I had known her to have a few of these already. Once she had turned our kitchen into a dairy. Bags of cheesecloth suspended from hooks in the ceiling gathered curds and dripped whey into buckets on the floor. She and I had peddled the cheese in the back entrances of posh stores on Váci Utca until the Party secretary at Gusti's workplace had warned him we should stop. A few weeks before the Revolution, she had organized a nursery school in our apartment. When I came home from school in the afternoon, small children were marching up and down the corridors, eating little snacks of sugared tomatoes and *kolbász*. But when we came up from the cellar for good, the nursery school proved impossible to reinstate. At least half of the families involved had already left the country. And now Shoshanna was infected with the desire to escape as well.

She began interviewing the neighbours about the logistics of such a journey. The whole city was buzzing with rumours of flight. Gusti joked that if he were to believe everything he heard, the country itself must be on the move, a beast with countless legs marching towards Austria. Petőfi Néni had a brother whose sister-in-law knew someone who'd take us across the border if we gave the money to Petőfi Néni the day after tomorrow. Takácsos Néni knew of someone else who had already exploited the Petőfi connection and had made it to Vienna. The janitor's wife knew of yet another party who used fewer middlemen and consequently offered a better deal. But Gusti cited the case of a colleague at work who'd been turned back at the border. The guards were armed, or didn't Shoshanna know? The people who'd been refused were lucky to be turned back and not shot in the head.

Shoshanna took me to Blanka Néni, our pediatrician, because my throat was red. One could be frank with Blanka Néni. She scolded Shoshanna, "Crazy woman, why are you still here? Vera's in Canada. If I had a sister in Canada, you can be sure another doctor would be looking at Ilushka's tonsils today."

At home Gusti warned, "It's a long way from Blanka's Néni's office to Montreal."

Shoshanna also had a brother, Duved, living in London. When the mail service resumed, one of Shoshanna's doctors told her she must obtain a supply of streptomycin from her sibling in England. It was the only remedy against the terrible cramps that had plagued her for months. The pills arrived shortly after. Shoshanna took them. She went to the toilet.

When she came out, her face was white. Her eyes practically bugged out of their sockets. In the palm of her hand, on a square of brown toilet paper, reposed the long coil of a worm, a legacy of our Mátra summer and the feline hunters that had shared the cottage with us.

Though the worst aspect of Shoshanna's revolution appeared to be over, the bickering between her and Gusti about our possible departure escalated into the most bitter quarrels I had ever heard between them. The border with Austria was still open, and there people were streaming into refugee camps, waiting for word as to which Western country would accept them. It appeared that, for the time being, our government preferred to let the discontented leave, rather than keep them forcibly at home to instigate another insurgence.

Gusti refused to budge.

"My experience," he said loudly to Shoshanna – Gusti seldom raised his voice – "has always been this: if everyone's leaving by the back door, it's better to take the front door."

"Not so," Shoshanna said, throwing back her head. "The back door's open now!"

"I'll gamble on the front door," Gusti retorted. "I'll stake my life we can get papers legally from your sister or your brother when all this has passed."

"You love this accursed country despite everything. You have no intention of leaving!"

"Not now I don't. But there'll come a time when the front door will be wide open, you'll see."

Shoshanna narrowed her eyes. Her voice took on a taunting edge. "You're temporizing. What you are is just plain scared!"

"You're right, I *am* scared. I'm scared to take children over minefields and through barbed wire."

"You're scared, period."

"Have it your own way."

Shoshanna was right. Gusti was scared and he was temporizing. We crossed the border in May 1957, not across minefields or through barbed wire, but in a first-class compartment of the deluxe rail express heading westwards to Vienna. Final destination: London.

But Gusti had been right too. Our country was prepared to let us go at that time, provided someone in the West would take us in. Shoshanna petitioned Duved in London and Vera in Montreal. The sponsorship papers and first-class tickets arrived first from London.

We sat in the dining car, the table laid with sterling cutlery, the tablecloth starched damask. Shoshanna, her hair freshly permed, was wearing a generously cut tweed cape over a matching tapered skirt. Juditka and I were dressed in the look-alike sailor outfits Vera had sent from Montreal; we both carried new dolls purchased by Shoshanna especially for the journey. Our trunks held the barterable Hungarian treasures conventional wisdom decreed to be the coinage of the West: quilted, satin-covered eiderdowns and crocheted tablecloths. Cash, which would have been infinitely more useful, we were not allowed to take out of Hungary. My father's wallet contained the permitted £15 that Duved, on his schoolmaster's salary, had sent along with the train tickets. Dressed in his finest double-breasted suit, Gusti mustered a joke just before we arrived at the border. "Aga Khan takes his dear ones on a tour of Europe."

But once we crossed, once we surrendered our Hungarian identity papers at Hegyeshalom and were left with only the *laissez-passer* stamped with the dreary letters that spelled out "stateless," he turned to my mother with an expression of mournful gravity.

"This far, I have brought you myself. To the edges of my world. From here on, you're our captain."

Shoshanna's face was a study. Disillusionment, worry, and fear flitted over her features, a pair of permanent frown lines engraving themselves above the bridge of her nose. Then she tossed her head impatiently and fixed her gaze on the landscape: dusty, flat, and devoid of promise. Gusti was fifty-one, Shoshanna thirty-eight. The balance of power between them was about to change forever.

six

THE COLORATION OF THE LAND

It was all a jumble. I was speaking a language only my family understood, and I didn't understand the language everyone else spoke. Here "tea" was pronounced *tí*, although it was written t-e-a, just like in Hungarian. It came with milk, not lemon. Auntie Caroline served it on a little plate called a saucer with a biscuit on the side. We drank it in a room labelled the lounge, while watching a television program about a horse named Fury. The next day we were going to move into a castle. Apu had seen it already and it was amazing, he said. We were incredibly lucky. But today we were taking the Underground to Whitechapel to visit a lady at something called the HIAS. Uncle Dave had taken the afternoon off from work to escort us there. We were going to ride on a moving stair. Wouldn't that be exciting?

I visualized hopping onto a step suspended in space before being sucked down into the bowels of the earth. But then it wasn't like that at all. It was more like a rolling chain of stairs, wide enough for me and Juditka to stand on either side of

Shoshanna, clutching onto her as we were swept briskly downwards. It *was* exciting.

A couple of steps below us, Gusti and Uncle Dave were chortling like a pair of schoolboys, leaning towards each other conspiratorially, my uncle's sandy head alongside my father's balding pate.

"And how am I to prove to this Mrs. Mermelstein" – my father turned a merry face to his newly met brother-in-law – "that I really am Jewish?"

"There's only one sure way," Dave responded, and they guffawed once more.

"What are they talking about?" I asked Shoshanna.

"We're applying for assistance from a Jewish organization," she answered, her brow furrowing at the mention of the Hebrew Immigrant Aid Society.

"What's so funny about that?"

"Nothing."

"How are we going to prove that we're Jewish?"

"I think," Shoshanna said, "that it's stamped on our faces."

The next day we made our way to the *kastély*, the castle that was to be our new home. But Monahan Avenue, in the suburb of Purley, the place that Apu had brought us to by a succession of double-decker buses and by train and now, finally, on foot, was a mere street, not the grand park that should surround a real castle.

I sounded out the cream letters painted on a crossbar nailed to the squat forest green gate. "H-I-G-H B-A-N-K-S," I enunciated phonetically, making the appropriate Hungarian inflections.

"High banks," Shoshanna pronounced in English. "It means tall slopes." She pointed upward at the greenery that surrounded the wooden gate. A bushy cedar hedge grew high above street level. An embankment of grass rose between the street and hedge.

"That's the name of the house." Gusti's chest swelled with pride. "In England nice houses have names."

I didn't ask him why he was now talking about a house, when before he'd told us we were going to a *kastély*. I was childish to believe in castles. A clever nine-year-old would have understood right away that he had meant a nice house, not a real *kastély*.

"Go up?" Juditka asked tentatively. Gusti gathered her in his arms while Shoshanna unlatched the gate.

The name of the house was apt. It perched above us on a steep incline. Risers of tender green lawn separated tiers of bright blooms and flowering shrubs. A pair of stone stairs on each side of the garden scaled the slope. Great hedges separated the property from its ivy-clad neighbours. The house itself was of dour grey stucco with a pitched terra cotta roof. Curiously, the front door was set into the side of the house, not its front. There was a shiny brass knocker attached to it, slim and tapered, shaped vaguely like our mezuzah back home. At first I thought it might be an English variety, but Gusti demonstrated its function. I reached up and allowed it to clang smartly a few times.

From a huge key ring, Gusti extracted a large key and turned it in the lock. We entered a glassed-in porch, impatient as he searched for yet another key that would open the inner door. Inside we breathed the dust of long disuse. Sheets covered everything in sight except for a pair of porcelain vases that were almost as tall as me. The Persian carpeted staircase wasn't the sweeping spiral I had imagined, but it was satisfyingly grand with a landing built into its wide curve and a lovely carved banister. We made the rounds of dining room, lounge, and kitchen downstairs, and counted five bedrooms upstairs. Brass beds in all of them, a crucifix above one of the twin beds in the master bedroom. Gusti removed it impassively, opening a drawer in a small cabinet and placing it within.

"An unbelievable stroke of luck to get this place," he said wonderingly.

"A miracle that it should fall into our hands," Shoshanna agreed. "Somehow we'll have to make it up to her."

"I'll tell her to let the gardener go," Gusti ventured.

"You've never gardened a day in your life."

"Yes, but I've got nothing better to do with myself at the moment. And I studied gardening at school once upon a time."

Shoshanna frowned and was silent for a moment. Then she squared her shoulders. "Let's go buy some groceries and then you'll have to tell me how I'm to find my way to this place Ilushka and I are going to tomorrow."

ROW UPON ROW of two-storey red-brick houses with bow windows. This was East Dulwich, very different from Purley, the garden neighbourhood of the previous day. Monahan Avenue with its beautifully groomed gardens and imposing homes, its Rolls-Royces and Jaguars parked in front, was much grander than this street, ironically called Crystal Palace

Road. And High Banks may not have been a castle, but it was much nicer than this house. What were we doing here?

"On the weekend you'll come home," Shoshanna said at the threshold, putting her hands on my shoulders, her blue eyes holding mine with great intensity. "And you'll see me in the corridors. But it's not a good idea to talk to me *magyarul*. Actually, it's probably not a good idea to talk to me at all while I'm working here. Friday afternoon I'll take you home to High Banks. In the meantime you'll go to school with the other kids, and eat with the other kids, and sleep with the other kids. You'll have lots of fun and a great deal to tell Apu and Juditka on the weekend. And you'll see how fast you'll learn English this way."

Her words announced the worst calamity that had ever befallen me. A scolding for wetting the bed was nothing. Being slapped for bad behaviour was a picnic. Leaving country and family behind didn't rate on this scale of awfulness. It was such a shock that I forgot to cling to Shoshanna when she kissed me. I allowed myself to be embraced and turned in the direction of a small queue of girls about my age who were lining up in the hall.

I retain three memories of my sojourn in the orphanage on Crystal Palace Road. One is of being surrounded by a group of girls and boys in the playground of the school we attended up the street with children who weren't orphans. I was in the centre of a circle as if for a game of Farmer in the Dell. I stood alone. The object of the game seemed to be to point at my shoes, my totally unremarkable Hungarian shoes, the lace-up two-tone black and white boots I'd always worn. On their feet, the shrieking mob wore loafers or running shoes. They were jabbering to one another in the language I was supposed to be learning, while I remained mute behind the wall of my foreigner's clothing and locked tongue.

My second memory is of returning to the orphanage at the end of the school day and passing by a room where my mother, dressed in a white apron, was ironing sheets. She looked up at me for an instant and waved – it wasn't clear whether in greeting or as a signal for me to move on – and then addressed her undivided attention to the ironing board.

The third memory is of the dormitory. We were in bed: two rows of cots with high sides facing each other across the length of a broad room. It was late spring and inside there was a golden glow from the rays of the evening sun. It was as if I was literally beside myself, observing. I was making enough noise to keep several dormitories awake, not just mine. Matron came in, a dumpy little woman whose own grandson had the best spot in the room, the bed next to the window where the breeze blew the curtains in. Matron tried to reason with me in impenetrable English and in a progressively more exasperated register. The room had darkened and the front of my pyjama top was drenched by my tears, the sleeves wet from repeated swabbings of my nose. In the beds next to mine, exhausted children burrowed beneath the covers to shut out the sight and sound of me.

I remained obdurately inconsolable. I was pretty sure my mother would be coming back, though I was not absolutely certain. In Hungary she used to threaten me with the *Intézet*, but I hadn't yet had a chance to be sufficiently bad in this country to merit that fate. Nonetheless, she had put me in an orphanage. This was where she thought I belonged. She and Gusti and Juditka were to live in High Banks, and my place was here. And I never even told them of my disappointment with High Banks. I never said a word about it not being a proper *kastély*. Still, they must have guessed somehow and banished me for my ingratitude.

Shoshanna did indeed turn up in the morning. The other children were getting dressed, lining up for the toilet and washstands, flannels and towels in hand. I hadn't budged from bed, nor shut my eyes all night long. They were slits in my swollen face.

Matron marched into the dormitory, gesticulating, explaining, raising her voice at Shoshanna.

Shoshanna looked at me in consternation. She shook her head. "What am I to do with you?"

"Take me home."

"I can't take you home right now."

"When?"

Shoshanna furrowed her brow. She exchanged words with Matron. She turned back to me.

"If I promise you that you'll come home for good on Friday, will you promise me that you'll not carry on like this for the rest of the week?"

"'For good' means I never have to come back here ever again?"

Shoshanna nodded.

I nodded back.

On the way home on Friday Shoshanna explained matters to me in snatches. Although she had been commuting from Purley to East Dulwich all week, she kept verifying directions with passersby and their cockney instructions were

hard to decode. ("Yes, yes, luv, that's th' wy to th' stysh'n.")
Once we were on the Green Line double-decker headed for
Purley, the story flowed more smoothly. At HIAS a week
earlier, we had been offered clothes and kosher food, but
Shoshanna had demanded English lessons and a job instead.
"No charity! Work is what we want!" she had insisted. She
and I were supposed to be achieving both at Crystal Palace
Road, a home for children from broken families. "Broken
families" meant single-parent families, and because there was
only one parent – or sometimes two parents who didn't live
together – the families were poor. So the children were in an
institutional home during the week and went to their families on the weekend.

Yes, I was quite correct, ours wasn't a broken family. But
we were poor and we were a special case. We were Hungarian
refugees. I especially needed to learn English, so I could fit
in and excel in school as I had back home. There were two
hundred children waiting to get into this institution ahead
of me, but an exception had been made because I was a
refugee. And a job had been found for Shoshanna, since she
had demanded work rather than take social assistance.

"And now we're out of there, because of you," she
grumbled, but without much conviction. "It would have
been better if you could have liked it." She smoothed the
hair off my forehead and we sat quietly for a while.

"I didn't like how that Matron played favourites," she
added. "It's shocking the way she and her grandson dine on
meat while everyone else gets toast and jam. It's unjust, a disgrace really. And it was disgusting the way you all took baths
together, the lot of you wallowing in one another's dirt and

germs. I won't stand for such a thing. I've decided I'm not going back either. We'll just have to find some other way."

A week later I was off to Holy Cross Academy with Felicity and Joazina. We walked to the foot of Monahan Avenue, continuing down the green slopes of Purley Knoll to where we waited for a bus. Felicity and Joazina wore their school uniforms: olive green tunics called gymslips, braided belts named girdles, and green bowler hats with a tiny red cross embroidered in silk floss in the centre of the band. I made do with a long-sleeved white blouse and my wool mauve pleated skirt from Budapest, which was much too warm for late June. Black loafers had been procured from some unknown source, as I refused to wear my Hungarian two-tones.

Felicity and Joazina lived in a Tudor-style mansion higher up the crest of Monahan Avenue. We met them one morning when they were strolling down the hill with their mother. They were headed for the shops on Brighton Road, and Shoshanna and I were off to buy groceries at Sainsbury's. Felicity was about my age, Joazina a few years younger. Both had dark eyes and dark hair like their mother, a jowly lady whose thick legs and ankles drew critical comments from Shoshanna, even though she felt nothing but gratitude towards her.

Felicity and Joazina's mother also spoke with an accent, and Shoshanna later said that they had conversed as one immigrant to another, despite the fact that she was the wife of a Spanish diplomat and we were paupers. In no time at all, the diplomat's wife had offered to speak to the headmistress at Felicity and Joazina's school. After all, everyone in England

Shoshanna and I, 1948. My birth was the fulfillment of the seemingly impossible dreams of both my parents.

Jani Bácsi and Cirmi, with Georgetta, during the early golden years of their marriage in the 1930s.

Shoshanna, Gusti, Cirmi, and Gréti, Zoli Bácsi's wife, in 1946 at one of Budapest's thermal baths.

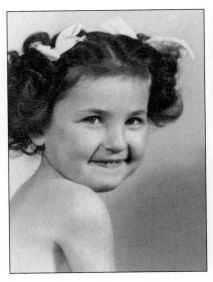

Hair curled and crimped for the photographer. A feather duster induced my smile.

Mancika in the pose in which she presided over our lives in Budapest.

"Loving you forever," Márton wrote to Shoshanna, on the back of this photograph taken around the time of their engagement.

"Aga Khan takes his dear ones on a tour of Europe," Gusti quipped as we left Hungary, travelling first class and dressed in our best. But he abdicated the captainship of the family when we crossed the border.

Shoshanna, Gusti, and Judy in the garden at High Banks, 1958.

In my English school
uniform and, as always,
with a book nearby.

Iszku and Nechama, in a suburb of Tel Aviv, soon after the State of
Israel came into being. The family's mad idealist, Iszku chose to work
on the land instead of practising law as he had been trained.

Shoshanna in the era when she played *Cinderella*, *Sleeping Beauty*, and *Briar Rose* in charity theatricals.

In the garden of the house in Beregszász: Apuka, Shoshanna, Mamuka, Lilli (pregnant with Tibike), Izidor, Magda.

Rózsika, the eldest of Shoshanna's sisters: "Everything the best, but luckless." Her daughter was the first Juditka.

Magda, Vera, and Shoshanna, with Juditka in the carriage. Shoshanna loved babies. Mamuka had predicted she would have a dozen.

Lilli and Izidor on their
wedding day. They could have
yoked her to an ox and she
wouldn't have protested.

Lilli with Tibike. Lilli knit and crocheted all his baby clothes, but
Shoshanna faulted her for being tense and short-tempered with him.

Magda and Józsi at their engagement. There is always less to say about a rapturous union than about a miserable one.

A swimming party by the Vérke River. Shoshanna is in the foreground, with her beloved brother-in-law Józsi on her left.

Nagyapa, the family's patriarch, second from the left, on vacation with Apuka, his son, fourth from the left, at a spa, possibly in Carlsbad.

wanted to do their bit for Hungarian refugees. Almost certainly Miss Rutledge would be persuaded to waive the private school fees. That Holy Cross was not merely a private school but a Catholic private school had not escaped Shoshanna and Gusti's notice. And before dispatching me there for the first time, they offered a few preparatory remarks.

We were sitting around the wooden, country-style table in the kitchen. The kitchen was the only down-at-the-heels room at High Banks. Tucked into the shabby side of the house, in the shadow of the ivied walls of its neighbour, it was dank and lit only by an overhead bulb that hung from a long cord above the table. We were eating white bread toast with baked beans from a can, Shoshanna having heard a television commercial at Uncle Dave's that claimed this made a nourishing English tea. Juditka was complaining that Shoshanna hadn't yet served George, the imaginary friend she had acquired when we moved to High Banks. Juditka refused to eat until a place for George had been set beside her.

"Oh, quit whining, for God's sake," Shoshanna said, dumping a tablespoon of baked beans on a quarter slice of toast and putting the plate on the placemat next to my sister.

"Do you like it, Georgie?" Juditka asked. "He doesn't like it, Mummy."

Gusti ignored her and instead addressed me with the facts of our current situation. It was true that the English were trying their utmost to help Hungarian refugees. That was why we were living in an elegant house like High Banks, on a jewel of a street like Monahan Avenue. We were the guests of Miss Mabel Potter, the headmistress of the school where Auntie Caroline taught in London. Miss Potter had recently inherited High Banks, and under the terms of her aunt's will, she was not permitted to rent it out. As she had no need to live in High Banks herself for the moment (she might, perhaps when she retired, but for now she was happy in town, near the school where she taught), she was letting us use it for free for as long as we needed.

Now Miss Potter was a Church of England lady, as was Auntie Caroline. Uncle Dave was Jewish like us, except no one knew that he was Jewish, not even his sons. Certainly not Miss Potter. So he had asked us not to advertise the fact that we were Jews. Just the way he didn't advertise it, even though every morning he davened quietly to himself. Religion was a private business.

I didn't daven in the morning. The old rabbi to whom Shoshanna had taken me for a few furtive sessions of religious instruction back in Budapest – furtive because the Party frowned on such activities – had never had a chance to teach me the morning prayer. Shortly after our lessons began, a cadre at Gusti's workplace had taken him aside and said that the visits to the rabbi had better stop. I did pray every night though. Out loud in Hebrew, the way the old rabbi had taught me. And I shouldn't stop, Gusti now said, patting me on the head. Under any circumstances. I was to remember every word of the *Shema*, beginning with the word *Ve'ahavta*. Had the rabbi explained the words of the prayer to me?

I shook my head, no. He had simply drilled the sounds into me with a kindly, abstracted air as we stood by the velvet curtains of the ark and the flickering flame of the eternal light in his musty little shul. The *Ve'ahavta* was our most important prayer, Gusti pronounced. It meant, "Thou shalt love the Lord thy God with all thy heart, and with all thy soul and with all thy might." That's what the scroll in the mezuzah said, too.

"When are we putting up the mezuzah?" I asked.

"We can't put up a mezuzah here on Miss Potter's doorpost," Gusti said with a little sigh. "That would be advertising. But we will continue to be Jewish in quiet ways."

"The thing is," Shoshanna broke in, "they mustn't know that you're Jewish at this school. So don't tell them. Under any circumstances."

"I can't tell them anything," I pointed out. "I don't know how to speak English."

"But you will," Shoshanna said brightly. "Very soon you will."

My knowledge of English was nearly non-existent, yet somehow I understood perfectly when Miss Rutledge, the headmistress, took me aside on my first morning as the other children assembled for prayers in the auditorium. Miss Rutledge was tall and had a leathered, tanned face that contrasted dramatically with her shock of white hair. "Are you Catholic or Protestant?" she asked, bending from her great height to look into my eyes.

My heart started to pound. Somehow, with a worldly intuition I didn't know I possessed, I grasped that there were Protestant children at the school and that their morning worship was different from that of the Catholic majority. At this moment, in fact, a hush descended on the assembly hall.

With a swishing of gymslips and scraping of chairs, a hundred girls dropped to their knees. I felt my face flushing. Why, oh why, had no one briefed me on how I was to field this question? Was I to say that I was Catholic or Protestant? It was one thing to be quietly Jewish at home, as Gusti instructed, but what was I to be in this place?

This much I knew: a Jew must never kneel to pray. So it couldn't possibly be right to say that I was Catholic. But my parents hadn't told to me to say that I was Protestant either. Only not to say that I was Jewish.

I continued to stare blankly at Miss Rutledge, while my throat constricted and my mind raced furiously. She placed her hands on my shoulders: "Protestant or Catholic?" she repeated, not unkindly but with a slightly impatient tug.

It felt as though our gazes were locked for an eternity. Then the answer came to me. There were only four words I knew to string together in English. They now tumbled out to my rescue.

"I don't understand English."

Feigning ignorance wasn't advertising. Nor was it lying.

Miss Rutledge gave a small shrug and steered me in the direction of the Protestant girls. Relieved that I wasn't required to kneel, I remained sequestered behind my wall of silence.

"How did it go at school?" Shoshanna asked anxiously when I arrived home that afternoon sweating in my woollens. I replayed the incident with Miss Rutledge and with some pride reported my Solomonic response to her question.

"Oh, my God," Shoshanna shrieked, "you pretended not to know the difference between Catholic and Protestant?

Oh, my dear God! They'll think we're atheists. We'll be run out of the country for being Communists!"

I DON'T KNOW HOW my parents smoothed over my blunder, but we weren't run out of the country. I stayed on at Holy Cross for a few more weeks until the end of term, with the understanding that I would attend a public primary school in the fall. In the meantime Shoshanna found a job in nearby Croydon, at the Philips radio and television factory, and Gusti, who was still unemployed, took my English education in hand.

Gusti was tone deaf when it came to music, and pretty much the same with respect to the nuances of English pronunciation. He couldn't master the "th" sound or the general softness of English consonants by comparison with the emphatic sounds of Hungarian. Nevertheless, he applied himself diligently to the night courses he and Shoshanna were taking. He was at Level One, she at Level Three, in the *Essential English* grammar texts. And whatever he learned, he conscientiously passed on to me. Solemnly he would intone the English expression, and I mindlessly intoned after him: "A bearrd in de hand is vort two in de bush."

While my mother mastered the intricacies of the coiling machine at the factory, feeding into it fine wire off a spool to ensure clean, static-free sound in radio sets around the world, Gusti taught himself to iron, wash dishes, and run errands. It was he who took me and Juditka, with the omnipresent yet invisible Georgie in tow, to the red-brick Purley Public Library and enrolled me in the children's section.

I began to read in English without understanding most of the words. Liberated from the oppression of school lessons in an alien language and released from the stress of maintaining my family's cover, I flung myself at the cornucopia of books on the library's shelves with a kind of manic enthusiasm. At first I resorted frequently to our English-Hungarian dictionary, but as I found myself absorbed by story after story, I couldn't bear to stop to check precise meanings. It was some time, for instance, before I realized that "grim" and "grin" weren't the same word and that there was a difference between "tail" and "tale."

But perfect comprehension was beside the point. Suddenly there were all these alternative lives to be discovered: on the floor-to-ceiling shelves, in books of every size and colour, were children who rode horses, studied acting, engaged in swordplay. Children who lived centuries ago, who served as pages for King Arthur, or crossed the Rubicon with Caesar. My particular favourites were boarding-school adventures. It didn't occur to me to equate my short sojourn at the home on Crystal Palace Road with the scary and exciting things that happened in *Dimsie Maitland: Head Girl* or *The Abbey Girls at School*. Real life and book adventures were not of the same universe.

I lived to read. I read *Heidi* and *A Dream of Sadler's Wells* in a single week, and as my speed and understanding improved, I reread them in single sittings. Suddenly and strangely, I was ecstatically happy. It was like falling in love.

Gusti too was reading. Each morning he purchased the *Times* and plodded his way through the headlines and subheads – he wasn't up to the stories themselves – with the aid

of the dictionary. Every night, he seated himself by the telephone table in the hall and dialled Dave in London. "It says
here," he shouted, for he never grasped the idea that long
distance required no more than normal projection of voice,
"that the Commonwealth leaders have come to a joint state-
ment of concern over what happened in Hungary. Can you
tell me what that's about?"

He listened for a while, then asked deferentially, "Duved,
do *you* think this will be useful?"

He seemed to enjoy these evening conversations with
Dave almost as much as I enjoyed my trips to the library.
Together they tut-tutted over the picket line violence in
the national bus strike and communed over the meaning
of Khrushchev's ousting of Kaganovitch, Molotov, and
Malenkov from the Politburo. But whereas I was advancing
by leaps and bounds in my acquisition of English vocabulary, Gusti's progress was slow. Shoshanna moved up to Level
Six in *Essential English* before he made it to Level Two. Still
he continued to persevere, keeping ledgers of new words
found in the *Times*, with their Hungarian equivalents
inscribed in his even, elegant script.

IT WAS AROUND THIS TIME that the past surfaced in a curious
and singular way. Uncle Dave called one evening and said to
Shoshanna that a couple of her old admirers were eager
to pay us a visit. Shoshanna seemed pensive when she got off
the phone and stood for a long time in front of the mirror
by the phone table. It was an antique affair with bevelled
edges that threw back her image in weirdly distorted waves
like a mirror in a funhouse. She was looking careworn and

frumpy these days in any case, her permed hair unshaped since our departure from Hungary, her clothes a bit tight because of our starchy diet. Dissatisfied, Shoshanna turned away from her reflection.

"Duved says that Bandi and Nunny want to come visit us on Sunday," she called out to Gusti. "Finally a chance for you to meet Nunny."

Much hinged on this encounter. Nunny and Bandi were high school chums of Uncle Dave's, all three members of a group of six university students who had escaped from Hungary shortly before the war broke out and who had married and settled in England. Among them, Nunny had made good in the splashiest way. He was a frozen food magnate, owned a huge farm in the country, and was being touted for a knighthood. For someone with Gusti's farming background and experience, Nunny was a gatekeeper of almost mythical proportions.

"I shall make a lamb roast," Shoshanna announced grandly. "That is what the English consider a delicacy. But for dessert I shall prepare something I'm sure their wives would never make. What do you think they'd prefer, Gusti, apple or cabbage strudel?"

"I know I'd prefer both."

"And are you prepared to peel a pile of apples and scrape your fingers grating cabbage?"

"I don't suppose I have a choice."

Shoshanna looked so pretty on Sunday that it deserved comment. She had brushed her hair back behind her ears and parted it in the centre, plucked her eyebrows and pencilled them in in half-moons, and painted her lips so red that her teeth gleamed white in contrast. She wore a cream sundress with a pattern of pink cabbage roses that I didn't know she owned. "Oh, you look beautiful today," I said admiringly as soon as the company walked in. I was rewarded with a ferocious glare before she turned to her guests with a dazzling smile and embraced the two men in turn. Foolish me, for having forgotten her earlier injunction not to talk out of turn this time, for heaven's sake, and not to say anything embarrassing. But who would have thought a compliment was embarrassing? "Very embarrassing," she chastised me the next day. "They used to know me when I was beautiful without making an effort."

"What's your name?" Nunny Bácsi turned to me after he had shaken hands with Gusti. His Hungarian had a singsong lilt to it.

"Ilushka."

"I know that. But what's your *English* name going to be?"

"Most Ilonas become Helens here," Bandi Bácsi offered.

"Ilushka doesn't like Helen," Gusti chuckled quietly. "She says it's an old-lady name."

"Your older sister's name is Ilona, too," Shoshanna recalled to Bandi as she showed the guests to their seats in the dining room. "She was with us in the *Lager*. Dave says she likes it in Israel."

"It's not an easy life, but I think she's reasonably happy there."

"Duved tells me," Gusti addressed Nunny, "that you all originally intended to go to Israel – Palestine as it was then."

"And very lucky we were, too, to have England take us in instead. I've thrived in this country. I can't imagine what I'd have amounted to on a kibbutz. The English are very good to you, if you make an effort to fit in."

"The English have been very good to us also," Gusti agreed, his hand gesturing vaguely to include the mahogany dining table set with sterling and crystal, the china figurines on the mantel, the Chippendale desk by the far wall. "But not particularly because we fit in. They've been good to us because we stick out. They've befriended us on account of our refugee status."

"Yes, well," Nunny said, sliding peas onto the back of his fork, English style. "I recommend that if you want to get ahead, you try to fit in. Take on the coloration of the land."

"What do you mean?" Gusti asked. There was a touch of frost in his voice.

"Being a Jew is a social disadvantage in this country," answered Nunny.

"It was more than a social disadvantage in the country that I left. That's why I left it."

"This is perfectly delicious, Anna," Bandi broke in.

"Wait till you see what I've made for dessert."

After everyone had oohed and aahed over the two kinds of strudel, Gusti got up to make espresso. Shoshanna served it out on the terrace in the heirloom demitasse cups from home. Juditka scampered off to play with a friend from across the street. I dragged a slingback canvas chair off the terrace into the sunshine, out of range of adult scrutiny but still well within earshot should the conversation turn interesting. The grown-ups were discussing Bandi's jewellery store and the popularity of frozen turkeys at Christmas, and I soon lost the thread of their talk as I immersed myself in a new book about an imaginary land ruled by a young king called Carol. The hero wasn't the king but a boy adventurer, whose mission it was to stave off threats to the beleaguered monarch.

Something about the tone and earnestness of the adults' voices brought me back from the tribulations of King Carol. "And your sisters?" I heard Bandi ask in a tight voice.

"Rózsika went straight into the gas with her little girl and our mother."

"And Magda? I so looked up to Magda. She was just a couple of years older than me, and so charming, so attractive," Nunny's voice had lost its breezy confidence and nonchalance.

"Magda and Vera and I were together until September 1944."

"Anna," Gusti said quietly, "don't. You'll get yourself upset."

Shoshanna ignored him. She didn't sound upset, or at least not the way I knew her to get upset. "We were together until September 12. I still fast on that day every year. It's another Yom Kippur for me. That's the day the English bombed us in Gelsenkirchen."

Shoshanna's voice was flat, quite devoid of emotion, as if she were reciting a chronicle that didn't have anything to do with her. She kept repeating certain details over and over.

"Gelsenkirchen is in the Ruhr Valley, by the Ruhr River. We were transported there in June, I think. We were working in an oil refinery, collecting all manner of debris, hauling huge planks and bricks in chain gangs. We lived in canvas tents, it was autumn. I think they must have thought we were soldiers, the Allies must have thought that we were men. We looked like men. We were living in canvas military tents. Our heads had been shaved, and we wore some kind of grey pyjama.

"When the bombs started to fall, Magda, Vera, and I, we all ran in different directions. They were English planes, the planes had English markings, they came to bomb the plant. The planes kept on coming, one after the other. And at first, before the attack started, we looked up at the sky and shouted to the English, 'Come, come, come! Make an end to everything! Make an end to this war!'

"When they came, all three of us scattered in different directions. They dropped the bombs, but that wasn't enough. They landed and trained their machine guns on us, they threw rockets at us. We were darting this way and that, trying to avoid the guns, the rockets, trying to escape. It must have been because they thought we were soldiers. We looked like men. Our hair was still so short.

"Suddenly I saw my cousins. Klári lay on the ground, and Rózsi was sitting beside her. Blood was spilling out of Rózsi's eyes, as if she were weeping blood, and she howled at me to help Klári. Klári was lying on her stomach and her whole back was ripped open. I saw her insides, her kidneys looked like huge purple beans. Maybe I should have stopped but I kept running, and then I collided with someone, a person running right into me, with big dilated eyes, her face all black from the oil. It was Vera. I almost didn't recognize my own sister, but then I grabbed her hand, and we ran on together. And God gave me something, some instinct. It was as if He whispered in my ear and told me what to do, so that whenever the blast came, I knew to pull Vera down with me. Because if you were standing when the blast came, it was all over. Whenever I heard that terrible whooshing whistle all around us, I groped for Vera and pulled her down. And then we ran on again.

"And then it was finished. Maybe it took fifteen minutes, maybe twenty. The planes left."

Shoshanna fell silent. No one spoke for a while. Then Nunny said very quietly, "And Magda?"

"I started to call. Magda? Where is Magda? Did you see Magda? No one had seen her. I lifted up every head, every head detached from its body. I lifted every arm. Every leg. Every trunk. I lifted everything. Looking for Magda. I started to holler, I went completely crazy. And then someone said to us that they had seen Magda with an SS officer, following one of the SS who was taking her and a few of the others to some kind of shelter. The Germans had their bunkers for safety.

"But it wasn't true. Magda was killed in the attack, though we never found her body. The next day or the day after that, all the dead were cremated. We were seven hundred women and young girls, and half of us died in twenty minutes.

"When the English came the next day and the next, we stayed inside our tent. I lay on top of Vera every time the attacks started. I thought, If we're going to die, let's both of us go together, like one. And we never again said to the sky, 'Come, come, you English, destroy everything so it will be all over.' Now we knew what it meant if they came, what it meant to destroy everything. Everything was us."

SEPTEMBER CAME and I started at a new school. I had found a new name for the occasion: Elaine. It sounded like a proper

English name, the kind that Nunny had said I needed, but without the maiden-aunt connotations of Helen.

Elaine had class; I had found her in the story of King Arthur. She was the fair and peerless lady who married the most romantic of the knights of the Table Round, Sir Launcelot, and she was the mother of Sir Galahad, the good knight who retrieved the Holy Grail. What the Holy Grail was, I wasn't exactly sure, especially since the Grail was sometimes called the Sangreal and had puzzling associations with Our Lord's blood. I concluded that, like Guenevere and Merlin and Morgan Le Fay, the Grail was all about being English. And, in my regulation navy gymslip, white blouse, and plimsolls, I looked like a fair approximation of an English girl myself when Shoshanna and I arrived at Christ Church Primary School at the beginning of term.

The unassuming red-brick schoolhouse on High Street near Purley Station bore a discreet cross etched into its gabled face above a large arched window. But the cross didn't frighten or put me off. It was a plain and modest English kind of cross, seemly, unbedecked by a suffering Jesus. It was the well-mannered religious equivalent of green lawns and tea roses.

Shoshanna left me in the hands of Mr. Ireton, the headmaster, a florid-faced, dark-haired man, well-built and handsome, who escorted me to my class and introduced me to my teacher, Mr. Jack. I was surprised by the way both Mr. Ireton and Mr. Jack enunciated my new name. They said "EeLAINE," whereas I thought I was "ELLaine." I'd given myself a name I didn't know how to pronounce properly. There was so much I had to learn.

But I felt it would be safe for me to learn things from Mr. Jack. Mr. Jack was short, roly-poly, and bald except for the sides of his head, which were a grizzled grey. He wore a brown suit and a huge smile; his eyes were kind, and his broad, large nose gave him a jovial and slightly raffish air. He put a hand on my shoulder as he presented me to the class. They were to welcome me, he said, I was a Hungarian refugee. Would it be all right with me if I was assigned to St. Patrick's? Margaret Avery, my house captain, would be in charge of making sure that I jolly well fit in. I said yes to everything. Yes, I'd be happy to be desk-mates with Margaret. Yes, I would bring in a shilling the next day for a week's worth of hot lunches.

I took to Christ Church Primary instantly and whole-heartedly. Morning exercises in assembly, beginning with the Lord's Prayer and announcements. Games of rounders and netball in PT. Morris dancing on Friday afternoons. Daily diary writing – Mr. Jack let us use a Biro for daily diary, although for other subjects it was pencil or pen and ink. Arithmetic, nature study, composition, Scriptures, penman-ship, I was game for everything. I learned to skip rope in recreation, I was inaugurated into the serious business of swapping marbles.

A picky eater all my life, I developed a passionate appetite for the meals we were served in the assembly hall that con-verted to a cafeteria at lunch time. Part of the charm was being waited upon by our classmates, who took turns at being waiters and waitresses. Soon I was to have a turn, too. The food was dished up at the front of the room by lunch ladies wearing white aprons and hair nets. They reached into great steaming vats to fill our plates with mashed potatoes, greens, brown gravy, and meat that gave off delicious English smells (no garlic, no onions). And there was always something lovely for dessert, which was called pudding whatever the selection: blancmange, treacle, canned peaches, custard, or raspberry jelly.

NO JOB OFFER for Gusti came from Nunny, and he continued to haunt the labour exchange in search of work. Sometimes Shoshanna accompanied him, both for moral support and to make sure that his English was understood by the English. But Shoshanna was seldom able to keep herself in the background and soon began to hector the employment officers. "Look, my husband is willing to do *anything*. You *must* have something for him!"

"All I have this week, madam, is an opening for a dustman. We have to wait until a suitable position opens up for a gentleman of Mr. Kalman's calibre."

Shoshanna took a dim view of this reasoning, noting tartly for the benefit of the employment officer that her husband's calibre and his skills in English were mismatched. She decided to take matters in her own hands and made inquiries on Gusti's behalf at Philips.

Gusti began working at the factory in Croydon shortly after I started at Christ Church Primary. His job was to lift television consoles onto an assembly line and to keep a running tally on a blackboard of the models and numbers that he was processing. He was given a white lab coat and a piece of chalk. Much was made by both his supervisor and his mates of the fine quality of his penmanship.

It was around this time that he jettisoned the *Times* and began bringing home the *Daily Herald*, the tabloid read by his co-workers. His evening phone conversations with Dave became even more animated. "Russia's going to be in a position to dominate the world," he boomed one evening. "These two satellites are just a taste of things to come." He rattled on about Sputnik I and Sputnik II, then switched topics abruptly. He was amazed, he said, that an English paper would publish front-page stories about the love affair of Prince Philip's private secretary and a Mrs. Thompson. "Surely this Commander Parker has the right to a little privacy? Why should he resign because of a little fling? Explain to me, please, how such trash can appear on the same page as the satellite?"

He was quiet while Dave explained. Then he boomed once more, "But it isn't public, it's private! Whose private life can bear such scrutiny? I bet you Prince Philip's can't. Frankly, my dear Duved, if I were married to our Queen, I might want to break out a bit, too."

With both Shoshanna and Gusti working, I was delegated to take Juditka – Judy, as she was in the process of becoming – to nursery on my way to school. As the weather shifted deeper into autumn, the mornings were often murky with a choking kind of fog. Judy dawdled, kicking pebbles this way and that, while I tugged her arm impatiently. I was looking forward to getting to school, while she was dreading it. Miss Houghton, the head of the nursery school, owned the resident dog and Judy was petrified of it, skulking in corners to stay out of its way. But everyone was still kind to Judy. She was a serious little girl, her bangs cut straight across her forehead, her eyes levelly taking your measure. We were all enormously proud when she was chosen to play Mary in the nursery's Christmas pageant. Gusti joked that it was only fitting that someone on high had directed Miss Houghton to pick the only Jewish child in the school for the Saviour's mother. After all, this Christmas hoopla was all about a Jewish baby.

Everyone was getting ready for Christmas. At the factory a bevy of women had been newly hired as part-time workers, seasonal employees saving up for the approaching holiday. Shoshanna listened hard to their conversations at tea break and at the bus stop. Her English comprehension was increasing day by day, but she despaired of her accent. Dave, whose English bore almost no trace of his origins, had made her hyperconscious of her diction.

Dave was thin-skinned about pronunciation, delegating Auntie Caroline or one of their sons to answer the phone because he claimed that it exaggerated his accent. When Shoshanna dreamed out loud of teaching school one day, Dave discouraged her. "The English public will never tolerate a teacher with a Hungarian accent."

"But I'll be a kindergarten teacher, my students will be babies!" Shoshanna protested.

"All the more so," Dave replied. "The younger the children, the greater a teacher's influence. You're laying the foundations for all kinds of development, language in particular. What if they all learned to speak like you?"

At Christ Church Primary, we were also preparing for Christmas. In art lessons we drew pictures of the nativity story that we read about in Scripture study. New, ever more mysterious words were entering my vocabulary. Words like "frankincense and myrrh," "Virgin," and "Holy Ghost." In assembly, instead of the usual hymns — "Onward Christian Soldiers" or "Glorious Things of Thee Are Spoken" or "God Sees the Little Sparrow Fall" — we were practising carols in preparation for a service at the church up the street. There seemed to be hundreds of these Christmas hymns and they were all charming. I knew only one Christmas song in Hungarian, about an angel coming down from heaven to greet a bunch of shepherds. Although the melody was totally different, the text was similar to "While Shepherds Watched Their Flocks." Some days my favourite carol was "Away in a Manger," especially the line "Bless all the dear children in Thy tender care." It sounded so kind-hearted, so loving. Still, "Once in Royal David's City" was even better, with its poignant conclusion, "And He leads his children on, to the place where He-e-e's gone."

By coincidence, I borrowed *Little Women* from the library at around this time. "Christmas won't be Christmas without any presents," Jo declared by way of a beginning, and I began to fret that maybe we, too, were too poor to afford presents this year. In Hungary, the gifts had come on Mikulás Day, in the first week of December. I'd wake up in the morning and find my shoes and boots on the windowsill filled with Mikulás chocolates, a golden switch also resting on the ledge. Mikulás brought presents only for good children and whips made of twigs for bad ones. I mostly got presents. A small table that customarily sat by the tile stove was moved up to the window. It would be piled high with new clothes and toys, left by Mikulás when he entered by the window. The gilded switch was a reminder that I hadn't always been good during the past year, a symbolic warning to mend my ways, not to be taken too seriously with so much bounty at hand.

The tree came later, on Christmas Eve. Christian children believed that the *Jézuska* brought it, though I knew it was Apu and Anyu. Attila Takácsos still believed in the *Jézuska*, in spite of his advanced knowledge in other fields. While his family was trimming their tree, Attila would come up to our place so the fiction of the *Jézuska* could be maintained. Only after one of his older brothers came to fetch him did Shoshanna and Gusti haul our tree out from its hiding place in the back room, and then all four of us trimmed it together.

The Christmas before our departure we had two small trees, one for me and one for Juditka. It was right after the Revolution and trees were hard to come by. Both Gusti and Shoshanna had gone out hunting separately, and by coincidence each had found a tiny tree that no one else seemed to want. We put them on either end of the long dining room buffet and hung them with glowing candles, angel floss, garlands of silver ribbon, and *szalon cukor*, soft candies wrapped in red, silver, and gold foil.

This year we'd be going to Uncle Dave and Auntie Caroline's for Christmas: there would be no Mikulás, but Father Christmas instead. Who would supply the presents?

SHOSHANNA AND GUSTI were constantly conferring about making ends meet, putting aside money for Canada, where it seemed we were eventually headed.

"I don't want to go to Canada," I'd protest, "I like it right here."

Explanations would follow about the better life we'd have in Canada, about the greater opportunities for all of us, about Shoshanna yearning for Vera Néni, who was her only remaining sister and whom she hadn't seen since the end of the war.

"But I like it here, in Purley. I like my school. I love the library. I want to live at High Banks."

It was the weather, though, and tabloid news and the Cold War, as much as Shoshanna's ambition to find work as a teacher and to be reunited with Vera that eventually propelled us to Canada.

The frequent occurrences of fog that punctuated our stay in England culminated in a particularly awful episode in early December. School let out at the usual time, and Judy and I made our way safely home before an eery yellowish cloud swallowed the city. Shoshanna usually finished work at five and Gusti at six, but that day the weather released everyone at four. Their trip from Croydon to Purley normally took an hour by bus, plus a few minutes' walk from the bus stop. But the density of the fog was worse than anything they had experienced or imagined, and they had no way of knowing that we were fine.

Gusti and Shoshanna were lucky to get seats, for the bus was jam-packed. They held hands tightly the entire trip. Gusti stuck his nose to the window from time to time but could see nothing. Except for the occasional nervous titter, an awed hush reigned inside the bus, everyone grateful that the conductor was living up to his title. The driver drove, but the conductor led. On foot, on the road, in front of the bus. In his iridescent mackintosh, a miner's lamp strapped to his head, he was the vanguard upon whom their lives suddenly depended. He performed his duties admirably: it took six hours to reach the stop on Brighton Road, but he got them there.

The ordeal wasn't over. Gusti and Shoshanna clambered off the bus and were enveloped by the cotton batten haze. Holding on to each other, they groped their way to a street lamp. The bulb above them was completely obscured by the opaque cloud. The muffled and vague sounds of occasional passing cars were a source of terror; they could not expect to be seen by motorists, any more than they could make out where the cars were coming from. They felt their way home along the curving lanes that led to Monahan Avenue, relying on tactile memories of the neighbourhood in which they had lived a scant six months. The decorative spikes on the library's fence, the hedges of the fine homes on Woodcote Valley Road, the reassuring rise under their shoes that signalled that they were truly on our street. And then a miracle. When they reached the gate at High Banks, the fog suddenly lifted. The stars were out, the house lights were on, and our parents rejoiced, even before they saw us, in the knowledge that we were safe within.

Gusti didn't take his coat off before calling Uncle Dave. "We're all right, we're home!" But his radiant smile was almost instantly replaced by a stunned expression. He shuddered. "*Jaj, borzasztó* . . . Oh, how dreadful!" He said goodbye to Dave and turned to Shoshanna, who had gone completely white.

"It's not them," he said and took her in his arms. "It's not them, thank God. Duved says we must switch on the radio. There's been a terrible accident in Lewisham." Lewisham was the suburb in south London where Uncle Dave's school was located. Two trains packed with commuters and Christmas shoppers had collided in the dark. A railway bridge, struck by one of the destroyed carriages, had collapsed, derailing a third train that hung precariously over the crazily twisted wreckage and over the bodies of victims and rescuers trapped beneath the girders. That night the radio reported sixty dead; in the days ahead the toll mounted to ninety-two, with hundreds injured.

The great fog and the railway disaster it caused had a profound influence on Gusti. His obsession with weather, which would become more pronounced after he was subjected to Canadian snowfalls, ice storms, and freezing rain, began at this time. It was as if the blows that fate had hammered down on him in his earlier life were telescoped and transformed into a phobia of what was daily beyond his control. But he would try to regulate it by caution, by prevention. He began to study the handsome mahogany barometer in the High Banks dining room several times a day, tapping the glass over the dials thoughtfully. With each passing week he admired the calm, orderliness, and sangfroid of the English more and more. But he focused on moving his family to safety in Canada with an intensity he had not possessed before.

CHRISTMAS FINALLY CAME. A few days beforehand, the entire student body of Christ Church Primary School trooped in a neat file to the nearby church for the carol service. I'd never participated in anything so ceremonious, never been inside a church except illicitly. It was wonderful. Our hearts were in our voices as we let soar the hymns we had been practising for weeks. We sounded exalted and solemn and joyful all at once, accompanied by the majestic strains of the organ. I was uplifted in a way I had never felt before, certainly not on my few visits to synagogue in Budapest, had I thought to make the comparison, which I didn't.

The next day, Gusti and Shoshanna and I attended the nursery Christmas pageant, beaming when Judy appeared in one tableau as an angel, in pink pleated skirt and white jersey, holding a wand with a star at its tip. But the high point came later when she was Mary, demure in a floor-length robe, a long silk head scarf billowing to her shoulders and held in place by a gold headband. She had no lines to speak but sat silent on a stool, her skirts draped around her, the picture of graceful and bewildered piety.

On Christmas Eve we took the bus and train to Uncle Dave's. That night I was so keyed up I lay rigid in bed as each chime of the cuckoo clock marked off the slowly passing quarter-hours. In the morning we gathered around the tree, a huge English tree that lacked *szalon cukor* and candles but was bedecked with gold stars and tinsel and gorgeous glass globes with shimmering hollows, and a jolly Father Christmas on top. Auntie Caroline brought in the presents in a white pillowcase slung over her shoulder. I need not have worried: there was a new Abbey Girls book for me, and a comb and mirror set, and a green and white striped paperback note-book, labelled "Diary." Afterwards we sat in the lounge with our cups of English tea, squares of shortbread on our saucers, hanging on the Queen's televised words of greeting from Buckingham Palace. And after that there was the festive meal

with turkey – a fresh one, sent by Nunny from the estate –
and plum pudding and hard sauce. Only the Christmas cake
was a disappointment. It looked splendid in its coat of white
marzipan and silver beaded candy balls, but when Auntie
Caroline cut into it, she revealed not the airy torte we were
anticipating but a concoction that had the colour and texture
of a brick.

When term resumed after Christmas, we were introduced to a new teacher and a new classroom upstairs, for
we were now the senior students. Miss Lewis was quite
different from Mr. Jack, not funny and jovial, but still
awfully nice. She let me sit with my best friend, Anne
Windley, which Mr. Jack hadn't allowed as we always chat-
tered too much.

There was an intensity to Miss Lewis which shone from
her fine intelligent eyes, and which set her wispy hair flying
out of the elastic that contained it. She had high cheekbones
and a hawk nose, and may have been in her late thirties. She
was a very good teacher, perhaps the best in the school, and
it was she who prepared us for the eleven-plus exams that
would determine whether we went on to grammar schools
or secondary modern schools, whether in fact we would
attend university. Only the grammar schools readied English
children for higher education.

Despite the rigours of the eleven-plus and her enthusiasm
for mental arithmetic and spelling drills, Miss Lewis had a
special love of the written word and neglected neither our
imaginations nor our spiritual development. Every day she
read to us from *The Wind in the Willows* or *Alice in Wonderland*
or *The Lion, the Witch, and the Wardrobe*. She told us to look

around when we were outside to appreciate the beauty and bounty of the natural world.

Scripture study assumed a priority in her class that it had not in Mr. Jack's. Miss Lewis made no secret of the fact that she was a devout and practising Christian, that Jesus was central to her life and ought to be central to ours. I don't know whether it was on account of her beliefs or the requirements of the curriculum that we were reading, writing, and talking about Jesus every day and memorizing the Apostles' Creed.

Jesus began to take on colour and assume a personality for me beyond the scary depictions on the Cross that had mesmerized yet repelled me when I had snuck into church in Budapest. Yes, he had performed awesome miracles like walking on water and multiplying loaves and fishes, but he had also told wonderful stories called parables, and he especially loved children.

I wrote laboriously in my Scripture study copybook – penmanship wasn't my strong point and the nib had a habit of splotching blobs of ink – "For God so loved the world, that He gave His only begotten Son, that whosoever believeth in Him should not perish, but have everlasting life." Jesus had led the exemplary life, Miss Lewis said; all we had to do was follow in His footsteps.

I wrote, "I am the resurrection, and the life: he that believeth in me, though he were dead, yet shall he live: And whosoever liveth and believeth in me shall never die. Believeth thou this?"

All we had to do, Miss Lewis declared, was believe. "Children," she said, tendrils of hair escaping from her bun, two spots of colour accentuating her high cheekbones, "if ever you're in trouble, if ever you feel overwhelmed, all you have to do is get down on your knees and ask the Lord Jesus for help. And He will. I *promise* you, He will."

IT WAS A WINTER of crime, or so it seemed to readers of the *Daily Herald*. My parents were terribly agitated by the murders in early 1958 of a couple of schoolgirls in the country-side. They said such things didn't happen in Hungary, despite its desperate politics, and surely wouldn't in Canada either. Gusti told Dave on the phone that he was beginning to revise his opinion of the English. Could Dave explain to him what Teddy-boy gangs were? Such a gang, dressed in Edwardian garb, had savagely knifed a fifteen-year-old London girl; what was the likelihood of this sort of gang in Purley? And didn't he consider the rise in the rates of drunkenness, sex offences, and crimes of violence among British teens quite shocking?

Other, more distant alarm bells were also ringing. A puzzling letter arrived from Montreal from Vera Néni. I was sitting at my favourite spot in the dining room, at the Chippendale escritoire whose cunning pigeonholes held a special fascination for me, writing in my green and white striped diary about Christopher Wilson, the handsomest boy in the class and the cleverest, who had chased me around the schoolyard that day. Gusti and Shoshanna seemed oblivious to my presence as they gingerly passed the blue aerogram back and forth across the table, as if it were some kind of booby-trapped device.

"She says we should do it before we come," Shoshanna said. "She says Protestant is better than Catholic, that the Protestant school system in Montreal is superior to the Catholic. They do accept Jewish children, but it will be easier if we're Protestant. I don't exactly understand what she means by 'easier.' Easier for the children, or easier for us, or easier for her and Péter? Anyway, she does say we could do it once we're there, but I get the distinct impression she'd like us to do it here beforehand."

"*Kitérni?* It's absolutely out of the question."

Literally, *kitérni* means to turn out. On my father's lips, pronounced with a mixture of disgust and outrage, the Hungarian word for conversion sounded like a recipe for turning a person inside out. He didn't raise his voice but spoke with a chilling finality. "I wouldn't convert on Nunny's advice and I won't on Vera's either. Or on yours, for that matter. I suggest you don't push me beyond my limits."

I don't know what possessed me to pipe up at this precise moment, addressing the green baize pigeonholes in front of me with the words of the Apostles' Creed. "I believe in God the Father Almighty, creator of heaven and earth and in Jesus Christ His son Our Lord. He was conceived by the power of the Holy Spirit and born of the Virgin Mary. He suffered under Pontius Pilate . . ."

"Oh, for God's sake," my father shouted, "not now."

I swivelled around and faced my parents. "Christians believe in Jesus and we believe in God. It doesn't matter what you believe, so long as you think it's true."

"Don't be ridiculous," Gusti said, a vein throbbing at his temple. "It most certainly does matter. They're filling your head with nonsense."

"I don't think it's nonsense."

"Oh, for heaven's sake! I'm not going to debate theology with a ten-year-old."

For a while it seemed we weren't going anywhere after all, because the letter had thoroughly spooked my father. Shoshanna went around with a long face; she wanted to see Vera, she didn't want to languish in an English factory forever. Then the Cold War heated up and Gusti began to tilt towards Canada once more. He didn't like the *Daily Herald*'s stories about H-bombs being transported by lorries through English towns and villages. The paper reported they were on their way to disposal, but a man who had Hungary in his blood wouldn't necessarily believe everything he read in a newspaper.

Certainly he believed it when the execution of Imre Nagy made the front pages in June 1958. "A decent, honest, and honourable man," Gusti wept, the paper clutched in his fist as he poured out his heart once more to Dave. To Shoshanna he said, "It's time to leave this accursed continent behind. If Khrushchev could sanction the murder of a man like Nagy, he's no better than Stalin, Twentieth Congress notwithstanding."

I sat nearby on the settee immersed in Noel Streatfeild's *Skating Shoes*. Shoshanna leaned down and gave my shoulders a benevolent squeeze. I looked up in some surprise; she wasn't usually given to displays of affection. Her eyes were glinting in excitement or merriment. "When we get to Canada, I'll buy you skates and you won't just read about skating."

"I'm not going to Canada."

I WAS IN MY ROOM UPSTAIRS, the small bedroom I shared with Judy. I had just come home from school and there was no one else in the house. The birds were making a racket outside, perhaps it was going to rain. I stared out the window. The view was of the unglamorous side of the house, the broken grey flagstones that led to our back garden, the kitchen of the house next door.

My room was modest, too; it held two brass beds and a wooden dresser, and the gas heater that generated almost no heat. I loved this room, I loved its view. I loved Christ Church Primary School. I loved Miss Lewis, who praised my compositions, my book reports, all the effort that she said I put into learning English. (It was no effort, the language stuck to me.) I couldn't bear the idea of leaving her and the house and the library with all the books I still hadn't read; I especially couldn't bear the idea of starting all over again, of being taunted about – what? Who knew what would be wrong about me in Canada? My shoes again? My burgundy and grey school tie? My National Health Service wire-frame goggles? My Jewishness, my troublesome Jewishness, that, conveniently, no one knew about here?

Miss Lewis's words came back to me. If ever I was in trouble, if ever I felt – what was the long word she had used? – if ever I felt "overwhelmed," all I had to do was talk to Jesus about it. I wasn't precisely sure what "overwhelmed" meant, but this sense of being stuck to a course that I knew was wrong for me, this feeling of having to go through with something very large and very bad, this might have been what she meant.

Very deliberately I faced the window and dropped to my knees. The window, because Jesus was in the sky, and this was the closest to Him I could reasonably get in the house. Behind my closed eyelids I pictured Him above the puffy clouds, looking sad but starting to smile just a bit because He was glad I was turning to Him and because He blessed all the dear children in His tender care.

"Dear Lord Jesus," I whispered, hoping this was the way to talk to someone who loved you and was waiting for you to love Him back. "Dear, dear Lord Jesus, please don't let this happen. *Please* let's not have to go to Canada where it will be hateful and cold and I won't know anyone and won't have the library."

It was embarrassing to admit to Lord Jesus that my heart would also break if I had to leave Christopher Wilson whom I loved. Although of course He knew everything anyway. So I just added some words about Anne. "If I leave, Anne will forget me, and I won't have a best friend."

I wanted to continue pouring out my whole soul, to say that I believed in Jesus, because my prayers would surely come true only if I believed. But the planks in the floor were hard, and there was also a hard lump forming in my chest that was not just about the irrefutable fact that we were going to Canada. Jesus couldn't smile under my eyelids because my eyes had popped open and refused to shut.

I was suffused with the knowledge that we would indeed have to leave Purley, if for no other reason than punishment for my betrayal of the God of the *Shema*. Even if Jesus did live in the sky, I still remained outside the reach of his tender care.

seven

A JEWISH EDUCATION

When we lived in Budapest, I used to pass by a pair of bungalows on Erzsébet Királyné Utja on my way home from school. They were handsome little houses in grey stucco with deep-set mullioned eyes and terra-cotta hats. Unusual for their neighbourhood, they occupied the same lot, though not because there wasn't enough land for two homes. They seemed meant to sit companionably side by side behind a wrought iron fence, cocooned by leafy trees and ornamented with peach-tinged roses that bloomed summer through fall. I loved the idea of their affectionate closeness and imagined them the residence of two sisters and their families. When Shoshanna told me that we were leaving Hungary, first for England, but eventually for Canada where Vera Néni was waiting for us, I pictured that's how we'd live one day. Side by side, the two families in matching houses sharing a common garden.

And in fact the street in suburban Rosemount where the cab deposited us in January 1959 was lined with red-brick bungalows, neat square homes with greystone accents that would have fit into my fantasy, had there been mature trees and rose bushes. But there were no trees at all, and what shrubs there might be were buried under piles and piles of snow.

What special brand of bravery or foolishness had possessed my parents to undertake this Canadian adventure in winter? First to endure the roiling grey Atlantic that heaved and tossed us about for seven days on the *Empress of Britain*. Then the encounter with a band of nuns in black habits and white wimples, who had escorted us from the harbour to the railway station in Saint John and, in parting, thrust a small plastic doll into Judy's surprised arms. And then the miles and miles of colourless terrain outside the train window, white fields, white-clumped trees and roofs, unrelieved expanses of whiteness save for the pasty sky, until we reached the outskirts of Montreal and the chain of sooty hovels that lined the approach to Windsor Station.

Shoshanna muttered under her breath, "Some New World. The most squalid hamlet in Europe looks better than this." But she stopped grousing when, on the platform, a petite young woman elegantly dressed in a plum winter suit trimmed with fox grabbed her by the waist and started waltzing. We all stood with our mouths hanging, surrounded by our trunks and belted valises, worried we'd get in trouble with disembarking passengers who were trying to weave their way between the two careening women.

"Vera, for heaven's sake," a nearby man admonished, at which point it dawned on me that the dancer was my aunt. With a huge, infectious grin, she suddenly veered towards me and exclaimed, "Let me look at your nice straight legs! Ilushka, my sweet, you're not a cripple after all!" She hugged me and my father, bent down towards Judy, who was staring up at her with round eyes, then addressed the disapproving man who had yet to say a word to us, "Come, Pierre, come, *tout le monde*, let's go home."

Despite Vera's ebullience, we were destined for a rocky start. My parents were shocked that, once we were dumped off at the house and our luggage ensconced in the basement playroom, Vera and Pierre returned to work. It was Thursday, they quickly explained, a long and busy day for them. My aunt and uncle owned two ladies'-wear stores. Vera ran the smaller one near Pie-IX and Bélanger, Pierre the larger one in a new shopping centre in Montreal North. But not to worry – they'd be back for a supper of stuffed cabbage later that evening. The hiatus would give us a chance to get acquainted with the children. And Rosa, the maid, was at our service.

Round-shouldered Rosa, who wore a squint and a permanently sour expression on her sallow face, resented us from the instant we crossed the threshold. Four extra people in the house could only spell more work for her. The fact that we spoke broken English and she, a recent immigrant from Italy, had a sketchy hold on French meant that she communicated with us mostly by grandiloquent gestures of the hands and extravagant shrugs of the shoulders. There were frequent appeals to the children for translation.

Alice, a gentle, honey-haired button of a girl a few weeks younger than Judy (who had turned five on the ocean crossing), immediately took my sister by the hand and began showing her the toys in her room. Philippe, who was nearly eight and spoke excellent English, announced that when his father wasn't home, he was the boss. This made Gusti smile and he asked the boss to give us a tour of the house.

Gusti's smile disappeared at the first stop of the tour, and his face settled into grim folds. In the small square living room, above a couple of Scandinavian-style armchairs, two oil paintings bore my uncle's scrawled signature, P. Bereki. One, a self-portrait in three-quarter profile in tones of ash, emphasized his winging eyebrows, hook nose, and high cheekbones. He was a handsome man, if he'd only look at you; even in this picture, his gaze was averted. The other, a stark depiction of the Crucifixion, was as arresting in style as it was in content. Semi-abstract, it showed Jesus at Golgotha flanked by the two thieves, his head drooping to one side, his silhouette, wounds, and the cross behind him prominent in thick black outline against a background of splotchy grey brush strokes. My parents regarded each other in mute consternation, and we shuffled off, subdued, to see the kitchen, the three bedrooms, the finished basement.

The subject of religion arose that evening after the stuffed cabbage had been consumed. The cabbage had sparked its own small crisis. When Vera and Pierre returned from work, Shoshanna pulled Vera aside at the front door to say that stuffed cabbage was much too heavy for her digestion. At seven in the evening, Vera didn't appear quite as young as she had earlier. She was in fact thirty-nine, just a year Shoshanna's junior, but her vitality and trim, muscular body made her seem more youthful. Philippe was clamouring in the kitchen and Rosa hovered nearby, trying to catch Vera's eye to vent some grievance. Vera listened with a distracted air to Shoshanna, who was trying to explain, at some length and holding her left side delicately, that after such a long journey and given that she hadn't yet fully recovered from a gallbladder operation eight months earlier, she had to be quite choosy about what she ate.

"I'm not a dietitian!" Vera spat out. "I can't cook separately for you." Shoshanna's lips set in a moue of automatic hurt and displeasure. Immediately Vera became contrite.

"I will find you something, I will find you something," she cried out, quite distraught, "if only my son would stop yelling!" Philippe, good as gold in his parents' absence, became a howler as soon as they walked through the door. Family get-togethers over the next few years were invariably punctuated by his tantrums.

The discussion about religion was carried on in Hungarian, a language Pierre had sworn never to speak again on account of what the Hungarians had done to him and his, a position Vera fell in line with. But since their second language was French and ours English, for the time being only the mother tongue was left for matters that required immediate resolution. Hungarian also had the advantage of being incomprehensible to Alice and Philippe, not to mention Rosa. Nobody seemed to mind about me and Judy.

While Rosa prepared our cousins for bed, the six of us sat around the kitchen table, Judy crumpled and dozing in my father's lap, the plastic doll from the Saint John nuns clutched in her hands. Talk of the pros and cons of Protestantism and Catholicism swirled around my head. It was a given that there were no pros to being Jewish. The question seemed to be: Could we see our way clear to shedding the existential liability of the religion into which we had all been born – for our own sake, as well as theirs? Or were we going to be as stubborn about it as our letters from England had intimated?

"I was born a Jew and a Jew I will die," Gusti declared, trying to catch Pierre's eye, which was fixed on the Arborite veneer of the kitchen table.

"Yes, well," Pierre said, "we have had enough of dying. There has been altogether too much dying. And it's not just about us. It's about the children. Maybe you should give a thought to your children and how they'll fare the next time a Hitler comes calling."

There was a long silence.

Vera said in a voice trembling with emotion, "I want my children to have a normal life. I don't want *anything* in their background to brand them as different. To brand them as *inférieurs*."

Then the conversation swerved in a different direction, to work. Where would Shoshanna and Gusti find jobs? They were welcome, both of them, in the stores, Shoshanna in Vera's small establishment, Gusti at Pierre's in the shopping centre. But if my parents were to accept these offers, they were not to parade their Jewishness publicly. As far as everybody in this city was concerned, Vera and Pierre Bereki were born Protestant. And the same thing applied to us children. If we were to attend the school our cousins did, we were to adopt the same alias as them. The Protestant alias.

And it did seem as if the word "alias" was the right one, because the longer the adults chewed on the subject of religion, the more it appeared that Jewishness was a stain that tainted every aspect of life, a sort of viscous cloud that stuck to and contaminated everything.

And yet they seemed to want us with them. We were to stay in their home as long as we wished. A livelihood was being offered, and a kindness that emanated from Vera's every generous pore. But there was uneasiness, too, and not just on their side but on my parents' as well. Was this generosity in fact a desire to keep us in check, safely shackled to them? Was it to hide us from the wider world, where our identity as Jews might tag them as well? Surely keeping us close to them could be even more dangerous. We might give them away in the store to the staff and to customers. Or at school to teachers and classmates.

Shoshanna and Gusti set out for their respective duties the next Monday. Shoshanna didn't have a preconceived notion of what her job was to be, but she did remember the family textile shop in Beregszász where Mamuka and Apuka had spent their days, and where Vera too had worked in the last years before the fall. Shoshanna remembered the great bales of cloth on dowels screwed into the wall. She remembered the young assistant who shouldered them down for Mamuka when the various town worthies stopped by to look at the latest patterns in *Vogue*. Mamuka chatted them up, fingering the shantungs and poplins and gabardines and taffetas. With unerring taste, laced with tact and a sober understanding of everyone's place in the town's pecking order, she managed to move the merchandise like no one else, while Apuka pored over the ledgers at her elbow and smoked a choice cigar. In the morning the assistant brought in the café au lait and crisp rolls from the bakery around the corner; at lunchtime they returned home for the midday meal and an afternoon nap. There was certainly hard work and fretting over bills, but also a dignified civility about how they earned their living.

Vera and Pierre were not Mamuka and Apuka. Or perhaps the difference was between Beregszász and Montreal. Here everything seemed to be about work, starting with the mad scramble in the morning to ready the children for school and the rush to the stores. Then there was the not-so-friendly competition at the end of the day, when the sales were tallied to see which of the two had done better.

Before the war Pierre had been a medical student. After the war, for a few heady months, he had studied art in Budapest. But once in France, he had had to reinvent himself, and he had fallen back on tailoring, his late father's trade. Working like animals in Paris – that's how Vera put it to Shoshanna, as they hustled out the door into the ferocious cold, a cold that forced the reply on Shoshanna's lips right back into her throat. Like *animals*, they had done piecework around the clock in their tiny apartment and hoarded the funds to come to Canada. Where, again, Pierre had slaved as a cutter in a garment factory to save up for first one store and then a second.

Which was all very well, Shoshanna thought, hard work was important, but work to the exclusion of everything else? In the store, Vera had no time for her, no time at all except to give directives. In the store Vera sold, and like Mamuka, she sold with her whole heart. She asked about the wedding at which the peau de soie two-piece had been worn. Had Madame made a splash in it? She sized up the customer who would look just right in that bouclé knit twin-set on special. She never pushed, never suggested a dress looked good if it didn't; in fact, she shook her head from time to time and clucked, "*Non, ce n'est pas pour vous.*" And still, in her hands, the merchandise sold like hotcakes.

All her attention was trained on the incoming traffic, ensuring that the sales staff stayed on their toes. (The staff consisted of a couple of brassily painted French-Canadian women who, luckily, had some English, for the French that came out of their mouths was not like anything Shoshanna had ever heard before.) Shoshanna was to stay on her toes, too, never sitting down, except for a half-hour lunch in the cramped room in the back. And she was to take her turn at swabbing the linoleum free of the brown slush shed by the customers' galoshes, just like everyone else.

It was the floor that finished it for Shoshanna, just as it had years ago with her sister-in-law in Mada. She could not abide the injustice and humiliation of mopping up after others. Why did she have to have her nose rubbed in the fact that she had been brought low, a nonentity in this new, supposedly better world? The saleswomen could do it, not her, not the sister of the *patronne*.

That night when the lights were turned off in the living room where she and Gusti shared the fold-out sofa (the Crucifixion mercifully invisible in the dark), she hissed at him, "Find out where the JIAS is to be found in this dump."

Located halfway across the sprawling island city, the Jewish Immigrant Aid Society, like its counterpart in London, wanted to heap them with clothing. And when they refused charity, demanding jobs instead, it shunted them to the Jewish Vocational Service. For Gusti there was nothing immediate, although there was some talk, given that he was a farmer, of obtaining government land somewhere in Ontario. For Shoshanna, inquiries would be made at the Jewish schools. No promises could be extended – it was the middle of the school year, after all – but they would do their best.

The next morning, early enough that no one had yet left for the stores, there was a call for Shoshanna. A day nursery in Mile End was interested in seeing her. Could she present herself at two that afternoon? It was a raw day in February with a wind that stung the eyes and sliced through lungs. Shoshanna had no idea where Rue Jeanne-Mance might be, but she said she'd find it somehow. When Gusti insisted on accompanying her, she gave in easily.

The narrow three-storey red-brick building in question stood on a street jammed with fretwork balconies piled high with snow, and with the winding exterior stair-cases that characterized the older sections of the city. Shoshanna and Gusti surveyed these stairs with horrified fascination. Why would people build in this eccentric mode, and who could climb up those icy treads without breaking their necks?

Luckily, Neighbourhood House was accessible at street level. Ruthlessly Shoshanna ordered Gusti to stay outside. She would not allow him to attend the interview, lest those inside think her the type who couldn't find her way in the world on her own.

A tall, square-set woman greeted Shoshanna and ushered her into a small office at the rear of the building. Seated behind her desk, she wore an air that was both commanding and benevolent. She had crinkly greying hair, a fleshy mouth, and huge eyes that swam behind thick lenses.

Articulating her words with slightly exaggerated care, she questioned Shoshanna closely. When had she arrived in Montreal? Only a week ago! How had she found her way here? By bus from the East End? What, all alone?

"No," Shoshanna admitted. "I came with my husband."

"And where is your husband now?"

"Outside. I told him to wait for me," Shoshanna confessed.

"On such a day! Whatever for?" The interview was taking on the aspect of an interrogation.

"I wanted to be independent."

"You mean, you wanted to *look* independent. Go and fetch him."

Miss Elsie Steinberg trained her considerable charm on Gusti. Such a gallant man, to escort his wife and to wait patiently for her in the cold. She wanted to know more about both of them and their circumstances before committing herself about the job. She was looking for a teacher for a clutch of three-year-olds.

Shoshanna started working at the day nursery barely two weeks after our arrival in Montreal. The chips of our lives then began to fall into place, clickety-clack, just like a game of dominoes. Judy would attend the same school, in the class for five-year-olds. She and Shoshanna left our apartment before seven every morning to open the daycare centre at eight.

For yes, we now had a place of our own, thanks to Shoshanna's proper job and a salary of $40 a week. Pierre — quite genial as soon as it was clear we weren't going to be on his hands forever — had taken Shoshanna and Gusti apartment hunting one evening. After the housing shortages of Europe, my parents were amazed that accommodation could be found, just like that, for the cost of a month's rent ($84) in advance. True, the location below the elevated Metropolitan Boulevard at 22nd Avenue and Dickens in Ville Saint-Michel was noisy and lacked charm. True, the mustard-coloured three-storey building might one day turn into a slum. But at that moment it was new, clean, and spacious enough for our needs: a living room, kitchen, bathroom, and two bedrooms, all smelling of fresh plaster and paint. And in fact the location was ideal, about halfway between Vera and Pierre's bungalow and the Montreal North shopping centre where Gusti would continue to work for Pierre. Gusti had thought over the business of the government land in Ontario. Farm with his bare hands at age fifty-three in a frozen land? With Shoshanna and two daughters for manpower? No, thank you.

I also found a way of saying no. One of the domino pieces that had clicked so neatly into place was the convenient proximity of a school, an angular brown box set down in a snowy yard directly opposite the apartment building on 22nd Avenue. It was perfection: an English-language Protestant establishment that, in Quebec's complicated and linguistically divided school system, accepted Jews without question, unlike the nearby Catholic schools, English and French, at which Jews had to pay. It was a school I could attend as a Jewish child at a safe distance for all of us from my Christian cousins.

Except that I dug in my heels. I wasn't going anywhere as a Jewish child. The swirling arguments in the Berekis' kitchen had carried weight with me, if not with my parents. If Judaism was optional for my aunt, uncle, and cousins, it could be optional for me, too.

"What do you mean?" Shoshanna exclaimed, thunder-struck. "What do you mean you're not going there as a Jewish child? You *are* a Jewish child!"

We were sitting in our own kitchen this time, at our own second-hand table, a singularly ugly item of Arborite and steel furniture trimmed in grooved metal and topped with a design of red and yellow concentric circles. The backs of my bare legs stuck to the vinyl padding of the chair. (Central heating was a new concept for us. Outside it was incredibly cold; inside we had to open the windows, it was so stuffy.) Shoshanna and I were alone in the apartment. Gusti had taken Judy grocery shopping at Steinberg's in the Boulevard Shopping Centre.

"I could be a Jewish child at home," I reasoned. "I could be a Jewish child in private."

"But why?" The V on the bridge of Shoshanna's nose furrowed. I could see she was really trying to understand, that she was paying full attention to me for the first time since we'd left England.

"I want to be like everyone else. I want to be Protestant at school. In England no one knew. Why do they have to know here?"

Shoshanna sat silent, pondering. Why did they have to know, she asked herself. The child would be happier, less resentful of leaving England, and Vera and Pierre would feel reassured, their secret pasts still hidden. Shoshanna decided to act without telling Gusti. It would only upset him, make him brood about the consequences of leaving his identity behind, the securely Jewish identity that was rooted in Hungarian clods of earth. How easily those roots could shrivel and wither.

The next day, Shoshanna took me across the street to register. I was immediately relegated to the fifth grade, it being general policy to put immigrant children back a year. While I absorbed this piece of news, Shoshanna was interviewed by the principal.

"And what is the child's religion, Mrs. Kalman?"

"I'd rather not say."

"I beg your pardon, Mrs. Kalman?" Behind her round glasses, the principal's eyes were frosty.

"I cannot talk about religion."

"Why ever not?"

"Because my child would like to be known as Protestant."

"*Is* she Protestant?"

"No."

"Well, what is she?"

"We are Jewish. But Elaine would like to be Protestant."

The principal laid her pen down on the desk.

"This is not Nazi Germany, Mrs. Kalman. You've come to a free country."

"I know that, Miss Peppler. I know that very well. But my child wants to be like the other children here."

"Mrs. Kalman, there are Jewish teachers on the staff of this school. No one will ever persecute your child here. But she can't be one thing on paper and another thing in real life."

Shoshanna swallowed hard. There was a brief silence. She blinked, then nodded, acquiescing.

"Another thing," Shoshanna said, her voice a bit husky. "Elaine is an intelligent child. Very intelligent. I brought you her English report card. Also I have a letter from her teacher in England. The letter tells you the exceptional progress she made there. You want to put her back a year. Everybody knows the English school system is the best in the world. I want you to put her ahead by a year."

"You mean into Grade Six?"

"No, I mean into Grade Seven."

SHOSHANNA AND JUDY sat together as the bus jounced along Boulevard Pie-IX. The child hoisted herself onto her knees, her brown rubbers dangerously close to sullying Shoshanna's coat. Judy was just starting to read on her own and she began sounding out the street names at each stop in her child's clear singsong voice: Jean-Talon, Belair, Bélanger, Saint-Zotique.

What kind of place have we come to, Shoshanna asked herself, not for the first time, where they named main thoroughfares after reactionary popes and obscure saints? Vera had explained that Pie IX was Pope Pius IX, but no one seemed to know the first thing about Saint Zotique except his proper pronunciation. It wasn't "Zotikew," Vera laughed at Shoshanna's attempt, it was "Zoteek."

Where have I come to and what have I done, Shoshanna mused, as she prompted Judy to say, "Bellechasse," then "Beaubien." What *had* she done? She was supposed to be making a new life, a fresh start, and she was encumbering herself with lies. Her daughter wanted to lie about who she was, and Shoshanna was close to abetting her. When had *she* ever lied about who she was, who she used to be? Once, when her life might have depended on it, Shoshanna was given the opportunity to deny her origins, and she turned it down. She turned it down flat.

IN THE FALL OF 1944, after the Allied attacks on Gelsenkirchen in which Magda perished, Shoshanna and Vera were put into the cattle cars again. They had no idea where they were headed since they were forced to sit with their backs to the doors. During the entire journey bombers strafed the cars. When the train finally stopped and the women tumbled off, they stared at their surroundings. They had left Gelsenkirchen in autumn sunshine but had been disgorged onto a deep winter landscape. They stood shivering, ankle deep in snow in their wooden clogs and grey sack dresses.

The town was called Sömmerda, home to the Krupp munitions works. Wooden barracks housed them this time, not canvas. One week they worked nights, the next, days. Their labour was vital to the war effort, no mistakes permitted. Shoshanna was to measure gunpowder into ammunition capsules. Even a small error in calculation would mean a defective bullet.

"Don't try to be smart. We'll wring your necks with our bare hands if you try anything."

The *Lager* was on the outskirts of the village, a fairy-tale town in Thuringia, spotlessly clean and orderly, with wide galleries on the two-storey timber houses. When the Jewish women walked the length of the main street to the factory in the morning, the German housewives were hanging their plump duvets and eiderdowns out to air on their balconies. The prisoners gaped upward and the German women stared back down, with curiosity and with no particular animosity.

At the factory, the prisoners worked alongside and under the supervision of German civilians, women as well as men. A woman at the same workstation as Shoshanna and Vera began to make a habit of bringing something every Sunday, a heel of white bread, perhaps, to share among the three of them. It may have been modest, but it was tantalizing to anticipate.

After she had filled her cartridges, Shoshanna placed them on a metal tray. An older man with a stoop took the tray from her and put the bullets on an assembly line. On Sundays, he would leave a gift on the tray for her: a piece of poppyseed cake, a turnip, a radish. Out of goodness or out of pity?

Later, it seemed to Shoshanna that this Thuringian interlude had been almost like normal life. They received only a bowl of soup and a husk of bread that had to be rationed to last the whole day. But from time to time a slice of onion would arrive with the bread, or a piece of wurst, or a smidgen of margarine. They were allowed to stuff rags into their clogs, and after a while, they were given horse blankets, big rough plaids out of which Shoshanna fashioned jackets for herself and Vera. They pulled long threads from the fabric for sewing, and Vera turned up a needle from somewhere. No one appeared to mind these small attempts at comfort. The Jews were needed for work, they were useful, let them subsist.

They started to fill out a bit. A dimple revived in Shoshanna's cheek. They had no mirrors, so Shoshanna had to take Vera's word for it when she informed her that her hair was growing in dark. She had always been blond, but Vera swore that it was jet black. The texture was different too. When she ran her fingers through the downy new tufts, she could tell for herself: the once bone-straight hair was growing in wavy.

One day a blue-eyed foreman with a pale face offered her something he called a *Knoblauch dragée*. Shoshanna popped it in her mouth and gagged. Sugar-coated garlic. She almost spat it out, then thought better of it. She worked it around with her tongue, trying to isolate the two contrasting tastes. She couldn't offend the foreman. Besides, it was food.

He began to make a habit of calling her over to his table under the guise of instructing her. One day he quizzed her about herself, visibly grappling with the discrepancy between the reality before his eyes and what he had been taught.

"But you, you're not Jewish like the others?"

"Of course I am."

"No, really. Jews are all cripples, degenerates."

"None of us here is crippled or degenerate."

"But the others aren't beautiful like you. Perhaps one of your parents wasn't Jewish?"

Stubbornly Shoshanna insisted. "I'm Jewish and so are my parents."

Back at the barracks, the other women scoffed at her. "You're mad," they said.

In their group was a sweet-tempered young woman, a pretty Christian girl married to a Jew whose fate she had somehow come to share. Seizing on the more humane treatment they were being granted here, her Jewish workmates spoke up for her with the camp command. The Gentile girl was immediately promoted from their ranks, given work in the office, and her rations increased.

With this example before them, Shoshanna's comrades berated her, "Why didn't you go along with him? Why didn't you at least tell him you're half Jewish?"

"Because I'm not."

Shoshanna thought it would be instructive to tell me this story.

I WASN'T RECEPTIVE to anything Shoshanna had to say to me after I found myself, first, in Grade Seven at Ogilvie School and, second, still Jewish. I had not been happy with the idea of being put back a year, but it was even more disconcerting to be among classmates nearly two years older. The girls in particular were intimidating. They wore pastel shades of lipstick, mostly mauve or coral, they had full breasts encased in bras beneath form-hugging sweaters, and, if they were short-sighted like me, their glasses were flamboyantly made to resemble sequined butterflies. Their hair was an especial marvel, set on jumbo rollers, then combed out into lavish pageboys or bouffants.

Shoshanna thought it immoral for thirteen-year-olds to sport lipstick and jeered at the suggestion of a bra for me. Whatever for? I had nothing to put into one. And what was wrong with my hair? Remember how thin it used to be? Just look at my thick brown mane now: simply push it behind my ears with a couple of bobby pins, it didn't need extra body from rollers. As for new glasses, the National Health Service wire-frame goggles, provided free of charge in England, would last me very well until I needed a new prescription.

I wrote letters to Miss Lewis and Anne Windley. It was horrid in Canada; I hated everything. I was way behind in French, which my classmates had been studying for four years. I couldn't do the arithmetic, here called maths. I missed Christ Church Primary and my friends, the library, and High Banks.

I succumbed to a nasty flu. My temperature soared, my back ached, my throat was red and spotty. But I was delighted because I didn't have to go to school. Before our move to the apartment, Uncle Pierre had allowed me to borrow anything I wanted from his bookshelf. Most of the books had been in French, but there were a couple of English titles. I left behind Thomas Merton's *Seven Storey Mountain*, not realizing it might have helped me in my spiritual quest, but the Duke of Windsor's *A King's Story* became the happy companion of my sickbed. Propped up on pillows and covered by one of the satin eiderdowns from Budapest, I luxuriated on the living room sofa, poring over royal family trees and sumptuous photographs by Cecil Beaton.

When I recovered, I was packed off to school. Every morning I developed fierce stomach cramps and begged to stay home. Shoshanna was pitiless: I belonged in school. She would coach me in French if I had difficulties, and Gusti would take me and my math problems in hand.

It was my good fortune to fall upon a fine teacher once again. A short, intense young man with a humped nose, prominent grey eyes, and a close-cropped brush cut, Mr. Tidy taught by joshing and cajoling. As in England I found myself held up as an example to my classmates. Here I was two years younger than everyone else, making a heroic effort in French and geography. And just look at my results in grammar and history.

We were – incredible stroke of luck! – studying English history. Everyone else wore looks of spacey resignation during history class: what possible relevance could King Canute or the Wars of the Roses have for Canadian school-children in the East End of Montreal? For me, shining in English history became the means of demonstrating fealty to my beloved England. I took immense pride in reeling off from memory the dates of the English monarchs from William the Conqueror to Elizabeth II. When we had to prepare a talk for a public speaking contest, I chose as my topic the genealogy of the House of Windsor and delivered it in a plummy English accent that no doubt underscored its complete incongruity.

In the meantime the religion issue continued to oppress me. Our schooldays commenced with morning exercises, a sort of participatory short religious service. We took turns reading snippets from a collection of inspirational texts collected by Mr. Tidy and then leading the class in the recitation of the Lord's Prayer. I loved the Lord's Prayer. I loved its solemn cadence and arcane vocabulary, I loved its archaic constructions.

Mr. Tidy, like Miss Lewis, was a strong believer. One day he spoke emotionally of walking home the previous after-noon and, in an astonishing late winter sunset of crimson and gold splashes, discerning the face of his Maker. When he uttered the phrase "the face of my Maker," I was convinced that he meant Jesus's face, not God's.

In the Saint-Michel apartment, I didn't have my own bedroom but slept in the living room on a threadbare grey velvet sofa bought at auction. I had never been a soft-spoken child, so my parents were accustomed to the sound of my prayers, the familiar *Ve'ahavta*, before I turned out my light.

One morning, out of the blue, Shoshanna asked, "How come you're not saying the *Ve'ahavta* any more?"

"I don't know," I said. "How come you're not saying it?"

I was used to Gusti muttering a morning or evening prayer unobtrusively as he performed his chores. I'd never seen or heard Shoshanna pray, except when she blessed the Friday-night candles in our Budapest home. She didn't do that here.

Although Miss Peppler had told Shoshanna that I had to be Jewish at school, no one else there seemed to know anything about it. Perhaps Mr. Tidy did, but he was too polite to say so. The fact that Miss Peppler said I had to be Jewish carried weight with me. I didn't like it, but I appeared to be stuck with it. True, I had stopped reciting the *Ve'ahavta* the very day Shoshanna had relayed Miss Peppler's decree, and by the time Shoshanna remarked on it, I barely remembered the Hebrew words. Yet I was also trying to shoulder the yoke Miss Peppler had insisted was rightfully mine.

But I really did love the Lord's Prayer. And surely its overall sense was the same as that of the *Ve'ahavta*. Both were about the greatness of God. It must be all right for me to add my voice to the seductive recitation of the rest of the class. Still, I knew one passage would be unequivocally forbidden. It couldn't be right for me to pronounce the short postscript that some of the kids (though not all) tacked onto the prayer before the obligatory Amen. It would never do to pledge "Through Jesus Christ Our Lord."

It was in these days of struggling towards what I wanted to be while remaining true to what I had to be that I noticed Gusti had changed. Formerly good-natured and forbearing, Gusti was increasingly irascible and impatient with everyone. Well, with everyone except Judy, for whom he always had a smile and a small gift on Friday evenings – not because he loved her more than me or Shoshanna, but because she was the baby. But with me and Shoshanna, Gusti seemed always exasperated. Gone was the dependable patience of my Apu, who had once taught me chess and been tolerant of my carelessness on the board. Now, in the course of tutoring me in math ("If two trains leave the station at the same time, each travelling at eighty miles an hour, and one is heading for City A and the other for City B, what time will each train arrive?" etc.), he regularly pounded the kitchen table with the flat of his broad hand, demanding rhetorically, "But why can't she understand? She's supposed to be so intelligent!" Every session ended with him stalking away from the table and me blubbering into my scribbler.

But Gusti wasn't picking on me alone. He was downright nasty to Shoshanna. Normally Shoshanna was scrappy and sharp-tongued enough to take care of herself, but this was different. These days she looked genuinely wounded when he found fault with her cooking or didn't kiss her goodbye in the morning. It's a measure of the kind of relationship I had with my father that, despite the friction between us, I felt entitled to come to my mother's defence. I chose my time carefully. For days I thought about how I would set him straight and bring about their reconciliation.

One crisp and sunny Saturday afternoon, the snow crunching beneath our boots, Gusti took me in search of the Rosemount Children's Library. It was a fair distance from our house, on Rosemount Boulevard, a few blocks west of Pie-IX in a municipal building that also housed an indoor swimming pool. We climbed the stairs to the third floor, breathing in the humid vapours of chlorine, ears cocked to the muffled cries of kids roughhousing in the water somewhere nearby. I was thrilled at the prospect of discovering the library and pleased, too, that Gusti was escorting me there, just as he had in Purley.

But the library proved a huge disappointment. A small room, it occupied a fraction of the floor space of the Purley Library, and a fraction of that space was dedicated to English books. When I scanned the shelves, naturally I couldn't find the girls' annuals and boarding school mysteries that I'd been craving. Disgruntled, I made do with a couple of Louisa May Alcott novels, and we began the journey home.

Gusti asked if I'd be able to come on my own next time. Absently I said yes, though I wondered if the trip would be worthwhile. Reading my mind, Gusti suggested that on subsequent occasions I might find new authors worth investigating. I warmed to him instantly and thought that this might be just the moment to broach the matter of his behaviour with Shoshanna. In a voice I thought to be the epitome of gentle reproach, I observed, "I don't think you're being very nice to Mummy these days."

He dropped my mittened hand as if he had been holding a cobra.

"I'll thank you to mind your own business."

Of course he was right. I had no business meddling in my parents' quarrels. And yet I was totally unprepared for his curt tone and flat rebuff. I had imagined he would be taken aback by my mild criticism and would ask, What ever do you mean by that? I would then reel off – like the list of kings and queens of England – the long litany of his mis- deeds regarding Shoshanna and point out that she really deserved better from him. As it was, we returned home in injured silence. The presence under my arm of *Eight Cousins* and *Rose in Bloom* was a minor comfort.

There are wrongs a self-important little girl of eleven can grasp and try to set right. And then there are grievances she begins to understand years later. Only as an adult did I appre- ciate that no matter how often my father extolled our life in the West, no matter how grateful he was to England for being the first country to take us in, and to Canada for sup- plying us with the oxygen in which we could breathe what he called the air of freedom, outside the borders of Hungary, he would feel forever emasculated. At eleven I couldn't know how much Gusti hated being under Pierre's thumb in the store. Or how it rankled that Shoshanna had again, as in England, found a proper job before he had. Or how it felt to be transplanted once more, to contend with another new language, when he hadn't yet properly mas- tered English. Or how profoundly disturbed he was by the religious split in the family.

With each move, each new workplace – Philips in Croydon, Bereki's in Montreal North – Gusti lost a bit more of his store of resilience, already depleted by the catastro- phes of his earlier life. And who was the agent of all this turmoil? Who had dragooned him into leaving Hungary and then shanghaied him to Montreal, the promised land of opportunity and family bliss? Who, indeed, but Shoshanna?

During the early months in Montreal, my parents' love life went through a prolonged drought.

Around this time Gusti spotted an ad for a bookkeeper's job downtown and made an appointment for an interview. He went alone and found the place all right, a brand new skyscraper with gleaming windows and sleek elevators.

"How did it go?" Shoshanna asked him, hoping for good news when he returned home.

"I didn't go in," he said heavily. "It was too grand a place for the likes of me."

Then Pierre intervened on his behalf and introduced him to the thankless servitude that was to be his lot for the next seventeen years. Exploited, unappreciated, and slighted daily by his employers, he worked as a costing clerk in a needle-trades company on St. Lawrence Boulevard, six days a week. With hindsight, it's clear he ought to have left and tried elsewhere, after gaining a year or two of Canadian experience. Shoshanna was to do exactly that when, a year and a half after starting at Neighbourhood House, she obtained a teaching job in the public system. But, fearing his age would count against him, Gusti settled for the devil he knew.

RELATIONS BETWEEN US and the Berekis improved as soon as Gusti left Pierre's employ and took up his new job in the summer of 1959. An informal weekly ritual evolved. Sunday afternoons we walked over to their place to enjoy the garden, share supper, and spend the evening together. We would stroll along 22nd Avenue, past little saltbox cottages, where I might nod at one or two of my classmates. At Jean-Talon, we'd cut through the Boulevard Shopping Centre, stopping to browse and find respite from the force of the sun beneath the narrow eaves over Morgan's shop windows. Judy might admire a doll carriage, which Shoshanna would warn her was much too expensive. "But you will have a birthday again before you know it," Gusti bent towards her ear to whisper, and her face lit up. I stood in silent contemplation of a record jacket. A young woman in a flounced blue dress danced in the arms of a suave gent in a tux. That summer Johnny Horton's "Battle of New Orleans" was big on the charts. So was Elvis Presley's "A Big Hunk of Love." Out of step with time and place, I dreamt of being swept off my feet in a breathless waltz.

Next we lingered for a few moments by the window of Vera's shop, commenting on the artfulness of the display. Vera had draped one of her own boldly printed silk scarves over the shoulder of an understated seersucker suit. The bathing suit on the full-size mannequin was a demure black one-piece, but on the floor at its feet lay several of the briefest imaginable bikinis, the tops unobtrusively stuffed with tissue paper.

The next stretch of the walk took us past seedy little pizzerias, *cordonneries*, butcher shops, hole-in-the-wall snack bars, and appliance stores with garish posters advertising perpetual liquidation sales. The last landmark before we turned our backs on the shabby bargains of Rue Bélanger in favour of the spanking suburban avenues of Vera's neighbourhood was the Orfanotrofio San Giuseppe, where, in front of a monolithic hulk of brown brick, nuns in swishing habits oversaw the rough-and-tumble play of scores of noisy children. The sight of these kids – more orphans – always gave me a pang.

At Vera's, Shoshanna put on shorts and a halter top and plunked herself in a garden chair. Judy and I changed into bathing suits so we could cavort beneath the spray of the garden hose with Philippe. Soon Judy and Alice were busy constructing one of their elaborate playhouses, dragging out kitchen chairs and draping blankets over them. Gusti rolled out the lawn mower and began cutting the grass. He said it was for the exercise – a doctor had put him on a diet – but really he was itching to perform anything that resembled a farm task. Pierre was not to be seen. Generally he made himself scarce as soon as we arrived, withdrawing to his room with a book and no excuses.

Late in the afternoon, Vera served a cold buffet in which familiar Hungarian tastes married with French dishes that quickly became new favourites. There was *kolbász* and a cheese spread called *körözöt* and *salade aux haricots verts* and Camembert with baguette. Vera was all affection on these occasions, pressing food on us, and jumping up every minute for some fresh delight or other, until Pierre ordered her to sit. Then she would laugh like a girl, her head thrown back, her neck smooth and tan. I loved the way she looked in her crisp cotton shirtwaist; I loved the spring in her step, her boundless cheeriness and energy.

Over Sunday dinner Vera and Shoshanna revisited their childhood pranks with considerable relish. There was, for starters, the time the two of them were romping around the kitchen back home when one of the older sisters' suitors was being entertained in the formal dining room. Shoshanna was riding piggyback on Vera — though a year older, Shoshanna was always the delicate flower, Vera the sturdy workhorse — and Vera made her laugh so hard that she peed down Vera's neck.

"Do you remember what happened next, Vera?"

"*Mais oui*, how could I forget? I took out the kitchen knife from the drawer and pointed it at your neck. And *j'ai dit*, '*Mindjárt temetés lesz!*'"

"*Qu'est-ce que tu dis, là, Maman? J'comprends rien!*" Philippe whined.

"She said, 'There's going to be a funeral here any minute,'" Shoshanna explained to him, with a distinct edge. She disapproved of the way Vera and Pierre handled Philippe. The child needed discipline and consistency. They were capable of neither.

The story of the kitchen knife was followed by the story of the ingested crochet hook and of the inhaled dry pea and of course of the adopted stray dog, Pityu, whom Shoshanna and Vera trained to rip the pants off a drunken one-legged war vet who paraded up and down the street. (This story ended badly, Pityu being impounded and put down.)

The story of the brick, the apex of the cycle, was recounted amid peals of laughter. It went something like this. Shoshanna and Vera were over at their friend Ica's. Ica lived up the street and had the best toys, being a fussed-over only child, while Shoshanna and Vera were the desultory afterthoughts of an already oversized clan. The two of them pushed the ancient rusted perambulator that had served the seven children of their family and that now chauffeured their ragamuffin dolls over to Ica's garden. Ica hauled out her new china baby with the pop-open eyes and corkscrew ringlets and – the pièce de résistance – a miniature tea set from Carlsbad that was gilded, so she said, with real gold. Then they set everything up for a doll's tea party.

Shoshanna alternated the lead roles of mother and German governess between herself, the oldest, and Ica, the proprietor of valued toys. To Vera she assigned the role of father. Both Mother and governess had the pleasure of looking after the babies, while Father was invariably despatched to the farthest reaches of the yard, near the outhouse, designated as the office. Here there was little to do but seethe. In a mutinous frame of mind, Vera found a pile of bricks, picked one up, returned to home and hearth, and slung it at Shoshanna's skull.

Shoshanna swept tendrils of hair back off her forehead, while wiping tears of laughter from her eyes. "See, Vera? I still have the scar."

After the story of the brick had been milked for its full dramatic effect – the gushing blood, the search for Mamuka at the store, the trip to the doctor by hired carriage, the poor injured head swathed in a thick white bandage for weeks – we were ready to move from the dinner table to the living room for drama of another sort.

Performing had been a way of life in my mother's family. All of them, including Mamuka and Apuka, had been musical. Friday nights in Beregszász were singalong affairs. "We weren't allowed to play the piano on *Shabbos*," Shoshanna explained, deliberately speaking in Hungarian so Alice and Philippe wouldn't understand, even though Pierre looked stern and Vera frowned as soon as the word *Shabbos* crossed my mother's lips. "The Orthodox aren't allowed to play on the Sabbath. But our parents had no objections to us improvising with makeshift instruments."

Apuka began the singalong, leading them at the table in Jewish songs called *zmires*. And after he had *bench*-ed – pronounced the grace after meals – he and Mamuka drifted from *zmires* into operetta, from *Prince Bob* and *The Csárdás Queen* to popular songs and Gypsy melodies. By this time the girls had run to the kitchen and hauled out the pots and lids to bang an accompaniment, while the two boys covered their pocket combs with tissue paper and coaxed out squeaking harmonies.

They were endowed with a good deal of dramatic flair as well as musical talent. Rózsika, the oldest, gave poetry recitations and performed in amateur theatricals. Magda could play the piano by ear, and was a wicked mimic. But it was teenaged Shoshanna who brought the family most fame, year after year taking the lead in community charity musicals, enchanting everyone with her convincing interpretations of Cinderella, Sleeping Beauty, and Briar Rose. And on sultry summer Sundays in a stuffy little Rosemount parlour, Shoshanna and Vera reprised these performances, Shoshanna still playing the lead and Vera taking all the other roles: the prince, the witch, the stepsisters, the courtiers of the royal court.

Vera was every bit as musical as Shoshanna, a contralto to Shoshanna's soprano, and her memory was prodigious. At times she even prompted Shoshanna in her lyrics.

"I was the little sister. I could also perform, but *mes parents* didn't want two in the same family. They say it is too much.

So then I was there each time when they *pratiquaient*, and I know the roles of everybody in the whole *opérette*. *Et puis j'étais aussi la claque*. Someone made up a poem about your mother. Because you know, your mother, she was *excellente*. She was the first of the first. So we clap and clap, and she pick up the flowers on the stage. And *nous*, the *claque*, we shout."

> Anna, Anna, the prima donna
> Anna, Anna, the belle of the ball
> Anna, Anna, *la vedette de* Hanukkah show
> Anna, Anna, *la prima donna*.

By this time Pierre was getting restless. He was dandling Alice on his lap, while Philippe squirmed beside them in the same armchair. "How about you dance for us, *beauté?*" Pierre asked Alice, grazing her gold cap of hair with his lips. Alice needed little persuading. While she went to her room with Judy to change into her pink ballet outfit, Philippe took the stage in the middle of the room.

Philippe was into humour that summer and required no prompting to unleash a barrage of knock-knock jokes. He followed them with peanut jokes, then elephant jokes, then riddles. To watch Gusti straining to grasp the wit in this display was the only amusing thing about it.

When Pierre told Philippe to cede the floor to Alice so she could dance, he began to howl, reaching crescendos that crossed the threshold of pain while Alice demonstrated the five ballet positions, which Judy, still in her smocked bathing suit, emulated next to her. Pierre hustled Philippe out of the living room to his bedroom, shutting the door behind them.

The muffled roar, akin to a wrecker's ball some two houses away, became marginally more tolerable.

It was at this point that either Shoshanna or Vera would ask me to perform something for the family. I was like my father. I had no forte. I couldn't sing or dance or tell jokes. I liked to read books and to ride my bike up and down the avenues of Ville Saint-Michel, hardly talents to display at living room concerts.

"No, no, I can't do anything. I don't want to do anything," I protested. It was just as well since the evening was degenerating. All Sunday evenings ended the same way, with Philippe still bellowing and his parents vainly trying to pacify him with declarations of love and promised treats. Pierre, as a last resort, administered a few whacks to the rear. Upon which a blissful silence descended on the house and we took our leave.

THE OCCASION OF MY PERFORMANCE, when it arrived, was for an audience larger than family. The school year was drawing to a close, and my turn came to lead morning exercises in Mr. Tidy's class.

There was nothing noteworthy about this particular June morning. After four months in the class, I still didn't fit in, but no one appeared concerned about it, not even me. Graduation was around the corner, with much excitement about our graduation exercises and dance at the end of the month. After the summer break we'd be off to high school, the great leveller, where all of us would be demoted from top dogs to lowest rung on the ladder, the poised popular kids as much as the misfits like me.

When Mr. Tidy called my name, I took my place at the front of the class behind his varnished blond wood desk, and trained my eyes on the Queen in her coronation robes and diamond tiara on the back wall. From the selection of texts Mr. Tidy had loaned me, I had picked Rudyard Kipling's "If," and I now read words that sounded so grand and important. I was perhaps hoping that their grandness and importance would rub off on me.

> If you can keep your head when all about you
>   Are losing theirs and blaming it on you,
> If you can trust yourself when all men doubt you
>   But make allowance for their doubting too,
> If you can wait and not be tired by waiting,
>   Or being lied about, don't deal in lies . . .

I delivered the final lines with a declaratory flourish:

> Yours is the Earth and everything's that's in it,
>   And – which is more – you'll be a Man, my son!

I found nothing absurd about this final assertion springing from my little-girl lips. Not skipping a beat, I intoned with a serious mien, "Let us pray."

Thirty-odd children – girls in shirtwaists, boys sporting brush cuts – shuffled to their feet, releasing as they did the usual adolescent odours of sweat, hormones, chewing gum, sneakers. Automatically, they bowed their heads and closed their eyes.

What possessed me then to say what I did? As I led the class in the Lord's Prayer, sliding my "r"s and pronouncing the "a" in "trespasses" the English way, it emerged from my mouth like a cartoon bubble.

"Through Jesus Christ Our Lord."

My face blazed hot with shame as I returned to my seat. The bargain with myself had been quite clear. The Lord's Prayer, yes, but Jesus never. Perhaps it was a profound wish to have been born otherwise, to have parents unbranded by the Jewish star, to be ordinary, mainstream, *free*. Invoking Jesus was my act, my pretense, my stab at another life.

I have no idea if it was a convincing performance for the audience in the classroom that June morning. I do know that in my own eyes I was an utter fraud. Never in my life have I felt more like an imposter, a child hollowed out.

THE IMPACT ON ME of Vera and Pierre's apostasy was potent and immediate, but the background to their abandonment of Judaism came to light later, in snatches of my parents' conversation, in questions asked and answered furtively and piecemeal over the years.

There was, first of all, the family legend of the Christian ancestress. My father used to twit Shoshanna about it from time to time, when she forgot the recipe for Passover *charoyses* or the holidays on which the memorial prayers for the dead were recited. Gusti would pat her on the bottom — a gesture that invariably raised her ire — and say slyly, "These lapses of memory must surely stem from the Christian great-grandmother."

No one could ever substantiate this legend, said to have originated with Iszku, my mother's oldest brother, the family sage and eccentric. But it ran something like this. In the town of Nagyszőllős — a town named for its splendid vineyards — some time in the early nineteenth century a whole congregation of Christians had converted to Judaism and one of them had married into Mamuka's family. Mamuka's exceptional intimacy with her Gentile clientele was attributed to this alleged lineage; so too was the fact that, before the war, both Vera and Magda had had Gentile suitors who, it went without saying, had to be turned down.

This bias for things Christian based on a vague bloodline of Mamuka's had a romantic tinge to it, but the main impulse for my aunt and uncle's conversion derived from malignant circumstances in Pierre's family. Pierre's father, Shoshanna said, had come from assimilated stock and was an atheist, and Pierre's mother took piety to extremes, to the point of shaving her hair after her marriage and wearing a wig. To spite his wife, Pierre's father sabotaged her efforts to raise their children as good Jews. On Yom Kippur, when Pierre's mother was beating her breast in synagogue, his father would take him to a restaurant and feed him pork.

Pierre was the sole survivor of the Holocaust in his family. His parents and his three siblings all perished. So did his mother's pious relatives. But on his father's side, all the relations who had converted to Christianity prior to the war survived. The conclusion that Pierre drew from this cautionary tale was that it didn't pay to be Jewish.

And yet he was not unequivocally wedded to the idea of leaving the faith. While he and Vera were living in Paris in the late 1940s, the state of Israel came into being. Pierre was a Zionist at heart, and he remained so in his own way to his dying day. When he and Vera began to talk about having children, he declared that the only place in the world he would contemplate having Jewish children was in Israel. Let her visit her brother Iszku there and see what she thought about making aliyah.

Iszku was the family's mad idealist. A brilliant young lawyer with a thriving practice, he had made aliyah to Palestine in 1938. In Palestine he fought in the Haganah, and after the creation of Eretz Israel, he declared that practising law was for weaklings and cripples. An able-bodied man ought to build the new country with the sweat of his labours.

When Vera arrived on his doorstep shortly after the end of the war of independence, she found him and his wife, Nechama, living in a hovel on a small plot of land, growing strawberries and oranges and husbanding a couple of goats. Vera hated it in Israel. She was terrified of Arab attacks, couldn't bear the heat, and was depressed walking the streets of Tel Aviv. In the faces of recently arrived *halutzim* she read anxiety, privation, and a long chain of suffering of the kind she herself was trying to forget. The poverty in which she found Iszku and Nechama was especially disturbing, what she imagined village life in Beregszász to have been at the time of the Christian great-grandmother.

Pierre had given her an ultimatum: Choose Israel if you want Jewish children, otherwise prepare to convert. She returned to Paris to face the inevitable. According to my parents, Pierre became a Christian out of pragmatism; they claimed that he was never formally baptized. They regarded his influence over Vera as Svengali-like mind control.

But it was more complicated than that. Although Vera had always been the headstrong daughter, the one who once caused her parents a great heartache, she had also been the most God-fearing of Mamuka's and Apuka's children. In the bombing attacks at Gelsenkirchen, Vera's faith had never faltered, and her cries of "*Shema Israel*" during the carnage had been among the loudest. She had been a believer as a Jew and, to become a Christian, she had to force herself into Christian belief. That meant the Immaculate Conception, the Holy Ghost, the Resurrection, the works.

It wasn't easy. No one knew the full extent of Vera's suffering when she undertook the study of Christianity in a Parisian Huguenot congregation. She was pregnant with Philippe at the time, and she claimed afterwards that she nearly lost her sanity in the process. When he emerged from the womb the child cried around the clock, a direct result, my parents believed, of the spiritual torment Vera had endured while carrying him. But once Vera passed through this private fire, she was forged in total conviction. She would believe unquestioningly in the Christian canon for the rest of her life. Pierre's conversion may have been one of convenience; hers was of the heart.

The family schism was a constant source of discussion and dissent among us. "Get over it," Judy and I would say impatiently to our parents as we grew older. "They may be misguided, but they have a right to live their lives the way they want. They're doing no harm to anybody."

Shoshanna didn't see it that way. "Their children are my parents' grandchildren just as the two of you are. But your cousins have no idea where they come from. They've no idea who Mamuka and Apuka were. They think being Jewish is like having the plague."

Gusti and Pierre had blazing arguments on all manner of subjects, but I don't think my father ever quoted to Pierre's face the passage from the Bible he often cited behind his back. My father knew virtually the whole of the Torah by heart, and when he recalled this portion of it, he pronounced it sternly, first in his old-fashioned Ashkenazi slur, then in guttural Hungarian for our benefit: "If thy brother, the son of thy mother, or thy son, or thy daughter, or the wife of thy bosom, or thy friend, that is as thine own soul, entice thee secretly, saying: 'Let us go and serve other gods,' which thou hast not known, thou, nor thy fathers; of the gods of the peoples that are round about you, nigh unto thee, or far off from thee, from the one end of the earth even unto the other end of the earth; thou shalt not consent unto him, nor hearken unto him; neither shall thine eye pity him, neither shalt thou spare, neither shalt thou conceal him; but thou shalt surely kill him; thy hand shall be the first upon him to put him to death, and afterwards the hand of all the people. And thou shalt stone him with stones, that he die; because he hath sought to draw thee away from the Lord thy God, who brought thee out of the land of Egypt, out of the house of bondage."

As he spoke these fearsome words Gusti's face set in furrows and his voice was dry and harsh. He was the picture of an ancient prophet, tongue-lashing his flock for their abominable sins.

"Tell me, how it is that Pierre can repay the Almighty, who brought him out of a bondage worse even than that of Egypt, by abandoning Him?"

Perhaps Gusti meant to send me a message, too, when he preached against Pierre. But beyond my father's strictures and warnings, something else deflected me from my flirtation with Jesus.

In the fall of 1959, soon after I began high school, my parents made visible preparations for Yom Kippur, the Day of Atonement, for the first time since we had left Hungary. In England, Shoshanna had lit holiday candles behind tightly shuttered windows, and she and Gusti had fasted surreptitiously, even as they went off to work at the television factory. Now they both had Jewish employers, and they could get off early in the day to prepare for the holiday. Once at home, they set to work together in the kitchen to make sure the pre-fast festive meal was prepared and consumed before sundown. There were remote tastes to be rediscovered: sweet challah from St. Lawrence Boulevard, boiled chicken with tomato sauce, quince compote studded with cloves.

We didn't have a synagogue to attend for Kol Nidre that year, but I remember my father laying his hands on our heads in turn, first Shoshanna, then me, then Judy, as he muttered the ancient blessing that his mother had bestowed on him and his brothers at this time each year.

That night as usual I went to bed in the living room. At the foot of the sofa on which I slept stood a low table, covered with one of our treasures from Hungary, a silk-tasselled Matyó-design throw, richly embroidered in primary colours. Six squat, metal-encased candles sputtered on it that evening. Judy and I had been sent out of the room when Shoshanna and Gusti lit them, because, Gusti said, those not required to mourn shouldn't even look upon the faces of mourners. My parents didn't know the exact anniversaries of the deaths of their loved ones, so every year they lit their memorial candles on the eve of Yom Kippur.

I fell asleep staring at the eerie patterns cast by the flames onto the ceiling, my throat and lungs heavy with the smell of wax. And then I suddenly woke with a jolt. Disoriented, I tried to make sense of the flickering patterns in the half-light. My mouth was dry and I propped myself on an elbow, vaguely thinking of getting myself some water.

From the other side of the wall, I heard a muffled noise I couldn't decode, the sound that must have roused me. My bare soles clung clammily to the linoleum in the hall as I pushed open the door to my parents' bedroom. All the lights were on, and I blinked like an owl at the sudden brightness. Still squinting, I tried to make sense of the scene. On the far side of the bed, Gusti's bulky form was curled into a fetal position. The choking sobs appeared to be coming from him, but I couldn't be sure because my view was instantly obscured. Shoshanna in a white nightie, her hair mussed, materialized in front of me. She held a finger to her lips and bent towards me as she pushed me back out of the room.

"It's all right," Shoshanna whispered. "Go back to bed like a good girl, okay? Don't worry, it's nothing. He does this every year. Every Kol Nidre he does this. Mourning his dead. All his dead from the war. Go back to sleep, please. *Please*. It has nothing to do with you."

I would like to write that, after this, all became clear for me and that my Jewish identity fell firmly into place. Actually, matters grew more murky with time, not less. What to make of the fact that, when we bought a house two years after our arrival in Montreal – in Ville d'Anjou, an eastern extremity of the island uninhabited by other Jews – my parents festooned our front windows with Christmas lights, out of respect for our Christian neighbours? Gusti, who had expatiated upon the passage from Deuteronomy about the fate of those who worshipped other gods, nonetheless held ecumenical views about Christmas. As I grew older, he often spoke about his great respect for the man from Galilee, a notable Jewish reformer and rabbi, whose disciples, he said, had twisted his teachings by deifying him against his own intentions. Gusti had no problem with a Christmas tree and Christmas presents to celebrate the birth of a great Jew, and saw nothing inappropriate in kindling the Hanukkah menorah at the same time as the Christmas lights winked in our windows.

Vera and Pierre were equally inconsistent. Every year at Passover, Vera asked my father to bring her matzo and matzo meal from St. Lawrence Boulevard so she could make *knaidlach* for a chicken soup that rivalled Shoshanna's in its "thousand tastes," as we say in Hungarian. And every year my uncle gave my father a generous cheque to pass on to the Combined Jewish Appeal – under Gusti's name, not Pierre's.

(When Pierre died prematurely in his fifties, Gusti had to endure belligerent calls from canvassers who berated him for the sudden unaccountable shrinkage of his donations.)

I shall never forget the sight of my uncle falling onto my father's neck in an entirely uncharacteristic display of affection during the mad euphoria of the Six Day War in 1967. "We've won! We've won! Jerusalem is ours!" Those were Pierre's words. And for once the two of them were in total accord.

Given the confusing range of adult opinion, behaviour, and emotion around the Jewish question in my family, it is not entirely surprising that for years I continued to skirt the territory between the Star of David and the Cross. My friends were exclusively non-Jewish until I was well into my twenties. I married outside the faith, eventually dragging my fiancé into Judaism, despite his patent unease with conversion to my religion.

Nonetheless something changed for me that Yom Kippur of 1959 when, for an instant, I glimpsed the brightly illuminated tableau of my parents' grief. At that moment, I stumbled on a core truth about my family. No matter what I did, no matter how much I wanted to, I couldn't divest myself of the albatross of our Jewishness. I could choose to regard the Jewish star as a tattoo of shame or a badge of courage. Either way, it was mine.

eight

BOYFRIENDS

In the back of my car, out of the blue and with no preamble, Vera dropped a petite conversational bon mot.

"I so much loved Mamuka. In the morning, I massage her shoulders and her back, before she gets out of bed."

For whom was this precious observation intended, I wondered? Shoshanna, sitting beside Vera in the back? Me, in the front passenger seat, next to my younger daughter, the driver? Perhaps she was just musing to herself, jogged by some stray brainwave taking her back to that other life, supposedly buried but, in fact, never far from the surface, its omnipresence betrayed by Vera's curious diction, her mix of past and present tense.

I craned my neck around to better follow the little drama in the back seat. Vera was patting one gnarled, nut-brown-freckled hand with the other, re-enacting the long-ago massages that ended with her rubbing lotion into Mamuka's hands.

But Shoshanna wasn't buying these reminiscences. In the grey pantsuit that brought out the blue of her eyes, she stiffened her shoulders, bristled.

"*You* didn't massage Mamuka in the mornings! Mari Néni did."

Mari Néni, the family's long-time housekeeper, roused the girls each morning with chirpy inquiries: "Sweet missy, what would you like for breakfast? Café au lait? Hot chocolate? Caraway soup with toast? Maybe a little sauerkraut?"

On this beautiful fall morning, the maple trees still thick with red and orange and yellow foliage, the sky a clear blue, my mother and my aunt were studiously ignoring the matter at hand. We were on our way to the cemetery for the unveiling of a headstone for Max, my mother's third husband. But they weren't talking about Max, dead a mere six months and buried on the western tip of the island of Montreal. They were arguing instead, con brio, about Mamuka's daily massages, sixty years ago and thousands of miles away.

"Maybe Mari Néni do it when we are small, but, *après*, I did it. *Mais c'est une chose étrange.* I loved my mother *beaucoup*, but I do not confide in her. I never get into bed with her in the mornings like you —"

"*This* I don't remember!"

"*Mais oui.* On Saturday mornings, when Apuka was in synagogue, you snuggle up with her in bed and tell her everything, *tout, tout, tout!*"

"I never had any secrets from Mamuka," the smile on Shoshanna's face was both complacent and nostalgic. "I used to read her all my letters, the letters I wrote – she said every one was like a novel – and the letters I received, even love letters."

"*Moi*," said Vera, "I love also *les parents* very much, I was very *fidèle*, but I never confide to them. *J'ai eu mes secrets.*

They know they can count on me, I will stay with them when they are old, I will be their *soutien*, but I can never tell them anything."

"Of course you were a very good child," Shoshanna agreed with a silkiness that implied the direct antithesis of what she had just said, "but *I* did everything they ever told me to. When they said I had to give up Imre, I gave him up. Even though I was wild about him and it broke my heart."

When Shoshanna married Márton, at twenty-three, she had already broken several hearts and had had her own heart thoroughly shattered twice. The first serious love of her life was Imre Schwartz. But she barely had time to launch into the story of her romance with Imre, the playboy pharmacist, before we reached the iron gates of the cemetery. Clutches of family members and friends gathered around the grave as the rabbi pulled away the rectangular veil covering the monument and began the five-minute speech that summed up a man's life.

Poor Max. The third dead husband. Shoshanna had met him while visiting Gusti in the chronic care facility where my father spent the last years of his life and where Max's wife was also institutionalized. One thing had led to another, and when the two sick spouses died within months of each other, there was nothing to prevent Shoshanna and Max from marrying. They had a few good years together, then some bad ones. Once more Shoshanna was saddled with responsibility for a debilitated and dependent partner. She came close to snapping under the strain.

Since then, for the first time in her life, she has been without a man. She spends a lot of time with Vera. They scrap a lot, the old quarrels over religion flaring high from time to time. But their confrontations don't run deep. These two are life partners in ways more irrevocable than marriage. They phone each other half a dozen times a day, and if the one doesn't pick up by the third ring, the other is on the verge of hysteria: has something happened to her? That inevitable loss is the one calamity each fears above all; it is the loss neither thinks she can survive.

During the Kaddish for Max, my mind drifted back to the conversation in the car. "I had no secrets from my mother," Shoshanna had boasted. It wasn't the first time I'd heard this refrain.

SHOSHANNA STOOD FRAMED by the door to my bedroom in the house in Ville d'Anjou. She addressed my back.

"I used to tell my mother everything," Shoshanna declared, "everything. She loved it when I read my letters out loud to her. She used to say that I should be a writer, that what I wrote was as interesting as any novel."

I hunched over my desk, shielding with my body the Hilroy notebook in which I kept my diary.

"My mother was my greatest supporter," Shoshanna continued from the doorway, undeterred by my lack of response. "She would say to me when I woke up in the morning that this was when I should receive my suitors. Because I looked prettiest then, my face flushed from sleep, my eyes shining. I had no secrets from my mother," she concluded on a non sequitur.

I wish you'd go away, I said to myself. I wish *you* had some secrets from *me*.

I was fifteen. I was in love. Shoshanna, as always, was plying me with details from her previous lives. She seemed to have more history than the proverbial cat. I had only recently stumbled on the full story of her first marriage. It was an appalling tale, or perhaps it merely appalled me. A marriage that had survived the cataclysm, the only marriage to have done so that I'd ever heard of. She had come back almost from the grave, and so had Márton. And she'd been unfaithful to him. With Gusti. With my ridiculously stodgy father. Here was this handsome man, this blue-eyed, curly-haired Adonis close to her own age, and she had left him for my old, balding, overweight father.

But no, she hadn't been the one to blame.

"It was you, *you*, who made up my mind for me."

The story had slipped out, as if by accident, though she must have wanted to tell me for some time lest I find out from someone else. The parents of one of my friends were divorcing and I mentioned it to her. Shoshanna said she too had been divorced.

We were folding laundry in her bedroom, a sheet pulled taut between us. My hold slackened on the corners in my hands.

"What do you mean?"

I knew she had been married before because there was a picture of Márton in her photo album. When, as a young child, I asked about it, she murmured that it depicted her first husband. I assumed that he, like everyone else, was dead.

Now, in a daze, I tried to process a tidal wave of unwanted information: Márton's disappearance on the Russian front in 1942, Shoshanna's return from the camps in 1945, her first encounter with Gusti, the discovery that Márton had been spared, the terrible predicament of loving two men and having to choose between them.

And then she exclaimed, "*You* decided for me. The fact that I got pregnant with you! That's why I didn't go back to Márton, though he still wanted me. Because you were Gusti's child, not his."

I dropped the sheet on the floor and ran from the room. My initial outrage was not over my purported role as the agent of my parents' marriage. Rather, my heart bled for Márton. She should have stayed true to him. I would have stayed true.

As the implications of her accusation sank in (only years later did the thought occur to me that her cry may have been less accusation than lament), I began to seethe. Right. I was to blame. Me, the zygote. (In biology we had just learned that the embryo was a zygote before it became an embryo.) Zygotic, embryonic me was responsible, because I had somehow managed to get her pregnant with myself.

These were thoughts – and images – best left unexplored. But instead of a veil of discreet obscurity settling over the past, I was being invited to tell Shoshanna *everything* in exchange for her unsolicited and unsavoury and quite superfluous reminiscences. No way.

Not that there was so much to tell. There was only one significant boy in my life, the boy who became the Boyfriend and later the Fiancé and then the Husband and ultimately the Ex. Yet onto the slim frame of this stand-in for the male of the species would soon be projected the doubts and fears posed by the romantic entanglements of the men in Shoshanna's circle — her brothers and brothers-in-law, not to mention the foibles and (mostly) failings of her own suitors and husbands. And upon the blank canvas of my barely formed life were splashed in bold lines and vibrant colours both the mundane events and the dramatic plot twists that characterized the romances of Shoshanna and her sisters. It didn't leave much space for an original stroke of my own creation.

There were two subtexts to the tales that were part of Shoshanna's didactic repertoire. Men are your road to money, status, and — indirectly, through the children they will give you — fulfillment. But one way or another, sooner or later, men will also be your downfall. For a long time I thought I had closed my ears to these stories of Shoshanna's. But I was probably listening all along.

"HE'S JEALOUS and he's possessive," Shoshanna hissed warningly of the Boyfriend. "I heard you crying last night when you were on the phone with him. My sister Rózsika's husband, Ernő, was insanely jealous of all her comings and goings. And he kept her on a tight leash. She married him because she loved him, but she could have had her pick of the finest our city had to offer. I'm telling you, you don't want that to happen to you."

Shoshanna had adored Rózsika. The greatest compliment she would ever pay me, years later, was to say that I resembled Rózsika in personality and, as I aged, in appearance. I didn't, it went without saying, resemble Rózsika in her youth, when she was the belle of the town. But if I did so however tenuously in maturity, it meant that Shoshanna was pleased, even proud of me.

Refinement, wisdom, goodness – these were the qualities Shoshanna ascribed to Rózsika. But they made her sound such an impossible paragon, when Rózsika was so much fun. She had the gift of mimicry. Rózsika acted out the drama of the fowl being fattened in the yard or performed what she called the symphony of the birds – her eyes dancing, her slender arms assuming the shape of wings – as she chirped, clacked, and twittered for the benefit of the family on a Friday night. No one could have been more delightful, more charming, more winsome than Rózsika.

The eldest had grown into the finest, someone on whom the parents relied. The younger children depended on her too, to broker their ambitions and defend their causes. It was Rózsika who noticed how Duved pined when he was taken out of school and brought into the store, instead of being sent to *gimnázium*.

"The store is not for him," Rózsika had said to Apuka and Mamuka, and somehow it became possible for Duved to go back to school, and eventually to university in Brno, then to Prague, where he excelled.

And it was Rózsika for whose sake Ernő, the prototypical son-in-law to Mamuka and Apuka, put on phylacteries every morning and davened like a traditional Jew although he had grown up in an irreligious household. Rózsika brought out the best in everyone.

Why Rózsika had fallen in love with Ernő was a mystery in the way that affairs of other people's hearts often are. He wasn't a handsome man, nor rich, nor especially charming. And she – such a beauty that she made heads turn on the Korzó. Delicately built with a sculpted, graceful form, her skin was faultlessly translucent, her eyes a deep greyish blue, her thick dark hair worn in a wave over her left brow, in the style popularized by the actress Irene Biller. Manufacturers, mill owners, wine merchants all came asking for her hand, but the one who won her was Ernő Borenstein, a struggling law student. And he won her not by special merit but by the force of his obsession for her. Ernő latched onto Rózsika and wouldn't let her go. He threatened to kill himself if she accepted anyone else.

An overprotected boy from a neurotic family, he had been brought up by a high-strung mother and a German-speaking governess who still lived with the family at the time of Ernő's marriage. He would lean on Rózsika the way he had depended on the German *Fräulein*, at the same time controlling her like a petty despot. Even before their wedding, Ernő's need of Rózsika verged on desperation. When he had to take his final bar exams in Prague, he refused to go unless she accompanied him, a controversial request to make of a sheltered, unmarried girl. The story went that Rózsika had to push him through the door of the examination room.

The minute Ernő received Rózsika's dowry – 100,000 Czech crowns, a fortune for which Apuka had mortgaged the family home – and opened up his practice, his father closed the elegant men's-wear shop on Main Street from which he had made a living and declared it was now time for his son to start supporting his parents. Until Juditka, their daughter, was born, Rózsika and Ernő lived with his mother and father. Once, Mamuka and Apuka were invited to dine there and were scandalized to observe that Rózsika's portion was the *gargli*. At home the chicken's neck was given to the cats.

Rózsika's marriage became a familiar topic of family conversation in the days before the war overshadowed every other problem. How Ernő couldn't take a breath without her, how she managed his office, catered to his parents, did practically all her own housework. How simply their flat was furnished, not at all in the manner expected of a lawyer's household, and how he forbade mirrors lest Rózsika primp and attract the attention of other men. How he balanced the household books every night, and if they were short one *fillér*, he wouldn't go to bed or allow her to do so until the discrepancy was found. A *fillér* or a thousand crowns were one and the same, he claimed.

Despite his eccentricities, Ernő's law practice flourished. He bought land, a vineyard, a house. But if Mamuka hadn't clothed Rózsika and Juditka from the store, they wouldn't have had anything to put on their backs.

Erno was as tight-fisted with himself as he was with others. In labour service years later on the Russian front, his comrades knew him to have money hidden in his shoes. He could have made his life easier by converting it to food, but he hoarded it instead. Had he been better nourished, he might not have contracted typhoid. When he fell sick, the bills still lined his shoes. They were there still when he and the other diseased men were locked into a barn, and the barn set on fire.

Back home in Beregszász, Juditka woke screaming in the night. "He died, he died! Apu's dead!" Rózsika tried to talk her out of it as she comforted her, but secretly she accepted the child's nightmare as a prophecy.

THE ONLY SIBLING Shoshanna could never speak of without choking up or bursting into tears was Lilli. Which was odd, since Lilli was the sister she was least close to. She couldn't say why exactly, couldn't explain it even to herself. The summer that Lilli had married and moved to the nearby town of Munkács, Shoshanna was sent to her home to convalesce after a kidney irritation. Shoshanna was always thin as a reed, but the one time in her life she was chubby, it was as a result of Lilli's care. Though she had a reputation for stinginess with food back home, Lilli kept tempting her with delicacies, stuffed her until she was plump as a capon.

And yet as a teenager Shoshanna resented Lilli and felt herself resented by Lilli. If she had had the words for it, she might have thought Lilli was jealous of her. But what was there to be jealous of in a little sister when you were a stunning newlywed in the full flower of your beauty? Lilli really was gorgeous. Taller than Apuka, taller than the man she eventually married, and statuesque. She had green, slanty eyes like a cat and golden hair that she maintained by rinsing it with camomile tea. Forever on a diet, she lived on green apples that would pour out of her dresser drawers when you snuck into them in search of a pair of silk stockings.

Lilli was artistic, with a flair for fine handwork. Instead of sending her trousseau out to be monogrammed, like her sisters, she embroidered all the items herself, the curlicues of her initials taking on fanciful shapes. She knit, crocheted, wove rugs that she decorated with heavy Kelim stitchery. She mounted petit point cushion covers onto velvet backing and fashioned one-of-a-kind lampshades bedecked with gold tassels made of heavy silk.

Still, it was easier to admire the work of Lilli's hands than to love her. After Rózsika married, Lilli took over the role of the household's "big girl," the senior daughter, a kind of apprentice homemaker who acted as Mamuka's deputy when Mamuka was at the store. A natural cook and a wonderful baker, Lilli relished this supervisory capacity over her siblings. She was good at policing.

Of course, without someone setting limits on the consumption of the delicacies that were produced in that kitchen, there would have been nothing to sit down to at mealtimes. The children had hearty appetites and were given to snatching whatever emerged fresh from the oven, even before it cooled. Fridays were the most rewarding days for such filching, on account of the baking done in anticipation of the Sabbath: the brioches, the Danish pastries – chocolate, cinnamon, jam, walnut – the poppy-seed roulades, the cakes, the tarts. Lilli was determined to set a proper table for the Sabbath, with everything *comme il faut*.

Lilli might find hiding places for her confections, but the enticing odours of fresh baking gave the secret away. And then the discovery that she had been outwitted would send her into paroxysms of rage. Sometimes she remained in the dark. Iszku and Duved, for instance, were entirely capable of finishing off a five-litre jar of apricot jam between them, swilling it down their gullets of a Friday afternoon like water, then tossing the jar onto the waste heap at the back of the yard, so the evidence of the empty container wouldn't give them away.

Though her stern face in the kitchen and harsh scoldings made her unpopular with her siblings, Lilli had many friends. One of them introduced her to a young man for whom she fell hard. Good-looking and comfortably rich, Menyush Klein lived in the neighbouring town of Ungvár. He began to visit the Schwartz household regularly on Sundays in the manner of an eligible suitor, and in his honour festive dinners and outings to the family vineyards were organized. Shoshanna and Vera in particular profited from these occasions. The chocolates that Menyush brought for Lilli invariably fell to the younger sisters, as, unknown to him, Lilli wouldn't touch them.

Always beautiful, Lilli now shone with new-found happiness. She was twenty-one, a perfect age for engagement. The match was assumed by everyone to be a certainty. But then Menyush suddenly stopped coming around. It appeared that his widowed mother opposed the union. Lilli's family wasn't rich enough, her dowry wouldn't do.

At this vulnerable moment in Lilli's life, her brother-in-law, Ernő, stepped in. Though Mamuka and Apuka disapproved of the state of Rózsika's marriage, they deferred to Ernő and respected him for his position as a successful young lawyer. They trusted his judgment and so they heeded his advice when Lilli was jilted. Ernő counselled, "Strike while the iron is hot. I have just the suitor for Lilli."

Enter Izidor Weiss, an older cousin of Ernő's, a business-man in Munkács. A good ten years Lilli's senior, he was not especially handsome, a tad shorter than Lilli when she wore high heels – and she never stopped wearing them, not even on her wedding day. He enjoyed a wide social circle and had just ruptured a long-standing relationship with a girl from a reputable family. Affluent and well travelled, he could ensure that Lilli would have a good life.

"Both of them are ripe for it and the time is ripe too. Strike while the iron is hot."

Lilli was not so much ripe as somnambulant, almost apathetic. They could have yoked her to an ox and she wouldn't have protested. If she couldn't have Menyush, she didn't care whom she married. A short courtship ensued. By the time the wedding pictures were posed, however, she was smiling placidly, looking regal in a floor-length gown and veil and holding her bouquet in white-gloved hands. But the picture also hinted at another side of Lilli. She wore that veil with its crown of lace florets aslant, like a flapper's rakish beret.

For their honeymoon they cruised the Adriatic and the Mediterranean, and when they returned to Munkács, Izidor began building a beautiful, modern home (indoor bath-room! hot and cold running water! flush toilet!) on the banks of the Latorca River. He was making piles of money as a highway contractor for the Czech government. He began by quarrying stone, then he purchased a large quarry, and then he landed lucrative paving contracts. One ambitious project led to the next. He bought a snazzy sports car, and, not long after the honeymoon, they drove down to the Dalmatian coast and to Italy.

They led a feverish social life. When Shoshanna came to recuperate from her kidney problem, she marvelled at the goings-on in the house. Izidor spouted Zionist rhetoric and there was *treyf* on the table, which amazed her since one of Lilli's duties when she had been the big girl back home was the stringent supervision of the koshering of meat.

A certain demimonde flavour marked their life. A lesbian called Peppi who dressed in trouser suits was part of their circle. Night after night, they moved from cabaret to restaurant to private party. Izidor was forever showing Lilli off and boasting about her looks. "Don't you think my wife's the most beautiful woman in Czechoslovakia?" he would tack on to routine introductions, his arm thrown proprietorially over her splendid wide shoulders. On one occasion Izidor pushed Lilli to enter an impromptu beauty contest at the Csillag restaurant. She won.

Late one night when Lilli and Izidor returned home from a party, the noise and sudden light roused Shoshanna, who was sleeping in the bedroom adjoining theirs, a mullioned glass door separating the two rooms. Sitting up, Shoshanna caught her breath as she slowly pieced together the image framed by the square panes of the doorway. Izidor sat at Lilli's dressing table, his head clutched in his hands, his shoulders racked by bitter sobs. Shoshanna never questioned Lilli about it but never forgot the scene either. Perhaps her sister's life wasn't as charmed as it appeared?

When Tibike, their son, was born a year later, Shoshanna, ever fascinated by babies, visited more frequently. As he grew from infancy into an energetic and rambunctious little boy, his father showered him with toys and novelties. Nothing was too extravagant or outlandish; even a pet faun was tamed for his pleasure in the country house by the river. But Shoshanna found Lilli tense around the child, and often short-tempered. Mealtimes became a battleground between mother and child, Tibike balking at the quantities of food Lilli pressed on him.

It was on these later visits that Shoshanna grew to resent Lilli for her high-handed ways. Just at the moment when the seven-year disparity in their ages ought to have counted for less and a true friendship could have grown between them, they rubbed fiercely against each other over small irritations. For instance, Lilli, whose own brows were plucked and artistically pencilled in, reprimanded Shoshanna sharply for blackening her eyebrows.

"You're not my mother to tell me what to do," Shoshanna flared. "I'm nineteen years old!"

Shoshanna had turned nineteen on August 30, 1938, just when darkness began to descend on their world, when drawing the line of an eyebrow wasn't as crucial an issue as it might have been a year earlier. In Hungary the first of a series of anti-Jewish laws had been passed in the spring. But Beregszász, Munkács, and Ungvár – the three Subcarpathian towns that bound Shoshanna's world – still belonged to the Czech province of Podkarpatská Rus. Since the end of the First World War, they had officially been known as Berehovo, Mukacěvo, and Uzhorod; Shoshanna had never known a time when they weren't Czech. She might and did call herself a Hungarian-speaking Israelite, but she was born Czech in Czechoslovakia, a democracy to be proud of. The father of the country, President Tomáš Masaryk, was a great liberal and champion of the Jews.

All this was true but soon negated by fresh geopolitical realities. A month after Shoshanna's nineteenth birthday, the Munich agreement was signed by Britain, France, Italy, and Germany, allowing the first steps in the dismemberment of Czechoslovakia. A few weeks later, on November 2, in return for Hungary's support during the Sudetenland crisis, Hitler awarded several Hungarian-speaking districts of southern Czechoslovakia, home to a million people, to Hungary.

It seemed as if all of Beregszász lined Main Street that November day, to witness first the withdrawal of the Czech forces and then the arrival of the much vaunted Hungarian cavalry in full military regalia on horseback, firearms ostentatiously slung from their shoulders. Perhaps it wasn't the whole town, but only the Hungarians, cheering lustily and mocking the retreat of the Czechs. Oh yes, the Czech government radio had bombastically declared, "*Berehovo, Mukacěvo, Uzhorod: ne dáme!*" We won't give them back! But in the end they had to.

While his neighbours clapped and hurrahed, Apuka stood in front of his store, tears coursing down his cheeks, and watched the cavalcade of Hungarian soldiers. Iszku, his older son, was already on his way, by some tortuous route or other, to Eretz Israel, and it was only a matter of hours or days before Duved, the apple of Apuka's eye, would flee through the snowy Carpathians on his way to free Czech territory in Prague. Knowing his sons could soon be forced into service, he preferred to send them abroad. Still, their departure was a devastating blow to Mamuka and Apuka. Once war was declared in September 1939, a wall of silence separated them from the boys – one a soldier in Palestine, the other in England – behind enemy lines. Not a single note or message managed to get through.

The change of regimes hit Izidor's business particularly hard. His fortunes had been entirely tied to those of the Czech government. When the Hungarians took over Podkarpatská Rus, the Czech government owed Izidor a million Czech crowns. Ernő mortgaged some of his properties to help Izidor with a loan of 100,000 crowns. Izidor hocked Lilli's two-carat diamond ring. From plenty they were suddenly plunged into near penury.

Enter an old friend of Izidor's called Bumi. A man without a last name in the family annals, Bumi, improbably, returned to Munkács from Palestine, where, even more improbably, he had amassed a fortune. A good-looking, red-headed charmer, home to visit his widowed mother, he looked up Izidor and proved a proverbial friend in need. He loaned Izidor money. Naturally he met Lilli.

Bumi became part of Izidor's immediate circle. On family visits to Beregszász, he accompanied Izidor, Lilli, and Tibike. He was introduced to Shoshanna, then began to visit Beregszász without Izidor. He expressed interest in courting Shoshanna, though, in light of later events, this may have been a ruse. In any case, Shoshanna wasn't biting. She was already involved with Imre Schwartz, the pharmacist, and sent Bumi packing.

In the meantime, Bumi was harassing Lilli. She complained about him to Izidor and to Izidor's brother: Bumi wouldn't leave her alone, Bumi was making demands on her. One evening Izidor found Lilli sobbing in the bathroom.

"What's wrong with you, for heaven's sake?"

"Bumi threatened to kill me."

"Don't be ridiculous."

"But he did!"

"A dog that barks doesn't bite," Izidor said, turning on his heel.

It was a troubled time. By the fall of 1940, Jewish men in Hungary were being inducted into labour service battalions. These units of the Hungarian army did dirty and dangerous work but were never armed. At the same time, more territory – in Transylvania – was returned to Hungary. Anti-Jewish legislation previously passed in Hungary was being applied to the annexed territories, drastically reducing the participation of Jews in economic, financial, and cultural occupations. Most Jewish voters were also disenfranchised.

Closer to home, Vera was pursuing a romance Shoshanna heartily disapproved of, and Magda was recuperating from an illness. Shoshanna spent as much time as she could with Rózsika, in whose company she felt soothed and comforted. When Izidor's chauffeur arrived at Rózsika's doorstep one afternoon unannounced and unexpected, he found the two sisters quizzing each other on English vocabulary in Rózsika's modestly furnished living room. They dreamt of escape, of possible emigration, of an early Allied victory. They were preparing themselves for some such happy eventuality by studying English together.

The chauffeur – Izidor had held on to some of the trappings of wealth – took off his visored hat and bowed.

"Madame Borenstein, Miss Anna, I apologize for bringing bad news."

Rózsika and Shoshanna sprang to their feet.

"What — what bad news?" Rózsika stammered.

"Something unfortunate has befallen Madame Lilli. Master Izidor asks you please to accompany me immediately to Munkács."

Shoshanna felt herself turn numb as Rózsika floundered for information.

"But what has happened to my sister?"

"I am not at liberty to say, Madame. But it is a situation of the utmost seriousness. Please to hurry. Master Izidor needs someone from your family, and he has asked for you."

Rózsika took Shoshanna by the shoulders. "Listen to me, are you listening to me?"

Shoshanna nodded.

"Take Juditka to my mother-in-law's for tonight. Don't breathe a word to our parents until the morning. I don't want them to worry unnecessarily. Maybe it will be all right. Don't say anything to anybody. Tell my mother-in-law that Lilli suddenly needed my help with something. If you don't hear from me by morning, it means that things are very bad. If you don't hear from me, tell Mamuka and Apuka that Lilli has had an accident and that all three of you are to come to Munkács."

"But — but how can I tell them that when —"

"Don't ask questions! I don't know any more than you. Just do as I say."

It was a terrible night for Shoshanna. She couldn't run to Vera or to her parents because Rózsika had forbidden it. Her mind kept buzzing around, trying to grapple with a horrible mystery: "unfortunate event," "utmost seriousness," "accident" – what had happened to Lilli? What was she to say to Mamuka and Apuka in the morning? And what was she to do about this unbearable pain that had settled in her chest?

"That's the third time you've gotten up tonight," Vera mumbled crossly from across the room in the dark.

"I'm refreshing my compresses."

"What?"

"I'm putting wet cloths on my chest. I have a very heavy feeling on my heart."

"That's a strange remedy for heartache."

In the morning there was no word from Rózsika. Shoshanna was trembling when she entered Mamuka's and Apuka's room and broke the news to them.

"Lilli has had an accident," she said. "Lilli is hurt and we must go to her."

The cab ride to Munkács, an hour-long excursion under normal circumstances, was more frightful for Shoshanna than the previous night's sleepless vigil. She had always believed her mother to be the stronger of her parents. Certainly Mamuka was the more ambitious and enterprising one, the initiator and facilitator who ensured that the girls as well as the boys were educated, that the store prospered, that the household ran like clockwork, that the family had a reputation – not entirely deserved – for wealthy stability. To all this Apuka contributed a quiet, cautioning influence. But Mamuka fell completely to pieces during their journey. That something had befallen Lilli – only twenty-eight, her precious darling – was unthinkable. Mamuka, who seldom raised her voice, was hysterical, her face tear-drenched and puffy, her uncombed hair escaping its bun.

"Ilonkám, Ilonkám," Apuka whispered, "my darling, don't —"

"If you don't tell me what's happened this instant, I'll throw myself out of the car!" Mamuka sobbed, reaching across Shoshanna for the door and managing to push it open. The driver screeched to a halt and threatened to turn tail for Beregszász.

Apuka assisted Mamuka out of the car and asked the driver for a moment's grace. They stood by the dusty shoulder of the highway, suddenly transformed into an old couple shrunken in their fall tweeds.

"My darling," Apuka said in a broken voice, but retaining his composure, "we mustn't give up hope."

But hope was dashed on arrival. Rózsika was standing at the gate of Lilli's house, watching for them since early morning.

"She is dead."

For Shoshanna, even the worst news was a kind of relief. The very sight of Rózsika in her checkered jumper and silk blouse with the bow at the neck, the outfit she had worn the day before for English lessons, was reassuring. It was the first step to righting the universe. It meant that Shoshanna's role as Cassandra was over. Lilli was dead, and the grown-ups were dealing with it. At that moment, Shoshanna, who was twenty-one, wanted nothing so much as to crawl back into the nursery. Give up the beaux, the strolls along the Korzó, the turned heads. If this was life as a "big girl" — and indeed, now it was Shoshanna who was the big girl at home – then Shoshanna wanted to stay a little girl as long as possible.

Piecing together what had happened was horrible and inconclusive. Lilli had left a note that Shoshanna didn't read, but the two sentences from it that the grown-ups shared with her stayed with her forever. They weren't profound or profoundly revealing, mere statements of fact, simple words summing up Lilli's final state of mind.

"I can't write any more. I'm very nervous."

When Izidor had come home the day before, Bumi's car was parked in front of the house. There was no sign of either Lilli or Bumi. Suddenly remembering every snatch of conversation, including the one about dogs barking and biting, every innuendo, every misgiving, Izidor stormed through the house hollering Lilli's name. The bathroom door was locked. Fear and rage lending him strength, he slammed his whole weight against it.

He found both of them, in a heap on the floor. There was a neat circle in the centre of Lilli's beautiful brow; Bumi was more of a mess, streaks of blood from a head wound staining his freckled cheeks. A black revolver lay stark against the white tiles of the floor.

The tragedy was one thing, the disgrace another. In Shoshanna's mind, grief and shame for her sister remained forever fused. The rumours and slurs began with questions about the burial. Would Lilli be admitted within the boundaries of the cemetery in consecrated ground or not? Had Bumi killed her, or had she pulled the trigger herself? Izidor, overwhelmed with sorrow and guilt, spewed garbled confessions about her accounts of Bumi's attentions and threats.

Others testified that Bumi was deranged, that he had abused and beaten his own aged mother. These allegations implied murder, rather than suicide. But there was the note that Lilli had left. In it she had bequeathed her remaining valuables – a fur coat, a leather jacket, the few pieces of jewellery left unpawned – to her sisters. Those instructions implicated her in her own death.

The dimensions of the tragedy kept on widening. The night of the burial (in the end a plot was found in a remote section of the Munkács cemetery) Mamuka suffered a stroke. It proved to be a mild one, though she would always credit her recovery to the expeditious treatment of a doctor who stayed by her bedside all night long, attaching leeches to her neck to slow the blood flow to her brain.

The newspapers buzzed with conjecture, the house was full of shiva callers. The details of the racy life Izidor and Lilli had led, Bumi's business ties to Izidor, all became choice fodder for gossip. Had Lilli, the beautiful socialite, fallen for Bumi, or merely flirted with him, or deliberately led him on? Had she been the victim of Izidor's pandering, the decoy for the fat loans from a complaisant friend that were to save her husband from financial ruin? Had Lilli been scared off by Bumi's intensity, his threats that he would murder her and kill himself if she wouldn't run away with him? Surely she hadn't wanted to throw in her lot with his and leave her husband and her child? After all, if she had been willing to do so, she wouldn't be dead now. The most pernicious story of all was that Lilli's death was God's just punishment of Izidor, who had abandoned another girl with whom he had had a long relationship before taking up with Lilli.

In their agony, Mamuka and Apuka distracted themselves from the circularity of these speculations with other worries: How would they be able to marry off Shoshanna and Vera with such a scandal in the family? And then there was the little boy. What was to be done with him? Magda and her husband, Józsi, came forward and took charge of five-year-old Tibike, whom they adored and hoped to adopt.

There is always less to say about a rapturous union than a miserable one. In later years, Shoshanna rarely spoke of Magda's marriage, far less than Rózsika's or Lilli's, because Magda had made a love match and was blissfully happy with Józsi. Or would have been blissfully happy if only she had been able to bear children. She had undergone a hysterectomy while Józsi was still courting her; in fact he had proposed to her while she lay bedridden in hospital at the time of the operation. (Idle tongues claimed that cystic ovaries weren't Magda Schwartz's problem, but rather an ectopic pregnancy.)

At the end of shiva, Magda and Józsi took Tibike home with them. In short order Józsi had riding britches and boots made for the little boy, taught him to swear like a peasant by the dung heap, and would have turned him into a Magyar version of Little Lord Fauntleroy, had Izidor not reclaimed him a few weeks later.

Józsi was everything that Izidor and Ernő were not: handsome, gallant, generous to a fault. ("Do you want to take yourself to the movies?" he'd ask Shoshanna, opening his horseshoe-shaped wallet. "Help yourself to as much as you want.") His manners were not merely courteous but heartfelt. After every meal at Mamuka's, he would kiss first

Mamuka's hand, then her cheeks, then her hand once more, before swearing there wasn't another woman in the world to match her. (His own mother had died when he was a boy.) Almost certainly Izidor wanted Tibike back not only because a son's place is with his father, but because it would have rankled too much to leave his care in the hands of the favoured son-in-law.

But without a woman to look after the child, Izidor felt at a complete loss. He approached Lilli's parents, sounding them out as to whether Shoshanna would accept his hand in marriage. Mamuka and Apuka – not to mention Shoshanna – were horrified at the suggestion. Soon after, he found another candidate. To the family's great relief, the stepmother was good to Tibike, who continued to visit Beregszász during summer holidays right to the end.

Whenever she spoke of Lilli in later years, Shoshanna became tearful. She always referred to the destiny of this ambivalently loved sister as "Lilli's tragedy." By contrast, what happened to all the others was a series of events. Mamuka, Apuka, Rózsika, Magda, Juditka, Tibike, and the three brothers-in-law succumbed to a common fate: they fell victim to history. But what befell Lilli was tragedy.

IN THE WINTER OF 1968, when my boyfriend became my fiancé, we marked the engagement by breaking an old saucer with a red rose motif in the kitchen. That was our familial bow to Jewish tradition. To further underscore the momentousness of the occasion, Gusti uncorked the bottle of Tokaji Aszú that Nanush had sent us from Budapest through a friend who had come to Montreal during Expo 67. For more than six months the Aszú had lain expectantly in the rose-wood wine rack in the living room, awaiting just the right instant to be opened and consumed.

Aszú is a splendid, amber-hued fortified wine, sweet and heady. Famed product of the town of Tokaj since time immemorial, it was apparently held in high esteem by Louis XIV, who called it "the wine of kings and the king of wines." Shoshanna liked it too and recalled for us the first time she had sipped a glass in Irma Néni's house in Tokaj. We may have been celebrating my engagement, but inevitably her past attached itself to the moment.

Irma Néni was Mamuka's older sister, married to Pinchas Bácsi. They were prosperous merchants in Tokaj, like Mamuka and Apuka in the textile business. Their comfort-able two-storey house on the main thoroughfare — the shop was downstairs, the living quarters above it — was often a refuge or vacation spot for the family in Beregszász. Shoshanna was dispatched there during the summer of '39. Tokaj was the perfect place to recover from a broken heart.

It was a jewel of a town, sheltered beneath the slopes of the Zemplén Mountains, at the confluence of the Bodrog and Tisza Rivers. The balcony off Shoshanna's bedroom was at eye level with the hills where fields of staked vines basked and ripened in the sun, a sight that was balm for Shoshanna's soul when she flung open the windows in the morning. She loved Tokaj, loved its cobbled streets, its faded ochre buildings, its storks nesting on the tiled rooftops.

She had come to forget Imre Schwartz. She had chosen to give him up rather than defy her parents. They had her welfare at heart, and in her own heart she knew them to be right. But it was hard to turn her back on Imre. He was so dashing, so generous, such a man of the world, not like the boys who blushed to the roots of their hair when they asked her to dance and then trod all over her toes during the foxtrot. Nine years her senior, Imre was well established, with a good living from a drugstore, a fine home that she dreamed of reigning over, and vineyards too. At a time when only a handful of men in Beregszász drove automobiles, he owned both a car and a motorbike.

Imre showered Shoshanna with gifts, which in most cases (the thick gold chain, the charm bracelet, the bicycle) her parents made her return. Still, the oranges and the five-kilo boxes of chocolates she was allowed to keep. Vera invariably filched them, however, since Shoshanna took her time in sampling treats. When the craving hit her, Vera was capable of gorging herself until every luscious bonbon in the rose-patterned gold box was gone. To foil her, Imre attached a little lock to the bureau in which Shoshanna kept her treasures. But then Vera, the rascal, managed to outwit them after all by removing the drawer at the top of the dresser and reaching down through the hole for the chocolates. Oh, she was exasperating!

Despite Imre's charms, Mamuka and Apuka disapproved of him. He came from an excellent family, but there were rumours about these Schwartzes – no relation – that perturbed Shoshanna's parents. Imre's older brother cheated on his wife with the leading ladies of the theatre companies that toured the town, and his younger brother had been courting a lovely young girl from a poor family for years without doing right by her. In fact, Imre had a similar past.

Before he began to woo Shoshanna, Imre had been keeping company with Manci Hausman, his sister-in-law's sister. Sometimes when Imre came to take Shoshanna for a walk on the Korzó, his brows were knit in a frown of preoccupation. Finally, when she asked him what the problem was, he replied that Manci had claimed to be pregnant and was threatening to kill herself. Shoshanna was shocked. This was a detail she didn't confide to Mamuka. Her parents were sufficiently opposed to Imre without this bit of unwelcome news. And Shoshanna herself, though only nineteen at the time and studying for her exams at normal school, was now on guard. Her better judgment told her to steer clear of this situation. At the same time, she yearned to believe the best of Imre. Mulling these thoughts, she fretted, lost her appetite, became thin.

One day someone in their circle threw a party in the vineyards, the kind of lavish picnic that Shoshanna loved. On a golden Sunday afternoon, a group of friends hired carriages to take them to the slopes of the hills outside the city. There they left the horses behind to rest and continued on foot, the men carrying the wicker hampers and the girls setting out the food beneath the apple trees: great salted pretzels and *körözöt* with anchovies, buns and rolls, and sardines.

While they were arranging all this, throwing wormy apples out of the way as they laid tablecloths in the grass, Manci pulled Shoshanna aside.

"I don't think you realize, Anna," she began with an earnest expression on her rather plain face, "that Imre has been courting me seriously." Tears sprang into Manci's eyes.

"I don't think you know that Imre has promised marriage to me."

All at once the party was ruined for Shoshanna. She could barely wait for the afternoon to end. When she and Imre were finally alone, walking up Magyar Utca towards her house, Shoshanna refused to take his proffered arm and burst out at him right there in the middle of the street.

"You told me it was all over between you and Manci. You never told me you'd promised marriage to her! I bet you're still seeing her – she wouldn't be saying these things to me if you weren't! And you can't drop Manci anyway: you'll always be connected to her, she's part of your family."

They stood on the street arguing furiously. Imre was beside himself, gesticulating, pleading.

"She's a troublemaker, spreading falsehoods! Let me just get the three of us together. Let's have this out once and for all. Let's see if she'll repeat what she said to you in front of me, that bit about promising marriage."

The next afternoon Manci came to the house. Like a mature hostess, Shoshanna received her in the big parlour. She served espresso while they made empty chitchat, waiting for Imre to appear. She poured him a demitasse too, when he arrived, and studied his long fingers as they stirred sugar cubes into the black brew with a tiny spoon. She was still concentrating on the fine dark hairs on his knuckles when she heard him spit through clenched teeth at Manci, "Tell me, when did I promise you marriage? When was it – Before? During? Just tell me when. After?"

"Imre!" Shoshanna exclaimed, outraged. "You can't speak like that to Manci! Manci is an *urilány*."

And that was enough for Shoshanna. Her parents didn't have to intervene after that. If Imre was capable of humiliating Manci in front of Shoshanna by speaking to her as if she were a common whore – Shoshanna knew what "before, during, or after" meant – if Imre could address an *urilány*, a refined young woman from a good family, a kinswoman no less, so coarsely, he wasn't worthy of either Manci or herself. She was head over heels crazy for Imre and no special admirer of Manci, but Shoshanna told him right then and there, in front of Manci, "I don't want to see you again. I don't want to hear from you again."

Armed with a brand new wardrobe designed by Mamuka, who was all solicitous sympathy now that the dangerous liaison had been averted, she took herself off to Tokaj. There the young swains of the town swarmed around Shoshanna like bumblebees around the sweet grape clusters in the surrounding vineyards. Three or four young men came calling, each requesting permission from Pinchas Bácsi to show her the sights. Pinchas Bácsi was stricter about such matters than Apuka. More Orthodox than her parents, he didn't approve of these freewheeling Jewish boys who went around town bare-headed. Nor did he think much of Shoshanna's form-hugging wardrobe and her excessive popularity. But Irma Néni found ways to prevail upon him. Despite the fact that she was distraught at the idea of new admirers, Shoshanna decked herself out in her long scalloped skirts and close-fitting bodices and allowed herself to be led by the elbow up and down the embankment of the Tisza.

An exceptionally handsome boy won her favour. Sándor Kohn had warm dark eyes, olive skin, and an aristocratic bearing. One night, after he had escorted her home from a party, she woke to the strains of Gypsy music. When she ran to her window, she found a ladder propped against it. On the street the Gypsy was playing "There's Only One Girl in All the World," and Sándor was perched on the first rung of the ladder, a red rose in his hand.

By the time Shoshanna returned home, her heart was on the mend from Imre. Sándor had asked for permission to write to her, and she had said yes. He was called up for military service and posted far away to the opposite end of the country, in Transdanubia, but still the love letters continued to arrive. He spent his first three-day leave in Beregszász. He met Mamuka and Apuka, who liked him, and walked Shoshanna along the Korzó. She was conscious of every head that turned to stare at the handsome couple that they made.

On Sándor's next leave she met him in Budapest. Vera came along to chaperone, and the three of them had a wonderful time at the opera, the theatre, the movies. Sándor had an aunt and a sister living in the capital and made a point of introducing Shoshanna to them. When she returned home after the visit, her parents held it tantamount to an engagement and assumed the marriage would take place when he finished his service. Mamuka ordered the linens for the trousseau and Shoshanna began to embroider pillowcases and duvet covers, tablecloths and napkins, with her monogram.

Then came Lilli's tragedy, endured by Shoshanna with her head held high against the gossip. Imre made every effort to show his solicitude, an attentiveness that she appreciated, though she did not want to lapse back into love with him. Throughout it all Sándor kept writing. There were more trips to Budapest, and further visits to Beregszász. When the telegram arrived, Shoshanna and Sándor had been corresponding for two years. It read, "I am discharged. I'm on my way to you."

She expected him the next day, or the one after that. But he never turned up. She never saw him again. A couple of weeks later she received the explanation. Like so much else that had passed between them, it arrived by letter. He apologized for disappointing her. On the train that was to have brought him to Beregszász, he had met a girl who was the apotheosis of all his dreams. It was as if he had been struck by lightning.

Shoshanna too felt struck, as if by a resounding slap across the face. Even though she had broken with Imre more than two years earlier, she experienced Sándor's desertion as a second blow. First, to have been drawn into a sordid triangle by one man, and now to be jilted almost at the altar by another! It was horrible.

No more, she said. Never again. More precisely, no more long courtships and never again long-distance love. If a man was to win her, he'd do it snappily. She didn't want a prolonged engagement or drawn-out love affair. She wanted decisiveness and certainty. Which is how Márton Weinberger won her. Almost in a trice, and arguably on the rebound. Plus the times favoured quick romances. There was a war on. You wanted to snatch what happiness you could from life before the noose around your neck tightened even more.

The first she heard of Márton was through Magda. Magda and Józsi lived twelve kilometres from Beregszász in the village of Mezővári, where Magda was a teacher. A detachment of Hungarian soldiers were stationed in the village, and a young Jewish squadron commander was billeted in their home. Among Jewish soldiers who had been called up earlier there still remained the odd officer; Márton was in their ranks.

On the piano in Magda's living room was a photo of Shoshanna, Magda's favourite sister, in a silver frame. Shoshanna wasn't especially photogenic, but in this professionally taken portrait she looked lovely. It wasn't what she wore — a simple polka-dot shirtwaist with a white collar — but the limpid light in her eyes and the wide generosity of her smile. The tiny gap between her front teeth lent a touch of charming irregularity.

Márton approached the photo with almost religious awe.

"Who is she?" he murmured.

"That's one of my younger sisters, Anna."

"I would very much like to make the acquaintance of your sister. Could you ask her to come meet me here?"

Magda smiled. "My sister Anna isn't the sort of girl to pay me a visit just because a boy asks to meet her."

But on Friday night, when Magda came for the Sabbath meal at Mamuka's, she mentioned the conversation to Shoshanna.

"What does he look like?" Shoshanna asked.

"Blond, blue-eyed, and short. Quite attractive in uniform."

"'Blond, blue-eyed, and short' isn't for me," said Shoshanna carelessly. Magda knew she was thinking about Sándor and Imre, both dark and tall.

A few weeks passed. The Hungarian soldiers had long since marched away from Mezővári when someone rapped at Magda's door. It was the young squadron commander, this time in civvies.

"May I come in?" Márton asked Magda.

"Of course," she said. He explained that he had been demobbed but not yet called up for labour service. He was working for the Reismans, owners of a large forestry management company in Munkács. In the living room he didn't take a seat but headed straight for the piano. He took the photo in his hands and gazed into Shoshanna's eyes.

"I haven't been able to get your sister out of my mind. What is the likelihood of my meeting her in town, in Beregszász?"

"I've no idea."

"There's someone I know very well in Beregszász, Dr. Ernő Hartman. We served together; I was his commanding officer."

"Ernő was a classmate of mine in *gimnázium!*" Magda exclaimed in surprise. "He lives next door to my parents."

"Well, then this is what I'll do. I'll go into Beregszász. I'll look up Ernő and ask him to introduce me to your family."

On a Wednesday afternoon, Shoshanna was visiting her friend Kató. Sixty years later she was able to remember the two-piece outfit she was wearing that day when Vera came to fetch her. Large squares of blue and red against a background of cream wool. Plaid was the rage that season.

Vera was breathless from excitement and from her exertions in crossing town as fast as she could to get from the store to Kató's.

"Come along, hurry," she urged Shoshanna, who at first feared some calamity to do with Mamuka. Vera explained in short bursts, her face glowing with pleasure on Shoshanna's behalf. Ernő Hartman had been to the store with a young man, who very much wanted to meet Shoshanna.

"He's fallen in love with you from a picture. Isn't that just the most romantic thing you ever heard of?"

Shoshanna allowed that it was romantic. Even if they were meeting at the store with bolts of fabric on the counter, and her mother, father, Vera, the shop assistant, and Ernő Hartman all crowding around in curiosity and speculating about the outcome.

Magda had been right. He was short, blond, blue-eyed, curly-haired, not at all her type. But she liked him right away. Fancy him finding a way to meet her like that, when he knew only one person in town!

The next day her parents received a letter from Márton. Might he continue calling on her? He wanted them to understand that he had only honest and serious intentions regarding their daughter. The letter concluded, "*Sic itur ad astra.*" This is how we reach the stars. Mamuka and Apuka were impressed. So was Shoshanna. Ernő Hartman had told them Márton was resourceful enough to make a living off an iceberg. He hadn't said anything about his ability to quote Latin.

Thereafter, he turned up every evening, whether by motorbike, cab, truck, or bus. Based in Munkács, he toured the surrounding countryside selling off parcels of wooded land for the Reisman family. He was tough and capable. When Shoshanna met his parents – simple, good people, real rural folk from Mada – his father boasted that Márton was so hardy that even a bout of typhus hadn't stopped him from mounting a tractor and going out plowing. (Mamuka blanched when she heard this. Who would permit a sick boy to get out of bed, let alone climb up on a tractor?)

This exchange took place at Purim, at the engagement party in February '42. They had known each other about three months by then. There was no need of a formal proposal. In effect it had been made in that letter to Mamuka and Apuka when he had professed his "serious and honourable intentions." There was a war on and no time to waste. They set the date for an early June wedding.

From the day she first met him in the fall, until the moment beneath the *chuppah* when he slipped the ring on the index finger of her right hand, there were only two instances when Shoshanna felt any hesitation about Márton. Once when they were out walking, he told her that Jenő Reisman, one of his bosses, had asked him how much dowry Shoshanna would be bringing him. She could have responded that this was no business of his employers, but she knew that they treated him as if he were family and were protective of his interests. She could also have responded with the truth, which was that her father still owned two vineyards. One was destined to be her dowry, the other Vera's.

They were strolling arm in arm through the shaded courtyard of the bank building. She stopped dead and pulled her arm away.

"So what did you tell Jenő?"

"I told him I didn't know."

"I'm letting you know right now that there's no dowry. There's only me. If that suits you, fine. But if you don't like it, you're free."

She was testing him. He never mentioned it again.

The other incident happened precisely a week before the wedding. There was something in the way he kissed her that day that was half-hearted, lukewarm. "What's wrong?" she asked. "What's happened?"

Bluntly he told her he had been with a prostitute that afternoon.

"But why?"

"It's been a long while," he replied tersely. "Ever since I first saw your photo."

"Well, you could have waited another week," she said, making light of her disappointment, yet still managing, she thought, to convey disapproval.

She didn't have a tantrum, didn't call off the wedding, didn't tell Mamuka.

She didn't ask why he couldn't wait, because she didn't want to make a fuss. And because the matter really wasn't one fit for discussion between an *urilány* and her fiancé. But if she had asked, if they had had it out there and then, he might have explained that the prostitute was a safety valve, that he didn't want to overwhelm her with his gross pent-up drives, that he hoped to awaken her slowly on their wedding night. And if they had had this excruciatingly embarrassing conversation, she might never have fallen in love with Gusti.

Shoshanna stayed faithful to Márton when he dropped off the radar screen of her life a few months later, even though she was beset by candidates galore with whom to be unfaithful. She remained faithful when he disappeared into the vast Russian front, and when Imre immediately materialized at her elbow. She remained faithful even though she was declared a war widow a year later when Márton was reported missing and presumed dead. She held on to the hope that he was still alive when desperate men importuned her in the cattle car shipping them all to oblivion, begging her to give herself to them there, right there, while parched children wailed for water, while Adolf Bácsi, Ernő's father, raved like a madman for his long-dead mother. Shoshanna waved off these frantic, doomed suitors with the cry, "Get a grip on yourselves! I'm a *married* woman."

But when she met up with Gusti Weinberger in the village where Márton was born and grew up, she questioned her steadfast faith. By then she was an orphan, a lone poppy buffeted by many winds. When an older man, a balding man of substance and solidity promised to shelter her, she had only a shadowy memory of the young, handsome, resource-ful husband. What lingered was the pleasure of that husband's lovemaking – no one would ever make love to her the way Márton did, with tenderness, ardour, control, and a quite astonishing staying power – and a pang of distrust. That ardent, exuberant yet composed young man who had loved her so deeply had visited a prostitute a week before he married her. If he couldn't wait seven nights before he was joined to her forever in the spring of 1942, would such a man remain faithful to her for eternity, as she was convinced Gusti Weinberger would?

SHOSHANNA AND MÁRTON'S WEDDING was held at home, the simplest of affairs because of the war, but still a lovely wedding. Mamuka had a gorgeous dress made for her, a froth of organdy and lace, and the *chuppah* – decked with the orange blossoms and snowballs that were blooming in the garden – was set up between the plum and quince trees.

Jellied carp in aspic was the first course. Golden soup came next, followed by chicken poached in the soup. These were considered plain fare, but there was nothing plain about the sweet table of Mamuka's specialties: apple, cherry, cabbage, and walnut strudels, Gerbeaud squares, *fládni* rolled up with nuts and poppy seeds and smothered in chocolate glaze, Dobos torte, and rum torte. Yes, it was wartime, but "my Anna" – Mamuka always pronounced her children's names lovingly prefixed with either "my" or "our" – was getting married, and the best possible was done for the occasion.

They had made reservations at a tony resort for the honeymoon, but Márton abruptly changed his mind and declared that he didn't want to waste time travelling. He didn't say a word to Shoshanna before the wedding, didn't want to cloud her happiness, but he had received his call-up papers. He knew that he would be leaving on June 10. They would have one week of married life together.

After the reception they took a cab to the elegant and brand new Donát Hotel and spent their honeymoon there. During their week together they charted each other's bodies and introduced each other to new tastes. Márton liked beer with his meals and taught her to enjoy a Pilsner. Shoshanna had grown up on red wine and kept tempting him with her glass until he surrendered and ordered some for himself. On the second day of the honeymoon she woke up homesick for Mamuka's *turos béles*. So they crossed the street to Rózsika's place, and Rózsika walked over to the store and told Vera, and Vera went home and told Mamuka. And Mamuka, who had been about to leave for the store, stayed home and baked a batch of her cheese Danish for delivery to the hotel.

At the end of their week, she accompanied him to the station. Unable to take his eyes off the speck on the platform that she became, he hung out of the train window and waved and waved. Shoshanna stayed rooted to the spot long after the coach had disappeared, then trudged the two kilometres to Rózsika's, tears streaming down her face. She climbed the stairs, walked straight into Rózsika's arms, and cried uncontrollably.

She saw Márton a handful of times after that. He had been called up to Ungvár, which wasn't that far away. An uncle lived there and she was able to spend a few days at his house. On the Saturday afternoon of her stay, her uncle and aunt offered to let Márton visit and tactfully left them alone. Another time Márton bribed the janitor of the Hebrew *gimnázium* where he was billeted to lend him his bedroom for the night. The janitor fetched Shoshanna from her uncle's and smuggled her into his apartment through the back entrance.

She was supposed to come one more time to see him there but he sent word for her not to. She was beside herself with disappointment and worry. Later a buddy explained. In keeping with new rules affecting military service for Jews, Márton had been stripped of his officer's rank. Like all common labour servicemen, he had been ordered to have his head shaved. He didn't want her to see him bald. To steel himself for the ordeal, Márton had sat clutching her photo while his batman sheared off his hair in neat stripes.

Which of her photos was he clinging to, I wonder? There are no photographs left of Shoshanna from this period of her life. Not the photo on Magda's piano with which Márton originally fell in love, not their engagement picture in which she wore a white angora sweater set, not the wedding portrait. Shoshanna and Márton posed for several pictures together, but none have survived. Were it not for Shoshanna's stories, you would never know that the marriage had taken place.

WHEN I DEVELOPED A CRUSH and began going out with the Boyfriend in the spring of 1963, my family behaved predictably. Gusti and Shoshanna were bemused and troubled by my choice of a Gentile boy, one who was so painfully taciturn as to defeat all their attempts to draw him out. Judy adopted him enthusiastically as a species of older brother, cadging piggyback rides and enlisting his help with school projects. But Vera's response was a complete surprise. Despite the fact that after shaking hands awkwardly, he barely dared return her gaze and proceeded to stare at his scuffed shoes throughout the brief exchange between them, my aunt declared herself captivated.

"Ilushkám," she said, drawing me aside and beaming, "your friend is so *charmant. Totalement adorable.* He so remind me of someone I know a long time ago. I tell you more about this on another *occasion.*"

To objective eyes, the Boyfriend must have presented an eccentric sight. He was tall and had a kind of loping gait, head thrust forward, shoulders already slightly stooped at sixteen. He had an athlete's build, wide in the shoulders, slim-hipped, long-legged. His stovepipe dungarees were chronically abbreviated, revealing a good couple of inches of white tennis socks springing from his loafers.

But I wasn't drawn to him because of his athletic prowess, though he excelled at tennis, played on the football team, and skated like an angel. What stirred me was his academic performance. The Boyfriend had won the Birks Medal in Grade Ten for all-round scholastic excellence, and there was nothing I admired more in a boy than good marks. In this I was slavishly following Shoshanna's indoctrination. The moment I entered co-ed classes in Grade Ten, she quizzed me regularly on the identity of the smartest boy in the class. Being smart was the key to success in the world. Hence the question before every date, "What was his average last term?"

Still, the Boyfriend had a mystique for me independent of Shoshanna's ambitions. The Boyfriend was deep, he was idealistic, he had concerns about issues that I'd never heard anyone raise before. Not the Holocaust, not Israel, not the Cold War – the serious topics that were hotly debated in my home. The Boyfriend wrote essays that our English teacher read aloud in class, praising their originality of thought and cogent reasoning, essays about environmental protection, about the cruelty and selfishness of our predatory species. I was drawn in by his compelling description of small woodland creatures hunted down for sport or trapped for exploitation, of powerful chemical by-products destroying pristine waters. His sensitivity impressed me at least as much as the accomplishments measured by Shoshanna's yardstick.

The fact that the Boyfriend wasn't Jewish was ignored by my parents at first because they held him to be a temporary madness on my part, a high school flame that would burn out once I started university. When I entered McGill University in the fall of 1963, aged fifteen — a consequence of skipping grades in elementary school four years earlier — Shoshanna urged me to seize the opportunity to date Jewish boys. It hadn't occurred either to her or to Gusti that my anomalous upbringing in Montreal's East End would provide few common bonds with Jewish boys or girls reared in one of the most conservative and traditional Jewish communities in North America. When I encountered them, or rather when I viewed them from a slight distance — I was leery of face-to-face meetings — they seemed a race apart, the girls with their precise Vidal Sassoon haircuts and perfectly accessorized outfits (for the most part purchased wholesale, as I learned later), the boys incredibly brash and articulate. To my eyes they were all sophisticated, all apparently fortified by wealth, and all much better grounded intellectually than my crowd of ill-at-ease and slightly down-at-the-heels friends from Rosemount High.

The Boyfriend and I clung to each other in the overwhelming, alien environment of McGill. Our insecurities meshed beautifully. Neither Shoshanna nor Gusti would have dreamed that what I had heard at home drove me into the safe haven of his sinewy arms. All those complicated romances of Rózsika's, Lilli's, and Shoshanna's — all that heartbreak, who needed that? Who could *cope* with that? I didn't want the kind of trouble lots of men in my life would bring. Someone steady to love me forever was what I wanted. And I had found him. Wasn't I lucky to have found him so young?

Vera clearly thought that I was lucky and continued to defend us. And I found much to identify with in Vera at this stage. Vera lacked her sisters' reputation for beauty, but in the old pictures she has a healthy, well-scrubbed prettiness that is very appealing. She wasn't renowned for cleverness, yet she loved poetry and could recite Petőfi and Arany and Vörösmarty at will, better even than Iszku, who was the brainiest child in the family. Yet Vera had been overlooked and not cherished enough in a family that set great store by appearance. And although both my parents loved me almost literally to distraction and valued me for my purported intelligence, it never occurred to either of them to compliment me on my appearance.

Vera thought me pretty, or at least she said she did. At first the outfits she found for me in the store were what Shoshanna called *bovli*, items from the sale rack that no one wanted. But when business picked up and when I became less gawky and a more promising mannequin on which to hang the best merchandise, both she and Pierre showered me with fetching outfits in which I began to feel prettier. But never beautiful the way I imagined Shoshanna to have been. Never the type to be a femme fatale.

Vera hadn't been a femme fatale either, though she had found her own way to gratification. That was what she wanted to tell me about the Boyfriend. He reminded her of the first boy she ever loved. His name was Jancsi, and he wasn't Jewish either. It did Vera's heart good to see us together, the Boyfriend and me, she said. It recalled a very happy time in her life. She so wanted it to work out for me.

"I tell for you something, Ilushka, if you marry him, I shall be *ravie*. It will be like if I marry Jancsi."

She hadn't married Jancsi, so it had not worked out for her, though I didn't know how their romance had ended. Under the circumstances, it felt almost a blessing to have the details withheld and I didn't ask any questions. When Shoshanna got wind that Vera was encouraging my attachment to the Boyfriend, she quickly disabused me of any fantasies I might have had about Vera and her lost beau.

"He was a low-life, a nothing, a common little clerk at City Hall. Rózsika asked him to stop bothering Vera and he mocked Rózsika. He said he wasn't bothering Vera. He said Vera was running after him! And that the more Mamuka and Apuka forbade it, the wilder Vera would be, the more she'd want him! And he was right, because Vera wouldn't give him up. She sneaked around behind our parents' backs and caused them endless suffering. And just around the time of Lilli's tragedy too."

Perhaps because of this lesson from the past, Shoshanna and Gusti didn't forbid me to see the Boyfriend. Our home was always open to him, and over time they grew fond of him. But when it became apparent that he wasn't fading from the picture, Shoshanna stopped indulging me and addressed the central issue head on.

"You know what'll happen, don't you? He'll end up calling you a dirty Jew."

"Oh, Mummy, for God's sake! Please."

"Maybe he won't mean to, but when people are married, they sometimes have vicious fights. Vicious! And things come out of your mouth that horrify you. Look at Duved and Caroline."

"What about Uncle Dave and Auntie Caroline? They get along really well."

"They get along when they get along. All right, all right, so they get along. I will admit they had an agreement when they got married, an agreement that if our parents survived the war, Caroline would convert. Become Jewish."

But Mamuka and Apuka hadn't survived. And when we arrived in England, Uncle Dave was still talking, more than ten years after the event, about the devastating impact on Caroline when she found out what had happened to his family. How distraught she had been, how she had offered to convert anyway. But Dave said a deal was a deal. It wasn't for his sake that he had wanted his English bride to convert, but for his beloved parents'.

"Oh, sure, they dote on each other, Duved and Caroline. But I remember when we were in England and I surprised them once in the middle of an argument. Duved's face was red, I've never seen him so agitated. And later that night I wormed it out of him. He'd gotten mad at her for going on a shopping spree. So she'd called him a miserly Jew."

"But you're always saying Uncle Dave's tight with money!"

"That's different. He's tight because he's a miser, not because he's a Jew."

It felt as if we'd never get out from beneath the weight of these persecutions, these dark stories of what had happened in our family, or in someone else's family. Why, I asked myself, didn't it occur to anybody that a person like the

Boyfriend could break new ground, strike out in a fresh direction, do something original, put all that anti-Semitism to rest?

But the stories weren't designed simply to caution me. Passing them on was a kind of exorcism. Repeating them, reciting them, invoking them for an audience was Shoshanna's way of defusing their ghastly hold on her.

nine

HISTORY

In 1997, when my older daughter graduated with a degree in education, our family felt a sense of completion, a full turn of the wheel. My mother had been a much loved kindergarten teacher for many years in Ville d'Anjou. Jessica bears a striking resemblance to my mother, and like her she took a great interest in young children from an early age. Her choice of the family profession – Magda and Duved, as well as Shoshanna, had been teachers – seemed almost foreordained, or *beshert*, as we say in Hebrew.

When the family gathered to fete Jessica, it was also *beshert* that Shoshanna should revisit the story of her own graduation from teachers' college. I had heard this story – mostly with one ear – many times. But Jessica and her younger sister, Rebecca, who would likewise follow in her grandmother's and sister's footsteps, had not. I could barely contain my impatience and, let it be confessed, my rage that once again what ought to have been an occasion of untarnished joy was ambushed by Shoshanna's past. The girls listened with rapt attention.

My mother, physically frail in her early eighties but still handsome, still wilful, was confident as ever that the floor belonged to her and that even a remote situational hook posed an opportunity – as my sister, Judy, likes to say – "to lead all roads back to Rome." At the head of the table, blue eyes faded to grey but still sparkling, she launched into full-blown storytelling mode.

"When I graduated from teachers' college, it was a very chaotic world, a war-clouded world. I had matriculated from *gimnázium* in '38 and begun my studies to be a teacher. When the annual exams were given in May 1939, I was too young to take them: you had to be twenty to be a teacher, and my birthday wasn't until the end of August. In ordinary times I would have waited until the following May. Instead I took the supplemental exams in September 1939, which were usually taken only by those who had failed the May sessions."

Shoshanna had never actually attended teachers' college but had studied at home, rounding out her reading of the compulsory texts in teaching methods with private lessons in perspective drawing, violin, and music composition – all requisite subjects for elementary school teaching. In general, home study was frowned upon and the examiners in Pozsony (also called Bratislava), the Slovakian capital where the college was located, failed virtually everyone who took the private route.

Magda had attended normal school in Pozsony a few years earlier and knew the city well. She accompanied Shoshanna for moral support. They stayed at the pension where Magda had lived and took their meals at a familiar vegetarian café. Then, the day before Shoshanna was due to start the examination process, Magda was summoned home to Vári. Józsi had been called up in a general mobilization; she had to return to say goodbye.

"So I stayed on alone," Shoshanna continued, pausing dramatically for effect. "There was a blackout every night, and the sirens were going at full blast the whole time. These were the circumstances in which I took my examinations." Shoshanna paused again, savouring the memory.

"I can see myself, I was *so* beautiful. Mamuka had outfitted me lavishly for the occasion – a royal blue dress made out of muslin. Its skirt must have had a hundred tiny pleats in it. I wore it with new black patent-leather high heels.

"I had never been in a classroom, and they gave me a Grade Five arithmetic class to teach as part of the test. The examination committee sat on a raised podium at the front of the room, maybe five professors in all. I was terrified, because I had a real complex about math.

"I was told to quiz the children on the nine-times table. Mental arithmetic. I paced up and down the aisles, and you know, I had to keep discipline as well. I was pointing at the children, calling on them, 'You, and you, now you.' I didn't even know their names! And somehow all my nervousness melted. I felt as if I were on the stage on Purim night or on Hanukkah, when I had starred in all those theatricals. The whole thing went down beautifully. And I passed with flying colours, despite the blackouts and the constant sirens."

Hungary was readying itself for war and beginning to cooperate militarily with Germany and German-dominated neighbours such as Slovakia. Imre Schwartz, then riding the crest of his romance with Shoshanna, was also called up. He was to join a regiment in Kassa, a Slovakian town partway between Beregszász and Pozsony.

Imre offered to meet Shoshanna in Kassa, escort her home from there, then return to his base. His lavish attentions were as generous as ever: the day after Shoshanna's arrival in Pozsony, a five-kilo box of chocolate-covered coffee beans arrived by special delivery. But Shoshanna was in such a state of nerves, she couldn't touch them.

Another young man complicated her life while in Pozsony; this too was inevitable, it seems. A Gentile classmate at the *gimnázium*, Béla Sárady came from a distinguished but impoverished family. He was taking his exams following the same private method as Shoshanna. She particularly admired the way he played the violin, not just competently, as she did, but with soulfulness and passion.

"And this boy fell for me completely. *Completely.* In the darkened city, with the sirens blaring, we went dancing. I wouldn't have wanted this boy if he had been the last boy in the universe. But I felt a kinship with him. We lived on the same street back home; we had travelled to Pozsony for the same purpose; he was alone like me, and it was wartime. We were somehow bound together."

After the three-day examination, Shoshanna prepared to return to Beregszász. Imre's orders had been changed and he couldn't come. Béla would be her male escort, for protection. But, for some reason, he had run out of money for the journey. The morning of their departure he had to cross town to collect some funds that had been wired to him.

Shoshanna couldn't risk missing her train; she already had her ticket.

She hired a horse-drawn cab to the railway station. The coachman badgered her the entire way: in addition to her suitcase, she had a violin and a hat box. He kept jacking up the price, threatening to throw her into the street with all her luggage.

"I was going out of my mind. The train was in the station when I got there, and it was already packed. People were hanging from the coach steps. I was in despair. Then someone, a soldier, opened a window and pulled me up from the platform into the coach. He even got someone to hand in my parcels.

"Finally I saw Béla. I hung out the window to attract his attention, and somehow he too got on. We travelled on that train for three whole days. In the company of Slovak soldiers. The Slovaks are the ugliest anti-Semites in the world – I swear they're even worse than Poles or Magyars. And the Slovak soldiers wanted to throw Béla off because they decided he was a Jew. He was freckled and red-haired, for heaven's sake!

"I told them, 'He isn't Jewish, he's Catholic!' Which he was. Think of the irony: here I was vouching for Béla, in the meantime *I* was the one who was Jewish! But they didn't suspect I was Jewish, because I was fair at that time and had blue eyes.

"To distract them from Béla, I fed them the chocolates I'd received from Imre. They ate their fill – there were five kilos! – and Béla stayed on the train. But then they told us to play the violin. They *made* us play. For three whole days!

Tchaikovsky and Brahms and bits of Mendelssohn, and folk songs, and then all the same repertoire all over again.

"We arrived in Beregszász on the third day. It was *erev* Rosh Hashanah. And who do you think was at the station? Dr. Ernő Hartman, our next-door neighbour, the one who would bring me together with Márton two years later. He said he was waiting to see who would make it home for the holiday. He drove me to our house by carriage.

"I found Mamuka having palpitations on the couch. She looked something terrible. They didn't believe I would survive the journey. That was *my* graduation."

As Shoshanna stopped for breath, an oppressed silence fell upon the table, the girls reflecting on what they had heard and unsure whether more would follow.

"What happened to Imre?" Jessica asked.

"After I married Márton, he came home on leave. We were all in the ghetto by then. He was on the outside and we were inside, in the brickworks. He brought us *krémes béles* – mille feuilles – from the patisserie because he knew they were my favourites. He understood there would never be anything between us, that I was married to Márton, but he still loved me."

"No, I meant what *happened* to him?" Jessica persisted. "Did he . . ."

"Oh, yes, he died."

"And Magda's Józsi?"

"Magda's Józsi too. It was said that he died a hero's death. His soldiers were ill with typhus and he was carrying one of them on his back, and Józsi caught the typhus from him and he died. All my brothers-in-law died. Józsi, Ernő, Izidor . . ."

"Enough, Ma! Enough!" My knuckles were white, pressed hard against the blond wood of the dining room table. I pushed my chair back and jumped up. "Is it not possible, just once, to have a family celebration without the Holocaust putting in an appearance? Is that too much to ask?"

My girls stared at me, wide-eyed with shock. Such unseemly cruelty from their mother towards her mother, her elderly mother! And over the most hallowed subject, the event that is this family's most sacred touchstone.

But Shoshanna took my outburst in stride, barely acknowledging it. She was the same with my father. Gusti rarely lost his temper with her, but when he did, she would smirk in triumph, as if to say, "I did it. I got you to pay attention to me."

It gnaws at me that I behave badly on these occasions, when my daughters, by contrast, are able to listen with appropriate respect to the stories that pour out of their grandmother. When the girls were children, she censored herself in a way she didn't when I was a child. I resent that now, resent that she didn't hold back for the sake of my innocence and unclouded youth.

I chafe under the burden of the stories I've been listening to all my life with a petulance that I know ill befits a mature adult. As if, were she able to keep quiet, it would all go away somehow. The truth is that I have to recognize that the bony outline of Shoshanna's stories is my bedrock. It is what I am built on. Willing it to disappear would be to risk disappearing myself.

In the end, is what Shoshanna has asked of me so terrible? She has made me into her audience, subjected me to a chain

of words linked one to another. What I heard were anec-
dotes, attenuated memories – many I would rather have shut
out – but still only stories.

Yet the stories weren't stories when she lived them. They
were real life, her life, demanding to be remembered.

MY MOTHER WAS BORN Anna Schwartz on August 30, 1919,
in a period of confusion and turmoil following the First
World War. Beregszász was about to become Berehovo, a
Hungarian city turned Czechoslovakian.

Less than a year earlier, as Austria-Hungary prepared to
serve as a whipping boy after the Allies' victory, losing two-
thirds of its pre-war territory and two million people in the
process, a short-lived Bolshevik revolt broke out in Hungary.
It was fuelled by the hope that a last-ditch alliance with
newly Soviet Russia might salvage the territorial integrity of
the Hungarian nation.

It was at this time that Mamuka – Ilona Pollák Schwartz –
became pregnant with her sixth child, and Apuka – Sámuel
Schwartz – was taken hostage by the local dictatorship of the
proletariat, accused of being a capitalist exploiter of the one
assistant he employed in the family textile shop. Carrying food
to him in a covered dish she held close to her bosom, Mamuka
was jostled, spat upon, and cursed by the Madame Defarges of
the day who clustered on the steps of the courthouse.

This pathetic and ignominious incident gave birth to a
family story that was cherished across the generations.
Apuka appreciatively slurped the soup Mamuka had brought
and doubtless hoped for a little cheer and encouragement
along with it. But instead Mamuka burst into loud sobs. She

didn't wail about the women outside who had reviled her, didn't complain about the five children acting up at home or the one in the belly who made her throw up every morning. She didn't even ask when he'd regain his freedom.

"Shamukám, whatever will we do?" Mamuka cried. "The sauerkraut refuses to ferment!"

What they did was run away for a while. Somehow Apuka escaped his jailers, and somehow the seven of them – with Shoshanna safest of all inside Mamuka – found refuge with Irma Néni, Mamuka's older sister, and her husband, Pinchas Bácsi, the selfsame couple who would welcome Shoshanna into their home two decades later.

They spent a couple of months in Tokaj until the situation in Beregszász stabilized. Of course, they didn't know if it would stabilize, didn't know how they'd return. They were refugees, charity cases really. But once she was reunited with Apuka, Mamuka regained her equilibrium and her optimism.

They were always content when they were together. Irma Néni called them the singing fools; they sang and sang like a pair of larks. The world might be coming to an end – a world had come to an end, in fact – but what was the use in worrying? They sang Lehár, they hummed Strauss, they warbled tuneful Jewish songs that they taught the children with meaningless patter instead of words. Such haunting melodies, such tugging at the heartstrings. Forty years later, beneath a Christmas tree in a suburban London house, Uncle Dave led us in endless refrains of one of these atavistic tunes – me and Judy, my three English cousins, Auntie Caroline, Shoshanna, and Gusti. Most of us were blissfully unaware that we were humming a Hebrew liturgical song that had been swirling about the globe for hundreds, perhaps thousands of years.

My mother had a very happy childhood, and always said that her ability to go on with life after the war was grounded in the sense of security she was given in a home where the parents were devoted to each other and to their children. Part of this reassuring stability grew out of an unquestioned respect for elders. From the time Shoshanna and Vera were old enough to go about on their own, they were expected to pay homage to their sole surviving grandparent, Apuka's father, Nagyapa. A tall, silver-bearded gentleman of venerable appearance, Nagyapa used to stand in the doorway of his wholesale grain emporium, leaning on his cane, as she and Vera passed by on their way to school.

"*Kezét csókolom, Nagyapa*," they greeted him. I kiss your hand, Nagyapa. Then each of them planted a kiss on the back of his gnarled hand.

"*Szervusz, Surele, szervusz, D'voyrele.*" Nagyapa smiled as he returned the compliment with a mighty pinch to their cheeks. Nagyapa had over forty grandchildren, but he kept track of them all by their Jewish names. No one else called Shoshanna Surele, or Vera D'voyrele. It was Nagyapa's way of obliquely reminding them where they had come from: Polish Jewish stock that had settled Subcarpathia, either a very long time ago or just recently, depending on whether you thought two centuries was an age or a blink of the eye of eternity.

The Hungarian roots of the town in which my mother was born are ancient, going back to the eleventh century, when, according to legend, a royal prince of the House of

Árpád established a settlement on the banks of the Vérke River, where it still stands. Bearing the name of Beregovo, it belongs to Ukraine now but is still the only town in the region that has a Hungarian-speaking majority.

There was a Jewish presence in the area for hundreds of years, but Jews weren't officially permitted to settle until the late eighteenth century, when they were invited to ply their trades on the estates of the Schönborn counts. By 1795, there was an organized community with a rabbi and a burial society.

The foothills of the Carpathians where Beregszász nestles were known from time immemorial for a refined cultivation of the grape, but otherwise the area was a backwater of the Austro-Hungarian Empire, characterized by subsistence agriculture and an absentee landlord system centred on vineyards and lush forests. All this changed dramatically after the birth in 1918 of Czechoslovakia, which, for only twenty years between the wars, was a dynamic experiment in democracy, industrialization, and relatively harmonious multiculturalism. Beregszász was a successful case in point, a predominantly Hungarian-speaking town with a flourishing Hungarian-speaking Jewish community that coexisted with Ruthenian (Ukrainian-speaking) and Czech minorities. In 1927, of a total population of eighteen thousand, there were twelve hundred Jewish families, comprising five thousand people.

The vast majority of the commercial establishments in the main square – called by the Hungarians the Great Bazaar, and by the Czechs Masaryk Square – belonged to Jewish merchants. Four of the town's six banks had Jewish directors, the town's chief engineer was a Jew, and Jews participated actively in municipal politics and a varied cultural life. A medley of religious institutions served the community: four "regular" synagogues, five adjunct prayer houses, a Jewish elementary school, and two Jewish seminaries, a Talmud Torah with 160 students and a yeshiva with 100. Although there was no Jewish hospital, kosher meals were provided for Jewish patients in the town's general hospital. A women's auxiliary that sponsored the theatricals in which Shoshanna would star a few years later was particularly active. Sobering proof of the exponential growth of the community was a call that year for the enlargement of the cemetery.

For Shoshanna it was home, and very proud she was of its neat and orderly streets, its public school system (a large Hungarian elementary school, a *polgári* or vocational school, and a *gimnázium*; and a Ukrainian elementary school and *gimnázium*), the imposing public buildings (a city hall, a courthouse, the post office, the big railway station), the many churches serving a variety of faiths (Catholic, Protestant, Ruthenian Uniate), the public beach on the outskirts of town, and the wonderful vineyards up the slopes of the nearby hills.

Curiously, for one born into freedom, she didn't take it for granted. Every fall, when it was time to register at school, she was asked to state her nationality and her religion. For nationality, she described herself as a Jew; for religion, she said she was Hebrew. Whenever she did so, she felt her chest swell with the knowledge of her rights. Some of her cousins proclaimed themselves Hungarian or Czech, while professing to be Hebrew in religion. In a free country you could be whatever you wanted.

The Jewish minority tended to stick together, although they didn't necessarily love one another unreservedly. In Mamuka and Apuka's store, for instance, located in Masaryk Square on the ground floor of an elegant block of flats between the Rothman Patika, the largest pharmacy in town, and an exclusive milliner's, Jewish customers were far from the favourites.

"Stay put," Apuka would caution Mamuka under his breath when a Jewish matron, her nose in the air, sailed in. "Let the assistant serve her." They knew their customers, and the Jewish women were demanding browsers and comparison shoppers. They'd point to this or that bolt of fabric, finger it dismissively, and waste your time with pointless questions before taking their business elsewhere. Mamuka much preferred to do business with Gentile clientele. Her Christian customers came from two wildly divergent groups: the genteel Hungarian bourgeoisie and the street-tough Ruthenian peasants who came into town on Wednesday, the big market day.

Mamuka was on such good terms with her Hungarian customers that they were in the habit of dropping by the store, like Apuka's many relatives, just for chit-chat. A few comfortable chairs faced the long counter behind which the store's wares were displayed, and visitors would collapse into them, settling down for a good gossip. Apuka often stalked out on these occasions, in a snit over having to share Mamuka with a talkative customer and muttering about a casino being run under his nose. By casino, he didn't mean a gambling joint exactly, although there was an element of chance about what would go on in his absence.

Mamuka took a genuine interest in the affairs of the bankers' and teachers' wives, not to mention the priest's housekeeper, who routinely kept her posted on the marriages of children and the births of grandchildren, the abatement of a set of symptoms and the onset of new ones. While mulling over these events, the ladies might spot a bolt of fabric of a particular hue and ask to see it. Shanyi, the assistant, pulled it off the shelf and placed it on the counter. Then Mamuka would stand and drape the material over her shoulders, cinching the abundant folds at the waist with her hands. The effect was far more fetching than that produced by the stilted mannequins in the window. And if a client, seduced by some lustrous silk or taffeta, turned wistful and sighed over the cost, Mamuka would pat her arm, gaze soulfully into her eyes, and say, "You'll pay for it when you can."

Apuka would pull on his goatee nervously or hold his head when he heard this. Returned from the library across the street, he dumped a fresh pile of books onto the polished wood of the counter for them both to read. (They were avid fans of Jókai, Mikszáth, Gárdonyi, Zrinyi, Zilahy – the entire Hungarian canon.)

"But Ilonkám *édes*, don't you understand, they may *never* be able to pay?" Fortunately, most did.

The other source of profits for the store was the peasants from the neighbouring villages and hillside farms who visited on market day. A couple of blocks over from the Great Bazaar stood a more modest plaza, appropriately named the Small Bazaar. Surrounded on four sides by lesser shops and seedier apartment blocks, the Small Bazaar burst into life on Wednesdays. Farmers set up booths overflowing with fresh

vegetables, the finest heads of cauliflower, the biggest cab-
bages, fat brown eggs in baskets, vegetable marrows that
didn't grow anywhere else in the world. Others brought in
their geese and hens and chickens and ducks, thereby giving
the Small Bazaar its other moniker, the Hen Market.

On Wednesdays the town bustled and throbbed with
activity, assuming an almost midway-like atmosphere.
Typical was the regular appearance of a trained bear, a big,
brown, sad-looking creature, its head bent low as it loped
through the streets, led on a rusting chain by its owner. But
how that bear would brighten when a crowd of people
circled it in front of the Hungária Hotel. How it grinned
and leered as it dribbled a soccer ball, how it stomped a great
lumbering *csárdás* to the tune coaxed out of a mouth organ.

Wednesdays required the presence of Mamuka or Apuka,
preferably both, in the store all day long. There was no question of "casinoing," with the steady traffic of Ruthenian
peasants. For one thing, there was a language barrier, each
barely breaking the tongue of the other. For another, these
customers weren't above running off with the merchandise.
They tended to arrive en masse, so that it was impossible to
serve them all at once. Summer or winter, the men wore capa-
cious sheepskin coats called *subák*: leather on the inside,
sheepswool on the outside. In this get-up they all looked alike,
all sporting black hats and ferocious handlebar moustaches. It
wasn't uncommon for whole bolts of cloth to disappear in an
afternoon, and there were always one or two children from
the family on guard duty, eyes peeled to the action.

The relative prosperity of the peasants in the Subcarpathian
hinterlands was another source of pride to young Shoshanna.

As a teenager she sometimes accompanied Apuka on buying trips to Budapest. When the train rolled through the Hungarian countryside, barefoot children dressed in tatters were too common a sight, playing in front of hovels she thought unfit for human habitation. Yes, there was poverty in Czechoslovakia, she informed Apuka self-importantly, but not this kind of desperation. Czechoslovakia was the country of the future, where everyone had not only equal rights but a stake in the overall prosperity.

Apuka smiled sadly at her enthusiastic chatter. Unlike her, he had grown up Hungarian, and he and Mamuka harboured fond sentiments for the monarchy and for Franz Josef, the dead emperor. On Friday nights, after the family had sung its fill of Jewish songs and had come full circle with its repertoire of operettas and folk songs, he and Mamuka frequently became misty-eyed as they wound up with a rendition of "You Are So Beautiful, You Are So Lovely, O Country of the Magyars." Yes, it was a fine thing to live as a tolerated minority in this new successor state, but Apuka understood how the Hungarian citizens of Berehovo, formerly Beregszász, might very well resent the fact that though all the teachers in the *gimnázium* were Hungarian, the principal was Czech. Or that all the military officers in the town were Czech, as if soldiers of Hungarian origin couldn't be trusted with authority. Or that the taxes in this new country were so inordinately high that to pay them, Apuka said, was to be skinned alive. The Treaty of Trianon ending the Great War had been too punitive; there were those who lived for the day it would be revoked.

REANNEXATION BY HUNGARY came in 1938, and with it the tightening of an invisible noose around the necks of the Jews of Beregszász. A series of discriminatory laws restricted their rights to higher education, deprived many of their livelihood, and impinged on their day-to-day lives in ways both vital and petty. It became too dangerous for Apuka to travel to Budapest to buy merchandise for the shop. Hooligans were in the habit of pulling Jews off trains and ripping out their beards.

Jewish stores were closed down and replaced by Gentile, Hungarian-owned businesses. Sámuel Schwartz Textiles was among the very last to be shut. One of Mamuka's best customers in the "casino" days was the wife of the new Hungarian mayor of the city, a woman who hadn't forgotten the generous offers of credit in earlier times. But Mari Néni, the family's faithful housekeeper, was let go, much against her will. Gentiles were now forbidden to work as domestics in Jewish homes. Magda's teaching contract wasn't renewed and she was left without a livelihood. Graduating at a time when she was unable to obtain a position in the public school system, Shoshanna opened a small clandestine nursery school at home.

Simultaneous with the implementation of these measures, Hungary pursued a duplicitous strategy with Hitler. It joined the Rome-Berlin-Tokyo Axis in 1940 and aided the German war effort on the one hand, but it secretly sought peace with the West on the other. As the tide gradually turned towards an Allied victory after the German defeat at Stalingrad in 1943, the Jews of Hungary dared to hope for a reprieve. Early in 1944, the Red Army reached Ternopol in Ukraine, some

250 kilometres northeast of Beregszász, and seemed unstoppable as it advanced towards the Carpathians and Hungary. The Hungarian government desperately attempted to reach a separate armistice with the Allies, as Italy had done.

It was not to be. On March 19, 1944, the German army occupied Hungary. Official Jewish policy changed overnight from discrimination and exclusion to deliberate annihilation. Jews were to be segregated and concentrated in ghettos before deportation. Knowing full well they had lost the war, the Nazis were intent on eliminating Hungary's Jews, the one remaining Jewish community in their thrall, with assembly-line precision and efficiency. With the Red Army approaching from the east, Adolf Eichmann stipulated that the country should be "combed from east to west," to rule out the possibility of liberation for the Jews in the direct path of the Russians.

Nowhere else but in Hungary were so many people deported and murdered as rapidly and systematically. In less than two months, 147 trains carrying 434,351 people left the country, causing a near glut in the gas chambers of Auschwitz. The process began in Subcarpathia.

WHEN THE GERMAN ARMY made its move on Beregszász, Shoshanna lost her head. The convoy of jeeps, trucks, and marching soldiers snaking through the streets filled her with terror. She was convinced that the army lorries speeding up and down the Korzó housed mobile gas units of the sort that were rumoured to be operating in Poland. She begged her parents for permission to go to Magda in Vári, where, a short telephone conversation revealed, the Germans were nowhere in evidence. Not knowing what to believe, they acquiesced.

Magda sent a farm boy, a handsome lad she knew, to fetch Shoshanna. Mamuka tied a black kerchief over her head and made her put on a couple of dirndl skirts, in an effort to disguise her as a peasant girl. She rode pillion behind the youth the twelve miles to Vári, while he cautioned her not to return home to Beregszász. He would save her from the Germans, he said, giving her arm a squeeze from time to time. He knew all the hiding places in her parents' vineyard, in the press house or in the vintner's lodge; he would bring her food at night, make sure no harm befell her, no matter what happened to the rest of the Jews in town.

Shoshanna's sense of dread intensified when they reached Vári. Their arrival coincided with that of the German army. As vulnerable as she had felt in Beregszász, it was infinitely worse here. Beregszász, after all, was a fair-sized town, with a large Jewish population that would take some effort to round up. Vári had a handful of Jewish inhabitants, all known and easily accounted for. The Germans went from house to house, announcing their directives: Jews were to pack up their belongings in fifty-kilogram packages that must include bedding, two changes of underwear, and provisions for no more than fourteen days. A couple of officers knocked at Magda's door, then strode into the parlour. They noted the grand piano. They saw the two beautiful, cowering young women. They said they'd be back that evening for some music and entertainment.

Magda and Shoshanna stole out the back door under cover of darkness and pleaded with some farmers Magda knew to give them shelter for the night. No one dared take them in. Above all, however, they could not return to Magda's. They had no illusions about the entertainment in store for them with the musically inclined Germans.

They ended up in the cemetery on a moonless night in March, tripping over bushes and markers. They encouraged each other with stories of how Józsi and Márton would soon be back, about how the war was nearly over, about how, in ancient times, God had saved the Israelites in Egypt with a "mighty hand and an outstretched arm." Passover was imminent; perhaps there would be another miracle, as in biblical times. Shoshanna asked Magda about the boy who had offered to save her. Both were of the opinion that even if he was trustworthy (and they couldn't be sure), Shoshanna would have to be prepared to submit to his attentions. Shoshanna said she couldn't bear that, and moreover, no matter what happened, she wanted the family to stay together.

The folly of this day, the fruitless flight from Beregszász, leaving Mamuka and Apuka and the others behind, was an object lesson on just what she shouldn't do. Home was where she and Magda must go. And so, in their skimpy shawls and dirndl skirts, the two sisters huddled together amid the gravestones and the crosses, waiting for the sunrise.

NO MIRACLE OCCURRED. The Jews of Beregszász were forced into the ghetto on the first day of Passover, April 16. Just before, Apuka, along with several other prominent Jews, had been ordered to surrender himself as a hostage, to ensure that the rest of the community complied with the draconian proceedings.

Shoshanna proposed hiding him among the wine barrels in the cellar of a neighbouring tavern. As they sneaked through back lanes, Apuka observed quietly, almost as an aside, "It breaks my heart to leave your mother behind. We have been perfectly happy these thirty-eight years." He stopped abruptly in his tracks. "I'm not going to hide. It's just so much tomfoolery." He returned home and surrendered to the gendarmerie.

Ten thousand Jews — those of the town and of the surrounding countryside — were rounded up at the Váry brickworks on the outskirts of Beregszász. Because the brickyard belonged to Józsi's uncle, the family was accommodated in what were regarded as privileged circumstances. A rectangular space partitioned by heavy carpets separated them from their neighbours on the top floor of the factory. In these favoured quarters (favoured because of the comparatively generous space and the privacy afforded by the curtains) were crowded Mamuka, Magda, Shoshanna, Vera, Rózsika, Juditka, and Rózsika's in-laws, Adolf Bácsi and Nelli Néni, and Apuka's sister and brother-in-law, Juliska Néni and Lajos Bácsi, with their two children.

They slept on the floor. Bathing and toilet facilities were woefully inadequate. At first they ate matzo that Mamuka had prepared in the final days at home. When their own provisions ran out, they resorted to a slop-like gruel that Shoshanna and Vera carried from a communal kitchen to their room in large cauldrons. Mamuka improvised a fire outdoors to reheat the unpalatable mush.

A Jewish council was established on orders from the Germans. Composed of the community's notables, its function was to receive directives from the Nazis and implement them inside the ghetto. Because of her impeccable German, the council enlisted Rózsika to parlay with the occupying Nazis. She accompanied members of the council on trips to German headquarters in town and reported back to the family news of what was demanded. Each day brought a fresh requisition for items of value: the first day jewellery, the next money, the third silver. Hungarian gendarmes arrived on horseback to extort and search for valuables. With bayonets they slashed open the precious eiderdowns and duvets that had been carried from home. A cloud of feathers and down settled on the ground as if from a heavy snowfall. The gendarmes produced buckets and shouted, "Throw the goods in here, throw the money in here!" Terrified Jews stripped off watches and wedding rings and flung them and their remaining currency into the buckets to be whisked away.

The signs were ominous and life was miserable, but it was life still. Shoshanna organized activities for the young children, playing circle games with them, teaching them songs from operettas, and exhausting her repertoire of fairy tales. Vera and Shanyi Friedman, the son of the town's duvet maker, became engaged in the ghetto, to the great pleasure of their families. Finally a suitable boy for Vera!

Apuka was returned to his family a day before the deportation. When the order for departure came, they were herded onto freight cars, the gendarmes forcing them with whips. "To Kecskemét," the gendarmes responded to the hysterical cries of those who pleaded with them. "Don't fuss, for pity's sake! Don't carry on like it's some tragedy. You're going to Kecskemét, to pick apricots." Clinging to any hope, they took a measure of comfort in this information that they were headed for southern Hungary, even though the date was May 15 and the season for harvesting apricots not until August.

They all managed to clamber onto the same boxcar: Mamuka and Apuka, Rózsika and Juditka, Magda, Shoshanna, and Vera, Adolf Bácsi and Nelli Néni, Juliska Néni, Lajos Bácsi, and their two daughters. Wedged into a space designed to transport forty military personnel in better days were some eighty people.

The doors were bolted from the outside with a resounding clang. A bucket at one end of the car was the sole facility for the disposal of bodily waste. The stench from it became unbearable almost immediately. Shoshanna was in agony because she had begun to menstruate. All she could do was stuff her few items of clothing between her legs.

For three days they were pressed against one another in claustrophobic embrace. Shoshanna's leg went to sleep but when she tried to extend it to relieve the numbness, Juliska Néni shouted at her for kicking her. Ica sat nearby, squished beside her best friend's father. Shoshanna watched in horrified fascination as he began pawing Ica in an attempt to seduce her. Beneath the eyes of his wife, the husband of another girlfriend begged Shoshanna to be his, right then and there. "I'll do anything for you, wherever it is that we're going, I'll be your protector, just let me kiss you. Kiss me back, *please.*" His wife looked on with stony eyes before turning her head away.

There was no food, except for a few morsels hastily stuffed into pockets when the gendarmes had begun to corral them towards the waiting trains. Shoshanna shared with her niece Juditka a hard-boiled egg, the shell crushed into its flesh. After weeks of privation in the ghetto, children began dying on the train. Infants wailed feebly at their mothers' dry breasts.

Some time after the Slovakian border was reached at Kosice – all fantasies of apricot picking now abandoned – a bucket of water found its way into the wagon. Lajos Bácsi, one of the most respected elders, was elected its guardian. Shoshanna would never forget how he doled out the precious drops with such impartiality that his own children received not a sip more than anyone else.

As the train rumbled on, some perfected the art of peering through the cracks that admitted slim shafts of light into the wagon and deduced that they were in Poland. Once the train idled in a village and the inhabitants stared back at them. Some of the villagers moved their index fingers across their necks, leering as they communicated the universal cut-throat sign. At this stop or perhaps another, the body of a newborn baby was handed out of the car. It was then that Adolf Bácsi, Rózsika's father-in-law, lost his mind. For the rest of the journey, he alternately babbled, screamed, and hallucinated.

When the doors were unbolted on May 17, those inside tumbled out onto the ground like flotsam. They came to their feet and stretched their aching bodies, trying to make sense of their surroundings. A surreal scene met their eyes. Fresh air, sunshine, music, and men in striped pyjamas running back and forth. After the conditions in the train, this place seemed like heaven. How could they know that this was Nazi Germany's largest concentration and death camp, a railway hub in a part of eastern Poland that had been annexed to the Reich? Their destination wasn't Kecskemét but Birkenau, the annihilation complex of Auschwitz.

Mamuka said wonderingly, "Look, there are people working here. I will be able to work."

One of the pyjama-clad men held a microphone in his hand and was singing an aria. From some unseen source the sounds of an orchestra backed him up. More men, moving swiftly like characters in accelerated film footage, swarmed around the newly arrived passengers. Rózsika, Juditka, Mamuka, and Shoshanna were formed into one line, Rózsika holding Juditka by the hand. Apuka was slightly ahead of them, staring at a row of horse-drawn carts that drew up.

Apuka said, "Look, they're putting people onto the carts. I'm too weak to walk, I'll ask for a ride." Apuka was lifted onto a cart by the pyjamaed men at his own request. No one from the family spoke to Apuka, no one waved goodbye, no one had the slightest inkling that those on the carts were being taken directly to the gas chambers.

Mamuka kept repeating her mantra as she gazed at the uniformed figures. "Look at how many people are working here. I'm strong. I'll be able to work." At fifty-seven, she was tall and spare, and, despite the stroke a few years back, still vigorous.

The pace of events quickened. Shoshanna, Vera, Magda, Rózsika, Juditka, and Mamuka were shoved forward and marched to a point where an angel-faced SS captain, cane in hand and a German shepherd by his side, pointed a white-gloved finger to the right or to the left. Dr. Josef Mengele's beatific smile dazzled and disarmed them. Mamuka and the other women of her age filed off to the left. So did the young mothers with their children. Magda, Shoshanna, and Vera were directed towards the right. It all happened so rapidly that no one reacted, no one objected, no one suspected peril or disaster.

Marshalled by SS guards, the three sisters found themselves in a bathhouse. They were ordered to strip as water gushed down from spouts above their heads. Shoshanna felt so detached from reality that she barely noticed the SS officers lolling about the room. Camp-hardened women – Polish Jews – accosted them with straight razors, roughly denuding them of their hair, which cascaded onto the floor in long ribbons.

A startling apparition confronted Shoshanna at this moment. "Józsi!" she exclaimed. "What are you doing here?"

But it wasn't her brother-in-law; it was his sister, Klári. With her bald head she bore an uncanny resemblance to Józsi.

The Polish attendants, some of whom had been in Auschwitz for months or years, threw shapeless garments at the Hungarians. Those among the new arrivals who could muster a little Yiddish asked, in all innocence, "When are we going to see our parents?"

"Are you insane?" came the jeering response. "Are you out of your minds? What possessed you to come here? Why didn't you resist? Why didn't you fight back? Was our experience here of no importance to you? The whole world knows about it! 'When are we going to see our parents?' Your parents are burned to a crisp by now! And you deserve everything that's happening to you."

In that benumbed instant, Shoshanna had only one thought, "At least Mamuka didn't die alone. At least Rózsika was with her."

Assigned to Lager A with scores of other women, Magda, Shoshanna, and Vera were holed up in small, two-tiered cages. They sat, slept, and ate in those cages and waited. They had not been tattooed and were not assigned to forced labour; it was likely they were waiting for death. But the Germans had not yet decided their fate, so they did nothing, save get up very early, roused from nightmarish dreams into nightmare reality. A small, half-crazed woman ran through the barracks at two in the morning, yodelling in Yiddish, "*Uf shtaygn yiddishe kinderlach, uf shtaygn!*" Get up, Jewish children, get up. The unfortunate creature had witnessed the murders of her children on the journey to Auschwitz and had become deranged. She was the morning alarm.

It was still dark when they arrived shivering in the yard to stand for *Appell*. The chimney of the crematorium was sending up flares and smoke on the horizon, the stench of burning flesh so thick they could almost taste it. *Appell* could go on for hours, while they were counted up and down. If the SS didn't like the looks of a prisoner, they pulled her out and took her away, never to be seen again. Anyone who seemed sickly or whose belly showed the early signs of pregnancy was likewise plucked from the line.

Vera fell into apathy. She simply sat and stared at a point in front of her, refusing to speak, refusing to eat. In the beginning none of them had eaten. The first day raw, unpeeled beets had been thrown into their cages. The next day there was a soup that looked like slops, fit only for pigs.

They glared at it in disgust, then Magda pinched her nose with the fingers of one hand, raised the bowl to her lips with the other, and opened her mouth.

"I'm swallowing this so as to see Józsi again some day."

As the days wore on, Vera remained impassive. Shoshanna and Magda were terrified. A week earlier, Klári Schweger, who lived across the street from them at home, had begun to screech hysterically in the middle of the day. She was taken away. Magda and Shoshanna feared that Vera would be the next to snap.

Life was a round of boredom animated by terror. Two pregnant women in the bunkhouse next to theirs had managed to evade notice during *Appell*. When they started labour, the *Kapos* ordered the women in Lager A to sing and shout to drown out their screams of pain. Afterwards, the *Kapos* removed the babies so the mothers might have a chance at life.

It seemed the Germans still couldn't decide whether to dispatch their group to the gas or assign them to work. Occasionally they were sent to clean the latrines; a few teams were shipped out to toil in nearby fields. Once Shoshanna and Vera were ordered to carry some dirty laundry from one *Lager* to another, but instead of returning to base they wandered about outside, hoping to find someone they knew. Shoshanna spotted a boy from Munkács and waved to him.

The young man stared at them in panic. "What are you doing out here?" He shouldered them into a corridor of some sort, while a transport of freshly arrived Greek Jews and their guards filed past. "If you don't watch out, they'll nab you and shove you into the gas!"

After they had been there for so long they could barely imagine another form of existence, they were rounded up in a windowless metal hangar called the dressing room. They were told to remove their clothes, so their bodies and apparel could be deloused. By this time they had no illusions and were aware of the drill. They assumed it was the end. Yet holed up naked in this room for two days, they devised the beauty contest in which Shoshanna took the prize for best legs. In spite of all they had endured, they yearned to live and dared to hope.

When the *Kapos* returned with stacks of grey sack dresses, the women knew they had been spared. Once more they were put into cattle cars. Two days later, on a morning in early July, they were delivered to a large oil refinery at Gelsenkirchen in the Ruhr Valley. When they disembarked from the train, SS guards shouted, "Let the pregnant women step out, they'll be well and separately treated." Only one of the few remaining pregnant women among them kept her wits about her and stood her ground. The others stepped forward and were immediately shipped back to Auschwitz.

In Gelsenkirchen, Shoshanna took risks. Occasionally she sneaked into line a second time to get a little extra food. She smuggled the bowl back to the bunkhouse, counting the minutes until Magda and Vera returned from work. She was almost crazed with hunger, but she never touched the contents until the three of them could dip into it together.

Here they were assigned heavy labour, carting wood, lugging rubbish, passing bricks in relay. Sometimes they sang softly in Hungarian, to keep up their spirits. The SS guards let them sing, understanding neither the words nor their special significance. "Everything comes to an end; everything ends one day; the promise of every December culminates in May."

Once Magda stopped for a minute to catch her breath. A guard lashed her across the back with his whip.

"*Alte Kuh!*" Old cow.

Beautiful Magda, now bald and dressed in rags. That night she said dully to Shoshanna, "If Józsi should ever find me here, how could he love an old cow?" Magda's will to live faltered after that. The bomb attack that killed her came a few days later. She was thirty.

After the third bombing raid by the British, it was off to Sömmerda and the Krupp munitions works. In this village in east central Germany, the women regained some of their health and their hair started to sprout again. Their German workmates were good to them. Once, an older man who was in the habit of giving Shoshanna a small treat on Sundays brought her an onion. When she slipped the cherished booty into her blouse, an SS guard who had been ogling her for weeks, even greeting her with a "*Guten Tag*" as if she was a human being and not a Jew, observed her furtive gesture. He reached out and groped her breast.

By reflex Shoshanna slapped his hand. Then, realizing her folly, she felt herself congeal with terror. She expected to be shot on the spot. But instead of drawing his gun, the grim-faced guard ordered another young woman next to her to search her. Shoshanna understood that the SS suspected her of concealing a weapon, of plotting sabotage. When the girl pulled forth an onion, the guard flushed red. Shoshanna read shame on his face, not rage. He stalked away without disciplining her.

One day the freight train brought a load of potatoes. Vera and Shoshanna were on their rest shift, but word of the precious cargo spread quickly through the camp. Everyone rushed to the wagons on the pretext of unpacking the potatoes and transporting them to the kitchen. Shoshanna concealed as many in her bloomers as she could without having them scatter as she moved. Later that night the women roasted the filched vegetables by the little iron stove that kept them from freezing. Vera and Shoshanna stayed awake lest someone steal their hoard. Once, somebody had taken a crust of bread that Vera had stashed away. She cursed and hollered for the restitution of the bread, finally quietening when the lights were doused so the thief could return it under cover of darkness.

On night shift in the factory, they were permitted to dash out to the toilets to splash water on their faces to keep themselves alert. They were always sleepy on this shift. During the daylight hours they had to launder their clothes and occasionally their blankets to keep them free of lice. Shoshanna would stand outside, knee deep in snow, washing first herself, then her clothing – sometimes with a rare sliver of soap – in ice water. They hung the wet laundry by the stove and then the two of them snuggled together for animal warmth on the straw ticking in the bunk until their garments dried.

And at night at their workstations, as they filled the cartridges with powder, they sang the same refrain as in

Gelsenkirchen: "Everything comes to an end; everything ends one day; the promise of every December culminates in May."

BY THE END OF FEBRUARY 1945, the factories to which thousands of Jews from Auschwitz had been consigned were about to be overrun by either the Red Army or the Western Allies. Jews who had survived the selections of Birkenau and subsequent slave labour in work camps were now subjected to harrowing death marches as these sites were abandoned. In the last few weeks of the war, thousands died of exposure, starvation, bombardments from all sides, pitiless cruelty at the hands of their masters, and random depredations from German civilians. Hundreds of evacuation trains, trucks, and foot marches were set in motion, their destination the concentration camps at Bergen-Belsen and Dachau, Buchenwald and Mauthausen, Sachsenhausen and Ravensbruck.

The evacuation from Sömmerda began in mid-March. A battle raging in the nearby city of Weimar could be heard by the women some thirty kilometres away. They set out in wooden clogs – all they possessed in the way of footwear – Shoshanna concealing a loaf of bread under her arm. Night and day they marched, sometimes in circles, avoiding the cities burning on the horizon. After the bread was gone, they foraged for roots. Passing a field of turnips, they scrabbled for the sparse remains of the fall harvest.

They walked for three weeks. When the bombs rained down they were permitted to take temporary refuge in ditches, but they were under orders to keep moving. Filthy from their exertions and from the gutters where they sheltered, they never had a chance to wash. On they trekked, aimlessly, it seemed, even in their sleep. Shoshanna dreamed she was marching, but it was no dream: she was sleepwalking.

Eventually they arrived at a farmhouse and were put up in a loft. A girl among them fell through a hole in the floor boards and broke her arm. There was no one to attend to injuries; she simply continued on the next day. But the farmers were good to them here. They fed them and gave them water to bathe. By this time the women were swarming with lice; in the ditches, they had slept in the traces of retreating louse-ridden soldiers. That night, as they lay in fresh straw, the SS bolted the door. Outside, the sounds of battle thundered around them; if a spark landed on the barn, they'd never escape.

They moved on. More burning towns, more burning lampposts. The SS escorts conferred with their officers; the group was ordered to Buchenwald. In the confusion that reigned there, other prisoners told them they would be taken into the surrounding forests and executed, like scores before them. Instead they were led out of Buchenwald without a word of explanation.

The absurd wandering seemed pointless and endless. The Germans had only one plan, to stay out of the path of the Americans and the Russians, as the western and eastern fronts converged. Eventually the Sömmerda contingent split up, one group heading towards Theresienstadt, the other, including Shoshanna and Vera, towards Dresden. In the final days of the march, they had no food at all. One night they collapsed in the ruins of a bathhouse. A murky pool covered the cement floor. They were so exhausted they fell asleep in the stagnant water.

In the second week of April they reached Glauchau, a Prussian village near Dresden. The battle front moved with them. Their SS guards, in a state of complete disarray, shed their uniforms and changed into civilian clothes. They still carried arms and could have killed their Jewish prisoners with impunity. Instead, following the example of an older officer, they showed a shred of decency. They told the women to wave a white flag — anything white — and then they fled.

In the trench where they had taken cover from the American guns, the women looked in vain for a white garment. They were all covered in muck. Someone stripped off a shirt that may once have been white, and, holding it by a grimy sleeve, fluttered it overhead. It had no effect. Unaware that the German soldiers had decamped, the Americans continued firing. Klári Kahan was killed; Luci Prics took a bullet in her shoulder but survived.

For days, Shoshanna and Vera huddled side by side as shrapnel flew overhead and their dying comrades gave up the struggle. Shoshanna clutched a cabbage leaf in her hand like some sort of talisman and Vera held onto the stump of a carrot. Finally, during a lull in the crossfire, they crawled on all fours to a nearby building. They gained entry and, completely spent, lay down on a table in what appeared to be a workshop. Bullets ricocheted through the empty window frames. Shoshanna murmured the words of the *Shema* over and over until she fell into a state of exaltation she had never experienced before. Not only did she feel the presence of God, she felt inhabited by God, as if God had prised open her heart and lodged Himself within. She knew it was all about to end and her terrible fear subsided. Either they would die in the next moment or they would be liberated. How much time passed before the American soldiers entered the workshop she could not guess.

Shema Yisroel, Adonai Eloheinu, Adonai Ehad. Hear O Israel, the Lord our God, the Lord is One. It was April 14.

THEY REMAINED IN GERMANY under chaotic conditions until the end of May. Shoshanna was fearful of everyone she saw, cowering from the American soldiers who offered her chocolate bars, nylon stockings, and candles. Then began the nightmare journey home, clinging to the dream of home, of being reunited with everyone by some miracle, waiting for trains that didn't arrive, then did arrive, then started, then stopped, then started up again, then dropped them off in the middle of nowhere. On trains, on trucks, and on foot, they criss-crossed the length and breadth of Czechoslovakia, snaking through mountains and valleys, by the Vltava, by the Vistula, inching their way towards Hungary. Once in some nameless countryside they clambered onto open freight cars that were later boarded by a regiment of Mongolian Russian soldiers. "Jump!" Shoshanna shrieked at Vera, and they jumped from the moving train they had waited a week for, jumped for dear life, because they feared rape more than they had feared gas.

Days later they found another train; later still they ended up walking a highway in Slovakia. In a village along the way,

Jews greeted them with chunks of bacon and huge loaves of bread. There was yet another train, this time carrying Romanian officers who wanted sport. "One, two, three," Vera yelled, and they pulled their bags off their backs and leaped down on top of them.

Shoshanna and Vera arrived in Budapest on July 30. Vera took shelter with distant relatives who worked her by day and whose attentions she had to fight off by night during the week that Shoshanna travelled alone to Beregszász. Mari Néni was waiting at the station, as she had been every day since the war ended in May, to welcome the family back. She accompanied Shoshanna to the house on Magyar Utca, where a prostitute had set herself up in business. Looters had ransacked the property, hunting for valuables. Tiles were plucked from the roof, leaving gaps like missing teeth. Mamuka's garden was a shambles, flowers and shrubs uprooted, the woodshed in the back dismantled. The house had been denuded of all its fine furniture, Lilli's tasselled lampshades and petit point cushions, the Kelim carpets, the grand piano. In the cellar the wine barrels were empty. Shoshanna hired a wagoner and drove with him to Magda's house in Vári. She rounded up all of Magda's furniture and transported it to the family home. She turfed out the whore.

But by then the Russian army was making merry there as well. Carousing soldiers thronged the city. Alone in the house one night she trailed from room to room, howling like a wounded animal brought to bay. So this was liberation. This was what had become of home.

On the wall above the spot where the piano once stood, the portrait of Magda remained in place. She lifted the painting off the wall reverently, as if it were an icon, and began prying at the nails pinning it to the frame. By the time she was done, blood was coursing down her fingers, but all she cared about was getting the job done and keeping the picture clean. The Parisian artist had framed the completed work perhaps ten years before. It seemed several lifetimes ago. Shoshanna rolled the canvas carefully, gathered a few pieces of clothing, and fled Beregszász under cover of night.

EPILOGUE

F riday nights my family gathers at my home in West End
Montreal. Rebecca and her fiancé are present every
week; this time Jessica too, visiting from Toronto, has joined
us. My mother and I kindle Sabbath candles; the man with
whom I share my life chants the kiddush.

After supper, I have a surprise for Shoshanna. Earlier in
the day I discovered several Beregszász heritage sites on the
Internet and printed off facsimiles of vintage postcards and
a few more recent photographs. For all her intelligence
and sharpness, my mother can't really grasp the concept of
cyberspace, but she is delighted by the images that I spread
out in front of her on the dining room table: the Great
Bazaar, the Catholic church then and now, the Protestant
church, the Vérke River, the courthouse, the railway station.
In a minuscule reproduction of one side of Masaryk Square,
Shoshanna points to a tiny portal with immense excitement.

"That's it, that's it! That's our store. Next to the Rothman
Patika – the pharmacy," she translates for the benefit of her
English-speaking granddaughters. Beyond the borders of

the image she jabs left and right at the printout. That was the way home from the store — less than a five-minute walk — and in the other direction, there was the Korzó, where the finest stores in town were located.

She is quivering with joy, animated by the sight of old haunts and by the corroboration of an up-to-the-minute, if alien source, that Beregszász really existed, and still does under the guise of another name.

"Ma," I say in my most persuasive voice, "what do you think if we went back together? You and me, and the girls —"

She stares at me, all the spark suddenly obliterated. "It would kill me, Ilushka."

So we haven't gone. Neither she, nor I, nor the girls. There is no need. Beregszász alone will not yield the essence of the story.

The enigma of my birth is part of that essence. Did my unexpected appearance force the issue of my parents' marriage? Would Shoshanna have been happier if she'd returned to Márton with me in her arms?

Through the decades, my mother always had news of Márton. Initially my father sent him greetings at every new year, ceasing only when Márton stopped responding. He and his wife had settled in Caracas, but as they prospered, they bought a condo in Miami. They never had children. When my parents wintered in Florida, mutual friends would find ways of relaying information about him. They made it clear that Márton too asked after Shoshanna: Was she well? How did she look? Had she and Gusti made good?

I'm convinced Shoshanna would have liked to meet him again, the way she occasionally rendezvoused with the friends of her youth in Boca Raton or New York or Tel Aviv. She cherished the illusion that he too longed to see her, but that his wife was jealous of the hold of the past on him and wouldn't allow it.

When Márton died, a year before Gusti, Shoshanna was notified by a brother who lived in Toronto. For a time she was inconsolable. She spoke about him constantly, travelled to Toronto to pay a condolence call on the brother, lapped up the details of the fatal heart attack. That she continues to this day to invoke his name and the part he played in her life is not only because of his centrality to the story but also because the opportunity for a final reckoning between them has passed forever.

In the ambiguous position in which Shoshanna found herself in 1947, how convenient to pin responsibility for her future on a chance pregnancy. But the letters that passed between her and my father during the previous summer, when she returned to work in Budapest and he remained in Mada, tell me yet another story. They were already lovers in all but one respect. On June 3, three weeks before they confirmed the relationship with their bodies, Shoshanna wrote to Gusti of Vera's opposition to the romance and her insistence that Shoshanna be faithful to Márton. Shoshanna begged Gusti to wind up his business in Mada and join her in Budapest "because I'm very alone here. I ask God to make it come out all right, that He should make me love Márton when he returns, if I must love him because he loves me. But now it is always of you that I think and how much I will miss you when I am with Márton. Come as soon as possible. Until now I haven't asked you to come, but now I miss you too much. My life is empty and it is not true that I love you only because I am alone. I really love you."

There was never a lack of love in my parents' marriage, even if it fell short of harmony and deep understanding. It endured through many vicissitudes and ended only with my father's death, forty-four years after they had first pledged themselves to each other. In the last eight years of his life Gusti suffered a long and debilitating illness. My mother nursed him devotedly for two years at home and to the point of depletion after he was institutionalized.

On the occasion of her marriage to Max in 1992, Shoshanna made clear her allegiances and he accepted them. When Max died five years later, she shed his name and became Mrs. Anna Kalman once again. One day, she will lie beside my father.